Après-coup

Jean Laplanche

Après-coup

Translated by Jonathan House

followed by

Time and the Other

and

Temporality and Translation

&

Debate on "Temporality and Translation"

Translated by Luke Thurston

New York:
The Unconscious in Translation

1050 Fifth Avenue, New York, NY 10028
ucsintranslation@gmail.com

First Edition

Après-coup was originally published as *Problématiques VI: L'après-coup*
ISBN 9782130555193

6, avenue Reille, 75014 Paris

Cover art: *Spiral,* by Jie Gu 2016

ISBN 978-1-942254-09-6
Library of Congress Control Number: 2016960161

CONTENTS

Preface

The lectures on après-coup were delivered in the academic year 1989–1990, the midpoint of five years that may have been the period of Laplanche's greatest synthetic creativity. Not only are they at the center of those years, they are also of central importance in that they point to unfinished aspects of Laplanche's theorizing, his unfinished continuation of what he called Freud's unfinished Copernican revolution.

These five years of explosive creativity began with the publication of *New Foundations for Psychoanalysis* in 1987, a year that also saw the publication of *Traduire Freud,* a collaboration with his fellow translators of Freud's complete works, of Laplanche's related essay "Spécificité des problèmes terminologiques dans la traduction de Freud," and of "Le mur et l'arcade." The lectures on après-coup followed in 1989–1990. "Implantation, intromission" appeared in 1990. Laplanche's lectures on sexuality, the seminar of 1991–1992, were first published in the journal *Psychanalyse à l'université* in the section *Enseignments,* later as a monograph entitled *Le fourvoiement de la sexualité chez Freud* and still later as *Problématiques VII.*[1] The classic essay known as "The Unfinished Copernican Revolution" was initially presented as the opening lecture of that 1991–1992 seminar and then in July of 1992 at the *Colloque international de psychanalyse* in Montréal. Completing the list of major works in this five-year period, in 1991 Laplanche published "L'interprétation entre déterminisme et herméneutique" and "Du transfert: sa provocation par l'analyste."[2]

---

1 The lectures were first published in *Psychanalyse à l'université,* then, in 1993, as a monograph *Le fourvoiement de la sexualité chez Freud;* the English translation by Donald Nicholson-Smith is entitled *The Temptation of Biology: Freud's Theories of Sexuality* (New York: The Unconscious in Translation, 2015). The monograph was republished in 1999 as *La sexualité humaine* and then, in 2006, as *Problématiques VII.*

2 "The Unfinished Copernican Revolution," "Implantation, Intromission," "Time and the Other" and "Transference: its Provocation by the Analyst" were translated by Luke Thurston and published in *Essays on Otherness* (London and New York: Routledge, 1999) a volume which also contains Philip Slotkin's translation of "Interpretation between Determinism and Hermeneutics."

New Foundations, which opened this quinquennium, is a synthesis of Problématiques I through V—his seminar lectures from 1970 through 1984—and of his previous conceptual research going back to *Life and Death in Psychoanalysis* of 1970 and, before that, to the works co-authored with Pontalis in the late 1960s. In his introduction to *New Foundations,* referring to Problématiques I through V, Laplanche writes, "Now the moment has come to show how my positions are connected with each other," and the book culminates in the first major presentation of the General Theory of Seduction. For the next quarter century, Laplanche showed the power of that synthesis deepening and extending it and pointing to the work that remains to be done.

When these lectures were first published in 2006, both the series name *Problématiques* and the format of the previous volumes of the *Problématiques* were retained. In other respects, this volume was an exception. All of Laplanche's previous and subsequent work, from the 1960s to the end of his life, was published immediately after being written. This was true for the lectures at the Sorbonne and at Paris VII, later collected as *Problématiques I* through *Problématiques V,* and also for articles and invited lectures presented elsewhere. In contrast, the lectures in this volume had to wait 15 years until, in 2006, they were published as *Problématiques VI*. Underlining the exceptional nature of this delay is the fact that the lectures on sexuality, given in the next academic years, were published immediately and by 2006 they had been republished in three new editions, only the latest of which is entitled *Problématiques VII*. In spite of this delay in publication, the lectures presented in this volume have an unpolished and, perhaps more precisely, an unfinished quality.

The problems confronting the translator of these lectures relate both to their importance and to their 'unfinished' state—I believe both factors contributed to the 15-year delay in publication. In the preface to this volume, as in the preface to every other volume of the *Problématiques,* Laplanche includes this sentence: "My spoken words have been altered only to the extent necessitated by their transposition to print."

Even a quick glance at any one of the other volumes of *Problématiques* reveals that, for those volumes, this claim is what Huckleberry Finn calls "stretching the truth." All those others have been carefully revised and edited, and it is clear by comparison that only the text of the present volume contains anything like an 'unaltered' Laplanche. What we find here are lecture notes, bearing few traces of later amendment. In all other *Problematiques*, Laplanche integrates questions from the audience and his answers to them into the body of his lecture, while here the interchanges remain as he had recorded them. The present text also contains detectable lacunae, missing passages, mostly bits of Freud, that Laplanche read aloud, often sight translating, translating from the 'open book'. His comments allude to passages from Freud just before and/or just after those included in the published text. I have "restored" such missing passages. In addition, the French text contains quite a few proofing errors—incorrect citations, paraphrases given in quotations, and so forth. Corrections have been made wherever it seemed wise and these are always indicated.

In a short passage added to the beginning of the last chapter of this book, Laplanche refers to the delayed publication as itself an example of après-coup. Like all occurrences of après-coup, the delay compels attention, both as to what was delayed and as to the delay itself – both are à traduire. Here is the beginning of the last chapter:

> We will finish today. But this "today," by a liberty I grant myself as I go over these notes from 1989 to 1990, is also a today in August, 2005. Probably, at bottom, little has changed since I gave this course. But the après-coup of these reflections on après-coup leads me to observe that since this course, very little has been "grasped" of what I have proposed as springing from this major concept in the psychoanalytic theory of time. In journals, colloquia, and review articles, the

> old "resignification," a barely modernized avatar of Jung's "retroactive fantasizing," seems to have been adopted unanimously. The sleep of very few clinicians or theoreticians has been troubled by the originality of a concept that signals an irrevocable double direction in relation to the arrow of time, an originality which had already been underlined in *The Language of Psycho-Analysis*.

Laplanche may be overlooking the significance of the delay in the development of his own work. Dominique Scarfone, who worked closely with Laplanche for many years, recalls urging him to publish the après-coup lectures in about 1999. "He showed me his files saying that they would require a lot of editing and rewriting, and that he could not find the time for that." My own view is that this work points to what is unfinished in Laplanche's theorizing: the nature of the urge to translate, an urge which is at the birth of the drive but is not itself a drive, does not have the economics of a drive, and is better understood as an instinct, a function. This was put clearly by José Carlos Calich in July of 2014 in his presentation at the week-long Colloque de Cerisy-la-Salle: *La sédution à l'origine : L'œuvre de Jean Laplanche*:

> Within the frame of the General Theory of Seduction, at the origin of the human psyche (or the human soul as Jean Laplanche prefers to say), the little human being receives messages infiltrated by the sexuality of his caretakers. The infant is endowed with the function of translation, that is to say with the ability and the urge to translate. Like other human functions, it is innate. It is that part of the infant's biology which seeks to translate the messages, to metabolize them, to integrate them, but lacks the translational codes necessary to fully satisfy the urge. Thus the sexually compromised message presents an enigma, it is an

> enigmatic message. A partial translation of such messages is made possible thanks to the functionality of translational codes supplied by the myths and symbols provided by the family and the broader culture, what Jean Laplanche calls "the pseudo-unconscious of the mytho-symbolic." The partial and incomplete translation of these messages creates different spaces in the human soul. It produces a vertical split that separates the untranslated elements from the translated elements and maintains them as separate reciprocally unknown. Thus creating the spaces that, depending on the topography used, are called systems or structures or instances: e.g. the repressed unconscious, the preconscious/conscious, and the enclaved unconscious as Laplanche described in 2003 in "Three Meanings of the Term 'Unconscious.'"

In 2005 Laplanche turned 81 years old. In addition to the ongoing work on the French translation of the complete works of Freud, Laplanche was preparing new editions of *Problématiques I* and *VII* for his publisher and he was writing a number of important works, for example—to choose only from those he included in his 2007 collection, *Sexual*, and only a few of those: "Levels of Proof," "The Three Essays and the Theory of Seduction," "Freud and Philosophy," "Psychoanalysis and Psychotherapy," "Incest and Infantile Sexuality," "Castration and Oedipus as Codes and Narrative Schemas."

But perhaps what had given him pause was not the amount of other work, but rather the power of what he had begun to unfold in these lectures: a return to, an unearthing of, Freud's notion of translation which began Laplanche's extension of the concept. This extension opened the way for Laplanche's writing on such major topics as the mythosymbolic, the death drive, psychoanalysis as an antihermeneutic, and the Fundamental Anthropological Situation. In another passage from the last lecture (perhaps it is also an addition from 2005[3]) Laplanche writes:

> Why then invoke a theory, a translational model of après-coup and, more generally, a translational model of the theory of seduction and even a translational model of the constitution of the human being? It is because there is no mental process that captures the double movement better than translation, the indivisible double movement of the "being carried forward" and of "referring back." The "being carried forward" is nothing other than what I designate as a "fundamental to-be-translated": a demand to translate the message of the other.

Elsewhere Laplanche speaks of a "translational theory of repression" and of a "translational model of a theory of seduction." Explicitly or implicitly, he also refers to translational theories of psychic trauma, infantile sexuality, and the constitution of the human being. In other words, the same moment of translation après-coup, the same urge to translate, the same exigency that Laplanche underlines in the Freud's letter of December 6, 1896, is central to the psychic mechanism at the origin of psychic trauma, repression, the Unconscious, and infantile sexuality; ultimately, it is at the origin of what makes the human subject a self-narrating, self-theorizing creature.

As his other writing shows, by 2005 all this was clear to Laplanche, but the thought of revising the lectures from 15 years earlier to take account of the conceptual power of the urge to translate après-coup, to articulate the conceptual power of the urge to translate après-coup, and to indicate all the avenues thereby opened up ... well, such a thought must have been daunting. Better to leave the lecture notes more or less unchanged.

---

3 Laplanche's notes, if they still exist, are stored in cartons that are currently inaccessible, waiting for a permanent home and for the work of an archivist.

This volume also includes two papers whose themes overlap those of the seminar and which were written at about the same time. The first, "Temporality and Translation," was published in *Psychanalyse à l'université* along with an addendum entitled "Debate" containing critiques by three colleagues and Laplanche's reply to each. Given that all this was published in the January 1989 issue, "Temporality and Translation" must have been written in 1988 shortly before Laplanche began the series of lectures eventually published as *Problématiques VI: L'après-coup*. As he writes in the first lecture:

> For this year's course, I had first suggested the title "Time and the Other" [*"Le temps et l'autre"*] but I then found the same title, but with quite different ideas, in a little book by Emmanuel Levinas. To avoid creating problems of precedence, I abandoned the title. ... In the context of this exploration of time, my specific approach will address something that I have spoken of many times but that I will take up again and refine (and here again you can see the spiral movement): the concept of après-coup. Another possible title for this year's course would be "*Nachträglichkeit* in the après-coup."

In 1991, Laplanche did use the title "Time and the Other" for an essay he published in *Psychanalyse à l'université* which is the second addition to this volume.

As these two essays complement *Après-coup* thematically and bookend it chronologically, the decision to include them was easy. The same can't be said for including "Debate." The exchange with Dayan, Laplanche's first intertlocutor in "Debate," will be useful to the reader, but that seems less likely to be true of the exchanges with Fédida and Gagey. The deciding factor was that Laplanche chose to publish all three exchanges not only in *Psychanalyse à l'université,* where "Temporality and Translation" was first published, but also in *La révolution copernicienne inachevée,* in which he collected his papers from 1967 to 1992.

Editor's Note

Conventions

- Comments by the translator are enclosed in square brackets: [---]
- Comments by Laplanche within quotations of Freud and other authors are enclosed in curly brackets: {---}.
- Citations to *The Standard Edition of the Complete Psychological Works of Sigmund Freud,* are given as *SE* (volume number): (page numbers)
- Citations to the *Gesammelte Werke* are given as GW (volume number): (page numbers)
- A bibliography of Laplanche's work is provided but, as so few authors beside Freud are cited, the full citation to other works is given in the footnotes. The index provides a cross reference.

Terminology

In the translations of Laplanche's work published by The Unconscious in Translation, decisions about rendering Laplanche into English have largely been left to each translator. For some terms, however, terminological consistency has seemed wise. Not all the terms in question appear in this volume, but for convenience—as much our own as that of readers who may simultaneously consult other works of Laplanche—we have reproduced and updated this note with each volume we have published.

With Laplanche's encouragement, UIT decided to publish the English translations of his work in more or less reverse chronological order. *Sexual: La sexualité élargie au sens freudien,* the first book published by UIT, containing his major work from 2000 to 2006, was the last volume of his work published in his lifetime. Laplanche was eager to be involved in its translation, and "Freud and the *Sexual*" benefited directly from his guidance. With one important exception, the decisions made for that volume have been carried forward to rest of the UIT series. The notes below address some issues we faced in translating key terms and offer brief explanations of the decisions made.

Âme, animique – psyche/mind, psychic/mental

Laplanche argued that the German *seele* has the same religious philosophical resonances as does the French *âme* and so *âme* and *animique* should be used for *Seele* and *seelisch* etc. We think the situation is different for 'soul' not only because its use in the sense of 'mind' or 'psyche' is less common in English than is the case for *âme* and *Seele* in French and German; although the adjectival forms 'soulical' and 'soulish' do exist, we think using them in these texts would be distracting, if not confusing. So, except in rare instances, such as 'apparatus of the soul', we have used 'mind' or 'psyche' and their derivatives.

Après-coup – après-coup

Freud's use of the words *nachträglich* and *Nachträglichkeit* is discussed at length in the book. As the reader will see, Laplanche suggested the neologism 'afterwardsness' for the English translation of the *Nachträglichkeit* and 'afterwards' for the *nachträglich*. In the years since Laplanche advocated 'afterwardsness', the word après-coup has become common in Anglophone psychoanalytic discourse. For that reason, we have decided to use après-coup as the English term for the concept.

Étayage – leaning-on

Étayage is the French translation of the German word *Anlehnung* which Strachey, in the Standard Edition, renders as 'anaclisis'—a cognate of the Greek *anaklinein* (ἀνακλίνω — leaning on). In translating Laplanche's work there is a long standing debate about the relative merits of translating *étayage* by 'leaning-on' or by 'propping'.

In his translation of *Life and Death,* Jeffrey Mehlman used 'propping' but often in the reflexive form. Laplanche preferred 'leaning-on' to emphasize the activity of the drive leaning-on the instinct, an activity which tends to be obscured. For this series, we have chosen to use 'leaning-on'.

Étrangèrité **– strangerness**

Étrangèrité is a neologism combining the meanings of *étrange,* 'strange', and *étranger,* 'foreigner'. We render it with the neologism "strangerness," which we hope conveys the same meaning and evokes the more or less the same associations.

Objet-source **– Source-Object**

By the time The Unconscious in Translation began publishing Laplanche's work, this word order was routine, e.g. in the translations by Luke Thurston and Leslie Hill in Essays on Otherness. While we see no advantage in one order over the other, we also see no reason to change the established practice.

Théorie de la séduction généralisée **– General Theory of Seduction**

Some translators have rendered the phrase 'theory of generalized seduction,' which is a reasonable choice but loses the echo of the distinction between Einstein's two theories of relativity. The first, known as the special theory of relativity, addresses a limited domain that is later expanded by the second, 'general' theory. Freud's (Special) Theory of Seduction concerned the origin of a specific group of psychopathologic entities: hysteria and other neuroses of defense. Laplanche's General Theory of Seduction is concerned with the origin of the sexual unconscious, and with the origin of the human subject as a self-theorizing, self-narrating creature.

Acknowledgements

First of all, I want to express my gratitude to Fondation Laplanche of the Institut de France whose support made this translation possible, then to those who have read and commented on various incarnations of this translation, especially to Gregory House, Tina Dobsevage, and Julie Slotnick. Copyediting of *Après-coup* was first done by Katie Herman. After substantial revisions, the translation was edited by Elise Yihan Chou whose editing led to substantive improvements. My translation of "Le pont Mirabeau" was improved by her suggestions and by those of Chantal Diebold

I also want to acknowledge others whose advice and encouragement has sustained me in the translating, the editing and all the other work of The Unconscious in Translation, these include Donald Nicholson-Smith, Dominique Scarfone, and Deborah Browning-Schimek. My friends who are my co-workers for Fondation Laplanche under the leadership of Christophe Dejours and Hélène Tessier: Maddy Brunot, José-Carlos Calich, Adriana Cinello, Gilbert Diebold, Udo Hock, Alberto Luchetti, Marcelo Marquès, and Francis Martens have been unfailingly supportive. The questions of my students and colleagues, both at Columbia's Center for Psychoanalytic Training and Research and at Columbia's Institute for Comparative Literature and Society, have been an important motivation for this work.

While Laplanche's work was and remains my primary inspiration, I am happy to have this chance to acknowledge the generous encouragement of Jean Laplanche and also Nadine Laplanche's inspiring enthusiasm about all things. Their memory gives me ongoing pleasure.

Jonathan House
General Editor

Après-coup:
Problématiques VI

Some Introductory Comments

Since 1962 at the École Normale Supérieure and the Sorbonne, and since 1969 at the Training and Research Unit (UFR) in Clinical Human Sciences (Sorbonne, University of Paris VII), my public teaching has taken a problematizing[1] and interpretative approach to some major axes of psychoanalytic theory. From the academic year 1970–1971 onward, my lectures have been collected in seven volumes under the general title Problématiques. The lectures have been altered only to the extent required for publication.

The themes of the successive years did not have a premeditated order; the path was set by the content and by the evolution of my own thinking. It was only afterwards, only après-coup, that I saw there was the possibility, without forcing things, to group my lectures into a series of volumes.

My annual course usually opened with a methodological introduction. These introductions are printed in italics at the beginning of each volume, so there is no need for me to repeat the ideas here. They give an account of an ongoing reflection about the methods of my approach as well as about its legitimacy "in the university."

Depending on their mood and their openness, readers may

1 [To problematize, in the sense owing to Gaston Bachelard, one of Laplanche's professors at the École Normale Supérieure, is to specify a truth or a concept *along with* the conditions for its emergence and persistence, to specify its domain and its articulations with what it does and what it does not address, and to specify the surrounding concepts and the historical context which limit, shape, underlie, and infiltrate it.]

react to this publication in two ways. The apparent classicism of the ideas, my frequent recourse to critical commentary on Freudian texts, and the repetitions and recapitulations (which are unavoidable when one is addressing a largely new audience every year) may lead some to dismiss these texts as an extreme example of the widely decried "Freudian exegesis." Others, I hope, will summon enough patience and generosity to get in step with the rhythm of my thought and will thus perhaps appreciate certain deepenings of my thought, certain breakthroughs I have made, or the way in which, by placing great weight on the turning points in Freud's thinking, I derive certain concepts. My approach is a way of making Freudian thought work in every sense of the word.[2]

Three models can help us understand both this way of making Freud's thought work and the "faithful infidelity" that guides my approach: *exigency, the spiral,* and *going astray*.

Exigency. Here the exigency is not primarily that of Freud the thinker, however rigorous he was; it is the demand that comes from the object of his thinking, that imperious object that fascinated him from his earliest work until the end of his life. The object that imposed this exigency was the unconscious: simultaneously undeniable and yet always impossible to grasp completely. We can, nevertheless, say certain things about this unconscious, notably that it is incontestably sexual.

The spiral. The spiral is a curve whirling itself around a fixed orienting point. At regular intervals, the spiral of thought circles back to the vertical of the same problem. At every turn, the problem is enriched or even changes its premises and, on each turn, the problem takes off from the previous turn and marks a progression.

---

2 [Laplanche writes:"*faire travailler*" *la pensée freudienne*—a phrase often translated as 'putting Freudian thought to work'. That translation seems to me to miss half of what is intended, to miss the sense of fixing something, of making something work that previously hadn't worked or hadn't worked well.]

* [See Editorial Note on terminology pages xix–xxi]

Going astray.[3] In the end, going astray is inseparable from the exigency of which it is a consequence: a mountain climber, drawn onward by a peak lost in clouds, takes a wrong turn and finds himself before an impasse. Should he impetuously continue or prudently retrace his steps to the last fork in the road? If so, at what cost?

Spotting and describing such goings astray yield a clearer account of fundamental problematics, which otherwise are often hidden in the labyrinth of concepts. This way of *problematizing* a doctrine rehearsed all too often allows another, more rarified *theme* to emerge, a theme I have baptized "the General Theory of Seduction," which I will develop in other books and articles.

3 [As Laplanche notes in the first sentence of this paragraph, "going astray" (*fourvoiement*) does not refer to a random error or sloppy thinking. It is a wrong turn inspired or dictated by the very object of thought. This is particularly important for Laplanche's analysis of Freud's account of sexuality, which he detailed in the lectures immediately following those in this volume. These were published as *Problématiques VII : Le fourvoiement biologisant de la sexualité chez Freud*. An English translation, by Donald Nicholson-Smith, entitled *The Temptation of Biology: Freud's Theories of Sexuality*, has been released by The Unconscious in Translation. See UITBooks.com.]

November 28, 1989

The teaching I resume today, one of the three courses required for the DEA [diplôme d'études approfondies],[4] *has peculiarities and difficulties. A DEA course must, in my opinion, be concerned with what is at the forefront of current research. If it were not, where else in the university would psychoanalytic research be taught? So this cannot be an introductory course, and those among you who do not have a sufficient familiarity with the conceptual background will not find the basics spelled out except incidentally. This course is a model, a sample of the research of the particular teacher, and therefore may not coincide with your interests or with the topic of your dissertation. It is a way of trying to convey my own ideas. In addition, it is part of the development of my own ideas, a development that I must presume that you know at least partially. Some of you have been attending my seminar for years, and others are here for the first time. Every year there are new students who, being only partially informed, have the problem of boarding a train that is already in motion. So in a course of this type, how can I reconcile my ambition to elaborate the latest aspects of what I am investigating with a desire to provide access to basics? To address this tension, I offer three thoughts:*

First, I hope you will find that my discourse is always clear, that when possible I give references and explanations, and that, as far as time permits, I am ready to answer questions and requests for clarification—even during my presentation but preferably at the end of class or at the beginning of the next class.

Second, I ask those who want a better understanding of what I will discuss to learn the basics of my thought. For what we will examine this year, that means reading certain articles in The Language of Psycho-Analysis, *articles which are quite old but still valuable, and two small books:* Life and Death in Psychoanalysis, *itself an old text, and* New Foundations for

4 [Roughly equivalent to the master's degree given to doctoral students after their first year or two of study.]

Psychoanalysis, *published two years ago, which is the starting point for my current thinking.*[5]

A third consideration touches closely on the subject of this year's course, namely my own connection to the theme, which is to say to time, to the time of thought. I do not conceptualize the work of thought, or any other work, as following the arrow of time (we will frequently refer to the idea of an "arrow of time"). The train of a thought does not travel in a straight line like an arrow. It follows a movement I call "spiral" but that, in reality, is a helix.

This means that the life of human beings, and especially the movement of their thought, is neither linear, constantly leaving one point to pass on to another, nor circular, constrained to repeat the same sequences. The movement of a spiral constantly distances itself from one pole, but at the same time, it is led to return again and again to points along the same vertical. Returning to a vertical, one is led to reconsider the same themes at another and higher level.

All of that is to say that there is nothing completely new in what I will say and that, like everyone else, I will be led to repeat myself and will even find, with astonishment, that I have said it all before, but in a completely different way.

THEORIES OF SEDUCTION AND THE THEORY OF TIME

I asked you to take the trouble of reading some texts and especially *New Foundations for Psychoanalysis*, which elaborates what I call "the General Theory of Seduction," on the basis of which, for the past three years, I have detailed the development of what could be called "elements for a philosophy of time." In German these might be called *Bausteine*, "building blocks," for a philosophy of time.

Why time, and why time based on the General Theory of Seduction? Well, in my thinking, there is an intimate connection

5 [A new English translation, to be published by The Unconscious in Translation, is in press.]

between the two. The theory of seduction is itself a thought about time. It is, as I will explain, a *translational* theory of time. Thus, it opens up a new conception, a new philosophy of time. Here, when I speak about time, I am speaking about time for the individual human being. Of course, I am framing it in relation to other types of time, for example cosmological time and biological time, and even historical time, but my focus is on human time, on time for the individual human, on the temporalization of the human being. Each human being temporalizes himself in the sense proposed by Heidegger. I am exploring that same domain but from a completely different perspective.

For this year's course, I had first suggested the title "Time and the Other" ["Le temps et l'autre"].[6] Titles launch themselves, leap forward, and then they work out or they don't. I will try to express what I wanted to say with that title as a hypothesis even though, for the moment, I won't develop it further. *The human being,* I would say, *temporalizes himself because—and to the extent that—he is in an originary relation to an other.* A philosophy of time arising from psychoanalysis must lead to this originary relation with the other. Of course, this refers to the other of seduction, the other who, from the start, injects the human being with enigmatic messages. I could say the same thing in another way: the engine of temporalization for each human being is the relation with the first other. To be clear, I am not referring to an abstract other. Let me emphasize that to use Other with a capital *O*, the Other in Lacan's sense, is entirely out of the question here. In the theory of originary seduction, the "other" is precisely the specific adult who was an "other" for the child—whom one can call "transcendent" if one likes, in the sense that he delivers enigmatic messages, enigmatic for the receiver *and* for the sender.

6 I then found the same title, but with quite different ideas, in a little book by Emmanuel Levinas. To avoid creating problems of precedence, I abandoned the title.

APRÈS-COUP IN THE HISTORY OF THE CONCEPT OF APRÈS-COUP

All this has been to highlight my thesis about "time and the other" as something that must be clarified but that I will not discuss at the start. My specific topic, in the context of this exploration of time, will be the concept of après-coup, something I have spoken of many times but that I will take up again and refine – and here you can see the spiral movement.

Another possible title for this year's course would be "*Nachträglichkeit* in après-coup." What do I mean by that? It is certainly not a play on words for the pleasure of doing so. Après-coup is the current translation of *Nachträglichkeit,* but to say "après-coup in the après-coup" would be tautological; what I mean is Freud's *Nachträglichkeit* understood in terms of the movement of après-coup. As a title, "*Nachträglichkeit* in the Après-coup" would touch on two points: the first point is that the history of the concept of *Nachträglichkeit* is inseparable from *Nachträglichkeit* itself. This is to say that its history, like the history of every concept, is a history of development within its après-coup. It is immersed in après-coup in many ways. One could fairly say that the history of *Nachträglichkeit* since Freud—its history since its beginnings in Freud and up to the present—is itself the best example of *Nachträglichkeit*. Freud once said that the example is the thing itself—a quite Hegelian formulation. Well, the history of the concept *Nachträglichkeit* is, as you will see, inhabited by and animated by *Nachträglichkeit* itself.

The second point is that my title is in two languages. While I could have said, "Après-coup in the Après-coup," using two languages serves to underline the essential function of translation in this history of *Nachträglichkeit*. The après-coup of *Nachträglichkeit*'s history is inseparable from its translational fate, from its translations—not only the translation of the word, but also the translation of the thought.

To say that *Nachträglichkeit* is a Freudian concept requires putting quotation marks both around "concept" and, equally, around "Freudian." Quotation marks around "concept" because, like most important concepts, it reveals itself only in its history, in its famous après-coup. What about the assertion that it is "Freudian"? It is both pre-Freudian and post-Freudian in so far as, coming from diverse positions, we create a usage of this Freudian concept après-coup. In Freud's own work, *nachträglich* and *Nachträglichkeit* are utterly caught up in a complicated history, a history of eclipses, with moments of erasure and with reprises. One can, at least initially, consider these eclipses and reprises as occurring more or less in parallel to the reprises and eclipses of the theory of seduction. But, as you will see, when we look closely—and we will try to examine them *quite* closely—it is not so simple as that.

There is a quasi-total eclipse, an obliteration of *Nachträglichkeit*, that hits the concept in the *Complete Works*[7] and notably in their indexes. It is absent from the indexes of the *Gesammelte Werke*, which are the complete works in German, notably the indexes of volume I, II, and III and also the general index, which is quite impoverished. The index of the English edition, the *Standard Edition*, is no better. This reflects an important truth: concepts cannot be indexed unless they are noticed. The new French edition of the *Œuvres complètes* aims to correct these lacunae, which first requires the working out of a view as to how concepts should be grouped; work that cannot done by a computer search or by a simple selection of terms.

Having closed this parenthesis, I return to the kind of eclipse or scotomization of *nachträglich* and of *Nachträglichkeit* in the indexes, even the German indexes. Such scotomization cannot be merely the fault of the editors. It is Freud's doing, not positive but negative; without hiding the concept, he did nothing to foreground it. I imagine that if Freud had been asked to make a list of his concepts for an index to

7 [Laplanche is referring to the various collections of Freud's works—in all languages—that had been published at the time this lecture was given.]

his complete works, *Nachträglichkeit* would have come very, very far after many others, at least during the last period of his thought. I have been told—I'd love to know if it's true; I haven't seen it—that there is an exchange of letters with Ferenczi on this point, which is to say a question from Ferenczi about après-coup.

THE REVIVAL OF APRÈS-COUP IN FRANCE

In any case, the first and the most important après-coup of *Nachträglichkeit* is its après-coup in France. It is an après-coup that is at the same time an après-coup of translation—and that has important significance. The author of this inaugural après-coup was Lacan, who, with his sureness of gaze, noticed, as he did so often, an essential point. It was his "Report from Rome"[8] of September 1953. (In a historical exposition like this, even if developments are parsed dialectically, the question of dates is interesting.) Nineteen fifty-three isn't yesterday. The second underlining of après-coup, also French, was the work of Laplanche and Pontalis, later continued by Laplanche alone. This occurred a decade later in "Primal Fantasy, Fantasies of Origins, Origins of Fantasy"[9] by Laplanche and Pontalis in 1964; *The Language of Psycho-Analysis*[10] in 1967, with an article specifically on après-coup and many other articles that refer to it; and then *Life and Death in Psychoanalysis*[11] in 1970. The contribution of this conceptual work—

8 ["Report from Rome" is the customary way of referring to "The Function and Field of Speech and Language in Psychoanalysis," which can be found in English in *Écrits*, trans. Bruce Fink (New York: Norton, 2006), 197–268. Except where noted, Fink's translation has been used without modification for all of the Lacan passages.]

9 [Jean Laplanche and J.-B. Pontalis, "Primal Fantasy, Fantasies of Origins, Origins of Fantasy" (including the 1984 postscript) trans. Jonathan House, in Dominique Scarfone, *Laplanche: an introduction* (New York: The Unconscious in Translation, 2015), 71; an earlier (problematic) translation, without the postscript, was entitled "Fantasy and the Origins of Sexuality," *International Journal of Psychoanalysis* 49 (1968): 1–18.]

10 [Jean Laplanche and J.-B. Pontalis, *The Language of Psycho-Analysis*, trans. Donald Nicholson-Smith (New York: Norton, 1973).]

11 [Jean Laplanche, *Life and Death in Psychoanalysis*, trans. Jeffrey Mehlman (Baltimore: Johns Hopkins University Press, 1979).]

Laplanche and Pontalis theorized après-coup completely differently than did Lacan—is the reinsertion of *nachträglich* into the theory of seduction, a contribution in which Lacan had no part.

All the same, we must remember this: a moment ago I said that the index of the *Gesammelte Werke* is impoverished, yet it was published in 1968. You can easily see that, up to the present day, neither Lacan's "Report from Rome" nor the work of Laplanche and Pontalis has had the slightest influence on the international development of psychoanalytic thought, or on the way Freud has been understood.[12] It is not completely false to say that the "return to Freud" is a French return.

LACAN AND HEIDEGGER

Now I'll remind you of and try to comment on that text by Lacan, which is extremely interesting for what he sees and proposes and is equally interesting for what there is to critique. It is a text on truth, on the historical truth of the anamnesis—the historical truth of a patient's story—and of course on the truth revealed by the patient's story and by the treatment. I will read you a few sentences from pages 212–214 of *Écrits* (for those of you who have other editions, it is in "The Function and Field of Speech and Language in Psychoanalysis"). In the course of the text, we will come to *nachträglich*, to après-coup, but I won't immediately go to that passage or to the problem of translation.

> The condition of continuity in the anamnesis, by which Freud measures the completeness of the cure, has nothing to do with the Bergsonian myth of a restoration of duration.

12 [On this point, see Jonathan House and Julie Slotnick, "Après-coup in French Psychoanalysis: The Long Afterlife of *Nachträglichkeit*: The First Hundred Years, 1893 to 1993," *Psychoanalytic Review* 102, no. 5 (October 2015): 683–708.]

(Lacan was never very pro-Bergsonian; in this he was perhaps justified in some instances and, in others, a bit unjustified. In any case, in France at that time it was mandatory to be violently anti-Bergsonian; now, perhaps, that is a bit less true.)

> Let's be categorical: in psychoanalytic anamnesis, what is at stake is not reality, but truth, because the effect of full speech is to reorder past contingencies by conferring on them the sense of necessities to come, such as they are constituted by the scant freedom through which the subject makes them present.

Clearly this text is extremely well put together. It is a text with a tight connection to Heideggerian thought, and in it one finds Heidegger's three temporal *ekstases*: past, present, and future. You can taste the flavor in that passage:

> . . . to reorder *past* contingencies by conferring on them the sense of necessities *to come*, such as they are constituted by the scant freedom through which the subject makes them *present*.

The sequence is well constructed, but what is amusing is the inversion of contingency that Lacan imposes on the terms for the past and the future, in the sense that contingency, which is usually attributed to the future, is attributed to the past, while necessity is attributed to the future. This is where the proximity to Heidegger can be felt, and as you know, in Heidegger the "necessity" to come is ultimately "being toward death" (*Sein sum Tode*). The past is not considered necessary, but subject to reworking.

What follows concerns the *Wolf Man*, and it is there that Lacan discovers *nachträglich*:

> The meanders of the research pursued by Freud in his account of the case of the Wolf Man confirm these

> remarks by deriving their full meaning from them. Freud demands a total objectification of proof when it comes to dating the primal scene.

Those of you who have read the *Wolf Man* know that one of Freud's objectives is dating the famous primal scene to the month and to the year if possible. I mean to say that Freud is more certain of the month than of the year since the month can be determined, but only with the possibility of displacement of a year. It is certain that the scene happens at Christmas time, and so the exact day is almost certain, but the year is less certain as Christmas comes every year. Indeed, this concern for dating is prominent in the text of the *Wolf Man*. Returning now to the Lacan's text, he writes:

> Freud demands a total objectification of proof when it comes to dating the primal scene, but he simply presupposes all the resubjectifications of the event that seem necessary to him to explain its effects at each turning point at which the subject restructures himself {note the terms "resubjectification" and "restructuring"} that is, as many restructurings of the event, as he puts it, *nachträglich*, après-coup.[13]

So here, in the *Wolf Man,* we have the introduction of *nachträglich,* the rediscovery of a Freudian discovery. In a certain way, Freud himself was probably rediscovering it before it was rediscovered by Lacan, who proposed the translation that subsequently we have not varied: "après-coup." Lacan relies on a text from 1917 (late in relation to the texts that we will soon discuss), which itself is situated in the *nachträglich,* in the après-coup of Freudian thought. In his

13 Laplanche's comments within quotations, as in this passage, are bracketed using braces: i.e. {}. In addition, here Bruce Fink's translation is modified; Fink uses "after the fact" to render Lacan's use of the term "après-coup." In fact, this is the only occurrence of the term "après-coup" in Lacan's "Rapport de Rome."]

footnote referring to the passage, Lacan comments on his own use of après-coup, calling it a feeble translation ["*traduction faible 'du terme'*"). Perhaps he thinks après-coup fails to contain all that *nachträglich* contains, and so he considers it a weak translation. I don't share this opinion and I will come back to that question; for now, let us continue with Lacan:

> What's more, with an audacity bordering on impudence, he declares that he considers it legitimate, in analyzing the process, to elide the time intervals during which the event remains latent in the subject.

That is Lacan's interpretation. Look at the text yourself. It is true that, in this case, Freud is more interested in the turning points than in the intervals of latency; *nachträglich* is precisely made up of active moments and eclipses. Yet here Lacan makes an explicit reference to his own article "Logical Time and the Assertion of Anticipated Certainty,"[14] which appeared in the same collection, to emphasize (perhaps unduly) the "decision to conclude" at the expense of what for us constitutes the essential feature of psychoanalysis: "the time of understanding." In this way too, Lacan remains very close to Heidegger and to what Heidegger called a "resolute decision" (*Entschlossenheit*). Lacan concludes this passage with the words: "This assumption by the subject of his history . . ." These terms are quite dated in the progression of Lacan's thought (for example, "assumption"); by the time of the matheme, Lacan would no longer talk that way.

> This assumption by the subject of his history, insofar as it is constituted by speech addressed to another, is clearly the basis of the new method Freud called psychoanalysis.

---

14 [Lacan, *Écrits*, 161–175.]

Thus it is "speech addressed to another" (which he has just called "full" speech) that permits the subject—in moments of meditation, concluding, and rearranging—to restructure and to reorder past contingencies. This terminology obviously raises questions. This is a philosophy that, without stretching the word, one can call hermeneutic; it is inspired by Heidegger, but, in a certain way, it would not contradict Ricœur, even his recent *Time and Narrative*. This is a philosophy in which speech plays an essential role—as one certainly expects in the "Report from Rome"—but notice that it is speech addressed *to another* and not speech addressed *by the other*. (Thus, there is nothing here concerning an enigmatic signifier.) The idea that time is heterogeneous is certainly crucial—indeed, it is essential. It is an idea which is not remote from or in contradiction to the idea of a spiral, since, conceived as a spiral process, time is not linear but cyclic and includes both eclipses and vivid moments; in such a spiral conception of time, there is an alternation between a past considered as factual and one considered as contingent—a meaning given to the past, a meaning to be constructed retroactively, a meaning serving to reorder a past that is considered factual. This is not the whole of Lacanian thought on historicity; nor—and I want to underline this—is it the whole of Freud's thinking on the subject. Here Lacan takes a snapshot of a single episode of Freudian thought, Freud's account of the case of the Wolf Man. In my opinion, Lacan always failed to pay adequate attention to the first Freudian texts, the texts of 1895–1897. Of course, he occasionally cited the letters to Fliess, the *Project*, etc. But, I am sorry to say, at the very moment that Pontalis and I started to elaborate Freud's thinking about it, Lacan lacked even a basic knowledge about Freud's "theory of seduction." Thus he necessarily didn't offer any reflections on it. The theory of seduction is absent from the Lacanian approach to Freud, at least at first glance, and in my view this is a significant lacuna. In this text, the lacuna ends up creating a dilemma of the same sort as that created by the "horrible debate" between hermeneutists and scientists.[15] Is the past a necessity and the future contingent, and thus is there an absolute determinism in individual history? Or inversely, is it the future that completely restructures the contingencies of the past? In a way, a text like this one is stuck in a dead end, which I will try to manipulate from different sides throughout this exposition on *nachträglich.* The dead end lies in the false dichotomy between two errors: reality as *raw facts* and interpretation as (in the end) *purely retroactive.*

FREUD'S WORDS

Now I come to Freud's *nachträglich*: Does he or doesn't he offer a solution? I will begin by speaking about words. Of course, I won't stop there; this is not a course on the German language. But I must go over a few words that are there on the blackboard and that have considerable importance in this story. Starting from the same root, these words, like most German words, display great richness. But to say that German is richer than French takes admiration too far. Sometimes it's richer, sometimes more limited. Sometimes it is difficult to express a nuance of French in German and vice versa; that is not the issue. It is certain, however, that the German language permits derivations from a single root in a way that the French language would have difficulty allowing.

Our starting point is the verb *tragen,* which means "to carry" and brings with it the idea of movement. Either a real movement or, still in a spatial sense but more metaphorical, a movement in the sense in which one speaks of how far a voice can carry, of the reach of a voice or of an idea. An idea that can go far, *weittragend,* is an idea that carries a long way.

15 [Cf. Jean Laplanche, "Interpretation between Determinism and Hermeneutics," translated by Philip Slotkin in *Essays on Otherness*, ed. John Fletcher (New York: Routledge, 1999), 138–165; and translated by Luke Thurston in *The Unfinished Copernican Revolution*, (New York: The Unconscious in Translation, forthcoming).]

The verb *nachtragen* adds the prefix *nach-* to the idea of carrying. *Nach* usually means "after" and "following," but in some cases it may mean "back" or "backward." Thus, the dictionaries identify three meanings of the word *nachtragen*. I hasten to say that, to my knowledge, the verb *nachtragen* is rarely if ever used by Freud. At least I have never encountered it. There are three confirmed meanings—and it's good news that there aren't more because if there were it would be hard to maintain continuity in translations. Each of the three is constructed both with a direct object—that which one carries: *etwas tragen*—and with a modifier specifying place or time, signifying backward or afterwards:

jemandem	*etwas*	*nachtragen*
to someone (or to something)	something	carry back

Or in a French that is a bit more correct [and in normal English]: "to carry something behind someone." From this, we get the three meanings. The first is quite literal, the second and third more complex:

1. "To carry something back to someone."
2. "To add one thing to another thing afterwards," in the sense of inserting an addition to a book, creating an addendum. For example, volume XVIII of the *Gesammelte Werke* of Freud is called *Nachtragsband*, a "volume of addenda" composed of articles that were not published in the series but is added après-coup.

And finally the third meaning, which is quite interesting, in which

3. "to carry something behind someone" (*jemandem etwas nachtragen*) becomes "to hold a grudge against someone about something."

If you like, for your convenience, keep in mind what Anglophone philosophers call "the arrow of time," which moves from the past toward the future, in contrast to the Seine, which, under *le pont Mirabeau,*[16] flows from the present toward the past. You can see that the games one can play with "*nachtragen*" may involve great ambiguity. No doubt my resentment, my grudge, goes in the opposite direction from the arrow, attaching me to a past injury, but the source of my grudge is well and truly in the past. In the same way, the volume of addenda is a collection of forgotten texts from the past, but the fact that their publication comes afterwards does not diminish the degree to which they modify what came before their publication. An addendum retroactively modifies the group of texts into which it has been inserted.

Then we have the essential term *nachträglich,* which is both an adjective and an adverb, and finally the substantive, quite rare in practice: the "concept" of *Nachträglichkeit.*

***

Question from the audience: Why do you speak of a philosophy of time?

Reply: Let's be clear. There is no "psychoanalysis of time"—indeed, that phrase has no meaning. On the other hand, psychoanalysis has made important contributions that upend all conceptions of time. Is it a "philosophy"? In my opinion, the word is not important, but it is necessary to be clear. What I am trying to do is not a continuation of what Heidegger did, but I am working in the same domain, the domain he explored in *Being and Time*. Clearly, I am starting out from different foundations and have a different perspective.

My perspective is that of the individual human, not of being in general. Mine is not an ontological philosophy but rather an anthropological philosophy. "Anthropology" not in the sense used by anthropologists (which would better be called "ethnology") but in the sense that the word has, for example, in Kant: a body of thought

16 [Laplanche refers to Guillaume Apollinaire's "Le pont Mirabeau." See Appendix 1]

about the essential foundations of the human being. One of these foundations, perhaps the most important one, is the fact of the little human's entry into a world of adults. Is this a contingent fact? On the contrary, it is a "universal" for human beings. And therefore, it makes sense to call it "the fundamental anthropological situation."

December 12, 1989

THE WORD *NACHTRÄGLICH* PUT TO THE TEST OF TRANSLATION INTO FRENCH

My approach to *nachträglich* is simultaneously recapitulative and après-coup. For now, I will continue to focus simply on words. After the verb *nachtragen,* we come to *nachträglich,* both an adverb and an adjective. At first glance, it seems *nachträglich* can be translated simply as "later," or "afterwards," or "subsequently"; as equivalents, German dictionaries give "*später*" and "*späterfolgend,*" which mean "coming afterwards," without mentioning the idea of going back. These definitions are in line with the "arrow of time," which, I remind you once and for all, goes from the past toward the future.

Freud frequently uses the expression "*nachträglicher Gehorsam,*" which he puts in quotation marks and which means "obedience après-coup"—for example, obedience to the dead father or to the superego precisely as a substitute for the father, etc. It would be interesting to learn why Freud puts these words in quotation marks as if it were a well-known expression or a quotation. I don't have the answer, but perhaps one of you will find out. Perhaps he was quoting himself but I don't think so. Perhaps he was borrowing from the domain of posthypnotic suggestion: as you know, one gives a command to the hypnotized subject and, once he wakes up, he "obeys this command après-coup." Thus, it's possible that *nachträglicher Gehorsam* comes from this technical vocabulary.

In fact, you can see that if it were translated using *später*—as *später Gehorsam,* as "later obedience"—there would be a loss of nuance. "Later obedience" is not "obedience après-coup." Obedience après-coup presumes that the past is represented in the present[17] and,

17 [Here Laplanche creates an unusual form of the verb "*presentifier*" derived from "*presentification*"—"the process by which an object is made present (in the form of an image)"—by prefixing it with a "re-," yielding "*representifier.*"]

inversely, also presumes that the subject puts himself back in the past situation. There is much more here than there is in a pure and simple *später*; as we noted in the last class in relation to Lacan, there is the idea of discontinuous time, a time containing blows and shock, moving in fits and starts [*un temps avec des coups ou des à-coups*] as the term "après-coup" suggests. What's more, the verb *tragen* in *nachtragen* indicates that these are blows that are *carried*. Thus a time with "carried blows" and, inversely, interrupted by latencies. Thus, the importance of the French translation and not simply the French discovery; or, more precisely, in the case of après-coup, the French discovery and the French translation are one and the same "coup." One could say the translation comes as a revelation, as a "test by the foreign" ["*épreuve de l'étranger*"], to take up the term Antoine Berman brilliantly introduced to the problematic of translation.[18] A body of thought can put itself to the "test by the foreign"—and here I am talking both about the "foreign" within Freud's thought and also about Freud's thought being put to the "test by the foreign" by its passage into French, a test that always entails discrepancy but also always provides revelations, since *tragen*, "to carry," is not exactly *"le coup"* of French.

In the end, you can see how the two terms are closely related and how "après-coup" is not such a feeble translation since, like *nachträglich* in German, après-coup goes indissociably in the two directions of the arrow of time. For instance, one can say "the scaffolding collapsed après-coup" which is clearly to say something quite different from "the scaffolding collapsed later." Similarly: "he revised his book après-coup" is not the same as "he revised his book later;" and "après-coup, I understood what happened" is to say that, après-coup, an event took on a different significance. We will necessarily stay with the question of translation, not only during this technical exposition of après-coup but throughout this year's course.

Compared with the German, the only weakness of the French

---

18 Antoine Berman, *L'epreuve de l'etranger* . . . (Paris: Gallimard, 1984).

is that initially there wasn't a substantive form of après-coup, only an adverbial form and possibly an adjectival form, as one can easily use the adverb "après-coup" adjectivally—the phrase "obedience après-coup" works perfectly well. In contrast, in German we have the substantive *Nachträglichkeit*—with a capital *N*, of course, and with the suffix *-keit*, which in German is one of the possible ways to form a substantive. Freud could have said *das Nachträgliche*, "that which comes après-coup," but with *die Nachträglichkeit* we have a mode of derivation that implies the term being coined is an independent substantive or even a concept. Is Freud the inventor of this "*Nachträglichkeit*?" I'd say that this is barely a meaningful question, as the German language owns the rights. Nevertheless, there is documentation of substantival forms for some words while for other words documentation is hard to find. Well, *Nachträglichkeit in Freud's sense* is not found in German dictionaries, at least not in the most recent dictionaries I have been able to consult. On the other hand, sometimes *Nachträglichkeit* is given two meanings of quite secondary importance, which, as you will see, do not have the same meaning as the Freudian term: sometimes it is defined as *Verspätung*, "delaying," and sometimes as "*nachtragendes Wesen*," which can be translated as "an unforgiving nature." You have seen that *nachtragen* can mean "hold a grudge," which, after all, is not without importance for our purposes.

In the case of *Nachträglichkeit*, French is compelled to undertranslate or to overtranslate: to undertranslate if one simply says "après-coup," ignoring the difference between *das Nachträgliche* and *die Nachträglichkeit*, to overtranslate if one adds something to "après-coup." As translators of Freud's *Œuvres completes*, even if we sometimes amused ourselves by coining neologisms we could not adopt a barbarism like "*après-coup-ité*." Thus, one is led to add a substantive and at that point it becomes rather arbitrary. In one period of our work, we chose "the effect *of* après-coup" ["*l'effet d'après-coup*"] and not "the après-coup effect" ["*l'effet après-coup*"]. One could also choose "phenomenon" or "process," terms that are certainly not contained in the *-keit* of *Nachträglichkeit,* or alternatively, "the factor of après-coup"— in one place, Freud uses the term *Moment: Moment der Nachträglichkeit* = "the factor of après-coup."[19]

Although these are everyday problems in the kitchen of the translator, the French translation revealed a major concept, and it was the translator who had the first opportunity, even before the German reader, to track the genesis of this nascent concept (precisely in its après-coup) by giving it a unique name.

AND IN ENGLISH?

What about English? We must give equal weight to this question because it is important for the history of the psychoanalytic movement, for the interpretation of Freudian theory, and for other questions that are just as current and just as important as the problem of interpretation. Although we will examine them in detail, these are not abstract questions and they are not the obsessions of a translator—the details lead to the essential. So, entering into detail, remember that *The Standard Edition* was first published between 1953 and 1966, that Strachey died in 1967, and that the index of *The Standard Edition* was published in 1974. Put these dates in relation to the dates I gave for developments in France; they are almost contemporaneous. The notion of après-coup was exhumed (a bad term), was put into relief, was given dignity first by Lacan in his "Report from Rome" of 1953, and then by Laplanche and Pontalis in 1964 and 1967. Although their work was more or less contemporaneous, one cannot criticize Strachey for not having read either Lacan or Laplanche and Pontalis. Given the

19 [The German word is *Moment,* which can be translated as "instance" or as "moment." In *The Interpretation of Dreams,* the sentence reads, "*Ich pflege mich der Anekdote zur Erläuterung für das Moment der Nachträglichkeit in dem Mechanismus der Psychoneurosen zu bedienen.*" Strachey translates *Moment* as "factor": "I was in the habit of quoting this anecdote to explain the factor of 'deferred action' in the mechanism of the psychoneuroses." *SE* 4:204–205.]

delay that exists in the interchange between English and French psychoanalysis, there is good reason for that ignorance, especially if one acknowledges that even today French psychoanalysis continues to be poorly known in Anglophone countries. However, that the Standard Edition's index of 1974 is so impoverished on the subject of après-coup is a serious fault.

In fact, Strachey did spot the term *nachträglich,* and it is indexed under "deferred,"[20] most often with "action"; the substantive *Nachträglichkeit* is rendered "deferred action." I will go a bit further into the details. Because he lacked an adequate translation and an adequate understanding—or should I say a sufficiently inclusive understanding?—Strachey missed the concept. I don't yet have the original source but at a meeting in London a German psychoanalyst told me that in the beginning Strachey (a man of refined insight who was not primarily an analyst—a good reason to credit him with refinement) had proposed a translation that didn't stick, namely: "retroactivity" or "retroactively." It was Jones who had insisted on the terms "deferred" and "deferred action." The idea of retroactivity reverses the arrow of time whereas deferred action follows the arrow of time; clearly that's a place one can find evidence that, as managed by Jones, *The Standard Edition* imposes a "scientific" conception—even a scientistic conception—against a certain hermeneutic interpretation of Freud's works. In addition, we must acknowledge that "retroactivity" would work in only four or five places, and that there are many places where using "retroactivity" would be impossible. To be clear, Strachey makes two errors. One is not following the concept's genesis in Freud's work, beginning with his everyday language. This is partially excusable since Strachey had no access to the correspondence between Freud and Fliess in which one can see the

20 [At this point in the lecture Laplanche said: "I don't know why, but in the *Vocabulaire de la psychanalyse,* [i.e. the French text] 'deferred' is written as 'differed,' an error which has never been corrected." He goes on to explain to his Francophone auditors the difference between the English words 'differ' and 'defer'.]

concept's gestation within the framework of the theory of seduction. The other error is to dissociate, partially according to the context, different meanings of the word—for they are often markedly different. These two errors combine to make the uniqueness of a signifier invisible, a uniqueness that is an essential guide for following the fluctuations of the signified.

Having eliminated the "retroactive," hermeneutic hypothesis on the suggestion of Jones, Strachey was left with the choice of a banal meaning that flattens out *nachträglich* into "later" ("subsequently," "belatedly"[21]) that is to say a meaning conforming to the arrow of time and to a unidirectional conception of the theory of seduction: what was inscribed in childhood remains latent until a later time when it exerts a "deferred action." This is what I call the theory of the time bomb, the second event being strictly determined by the first, of which it is the pure and simple consequence. And here let's underline the fact that, in spite of all the ambiguities which we will examine in detail, such a theory is never at work in Freud. The word "afterwards," which is very close to "après-coup," appears once, but only in Masson's translation of the Freud-Fliess correspondence. I will permit myself to legislate for the English language by proposing this specific and excellent term—at least for the English translation of some of my own writings. In addition, in English there is the almost limitless possibility of creating substantives with the suffix *-ness*. From this, I propose the pair of terms: afterwards / afterwardsness. I hope they will become the rule with all the theory they entail.[22]

---

21 ["Subsequently" and "belatedly" are in English in the French text as examples of Strachey's translations.]

22 [Since Laplanche gave these lectures and since his 1992 paper "Notes on Après-coup" in *Between Seduction and Inspiration: Man* (New York: The Unconscious in Translation, 2015) in which he makes the same suggestion, "après-coup" has become the standard English translation both of the German *Nachträglichkeit* and of the French *après-coup*. See the Translator's Note on page xv.]

IN FREUD: A SYNCOPATED HISTORY

Now I will spend some time on the complex history of *nachträglich* in Freud's writing. There is a simultaneous evolution of a body of thought and of a term; two evolutions that are in no way parallel, but can be seen as syncopated. "Syncopated"—we could play with this term, which comes from the Greek *kopto*, "to cut" [*couper*]. In French [as in English], "*syncope*" has two meanings. In cardiology it means a "momentary stop," a pause in the heartbeat, a temporary cardiac arrest—possibly a permanent arrest, but in principle it is only momentary—and then the heart resumes its rhythm.[23] The other meaning is musical[24], mostly in relation to rhythm, and is defined as follows (this is the best definition I was able to find): "a note begun on an offbeat or a weak phrase and continued into the downbeat." (I am many things but I am not a musician, so I am ashamed to use a musical effect as an analogy.) What is important is that in musical syncopation there are two times and that the note is played on the offbeat, let's say at the end of a measure, and further that the note is continued into the downbeat of the next measure. In jazz, the phenomenon of "swing" is nothing but syncopation. The "syn-", the "with" of syncopation, is essential, which is to say there is no syncopation if there are not two lines: the line of the underlying rhythm and the line of the melody, and then the play of one in relation to the other. The play of two rhythmic chains, one in relation to the other, the melodic chain played against and winning out over the chain of the rhythm of the regular measure. *Syncope* in the sense of a momentary arrest becomes musical syncopation precisely in the play of these two rhythmic chains.

---

23 [The American Heart Association defines 'syncope' as a "temporary loss of consciousness and posture, described as "fainting" or "passing out." It's usually related to temporary insufficient blood flow to the brain. It most often occurs when the blood pressure is too low (hypotension) and the heart doesn't pump a normal supply of oxygen to the brain."]

24 [In English, the use of "syncope" to mean musical syncopation is outdated, thus "syncopation" is used in what follows.]

LOCATING A CONCEPT

Already present in the evolution of the concept is its content, which is to say its parts, the doubled part, the two chains and, equally, the play between them. In Freud, this history also raises the question of what concepts can be called Freudian concepts, a question that has recently been revived apropos of problems of translation. "What is a concept?" Alongside explicit concepts, the translator is constantly confronted by the question of so-called *implicit* concepts. What constitutes an explicit concept? At what point can an explicit concept be said to exist? It's not so simple. If there is agreement that *Verdrängung* (repression) is a Freudian concept, terms as common as *Angst* (anxiety) or *Zwang* (compulsion) have recently been refused the status of "concept" in being refused a unique translation. Let's say that what makes a concept in Freud's work is the obligation to translate it in the same way, in a way that reveals the underlying continuity. Thus, in Freud, alongside explicit concepts—and a moment ago I cited one of the most obvious examples, that of "repression"—one comes across something like "quasi-concepts." There is something that, as we say, "makes a concept," and it always makes the concept après-coup. This is to say that it is in the après-coup of reading of Freud's texts, and, of course, equally in the après-coup of the development of Freud's thought, that something comes together to make a concept. An example is the notion of leaning-on [*étayage*] (*Anlehnung*). Many others turn up in the course of translating Freud: "overcoming" [*surmontement*] to render Freud's *Überwindung; Sehnsucht* translated as "longing" [*désirance*]. Only this morning, while leafing through the letters to Fliess, did I find '*Schnsucht*' wrongly translated as '*désir*' in manuscript J, one of the earliest manuscripts."

RETURN TO APRÈS-COUP

Even in Freud, the evolution of the notion of après-coup is syncopated, marked by periods of blackout followed by rebirth where one wouldn't expect it; the evolution puts more than one complex series into play, puts them into play precisely as syncopated in relation to each other. There is an evolution of the content in relation to the evolution of the signifier, by which I simply mean that at certain times the idea of après-coup is present although the term is scarcely used, and at other times the term appears when one wouldn't expect it. And then, within the signifier itself, there is another play of syncopation: between the everyday meaning or meanings, the *Sprachgebrauch*, and the tendency toward conceptualization, which is most marked by the formation of the substantive, *Nachträglichkeit*. But the concept can appear without the formation of a substantive.

This is extremely complex, but we cannot abbreviate it. As Freud wrote, "I would gladly do without all these complications, but, as you know, *Que messieurs les assassins commencent*." That is a phrase written precisely in this context, which is amusing to find there in the letter to Fliess on April 6, 1897.[25] It is quite well explained by Masson, the editor of the letters to Fliess, but until Masson's work, the phrase had only been spotted in *Civilization and its Discontents* in relation to aggression and the death penalty. Freud says approximately this: I agree with the representative in the Assemblée nationale who, in a moment of silence during a debate on the death penalty, stood up and said: "I would favor giving up the death penalty but let those gentlemen who are murderers start first."

What is particularly interesting here is that Freud's memory is in error. Apparently, this was not part of a real debate but rather a scene from *Les guêpes*, a novel by Alphonse Karr which was published in 1840. My scholarship comes from Masson and I won-

25 [*The Complete Letters of Sigmund Freud to Wilhelm Fliess, 1887–1904*, trans. and ed. Jeffrey Masson (Cambridge, MA: Harvard University Press, 1985), page 235.]

der if there was a debate about the death penalty before 1840. It is remarkable to see Freud transpose into reality, into a real session of the Assemblée, a sentence from a novel. Furthermore, the first time Freud uses this quotation, in the letter to Fliess, it is completely metaphorically, for an epistemological point along these lines: I would gladly relinquish all these complications if reality itself would start by not being complicated. Here I find myself in the same situation: if the reality were not so complex, I wouldn't be forced to give an account of so many complications.

THREE PERIODS IN FREUD

It is fair to say the explanation must be complicated because the reality is extremely complicated, and so I will try (rapidly when it is possible) to follow this syncopation, this après-coup of "après-coup," in texts of three periods:

1. The texts from before 1900.
2. A passage from *The Interpretation of Dreams* (*Die Traumdeutung*); only fifteen lines but extremely interesting.
3. The text of the *Wolf Man*.

Since I don't want to leave you completely at sea, I will clarify the issue—*falsely*, of course—by trying to distinguish the nuances of the terms from the beginning, but only in order to say that we will work over these nuances until they disappear.

The first meaning of *nachträglich*, I will call it *meaning A*, is simply the sense of "later," "added," or "secondary," a meaning following the arrow of time without questioning it. The major example is Freud's use of the notion of secondary consciousness [*conscience secondaire*], *nachträgliches Bewusstsein*, which is to say a conscious awareness après-coup. Such secondary consciousness is an awareness that is added to a mental phenomenon; primary consciousness is the awareness of perception.[26] We may have reason to come back to this point, but for Freud, it seems there is no causal relation between primary consciousness and secondary consciousness. In addition, there is no relationship of retroactivity, at least not in Freud's texts; Strachey translates such passages using the words *subsequently* or *subsequent*, indicating an awareness that comes later.

Meaning B is essential to Freud's seduction theory. I will call it a *deferred secondary effect*, which describes—and we will examine this in detail—a memory that acts après-coup with more force than did the event of which it is the memory. This theory omits any retroactivity, at least from the economic point of view. Later I will come back to this, the most economic aspect, the most mechanistic aspect of the theory of seduction. But it is only one aspect of that theory. Strachey generally translates this second meaning, which I call B for the present expository needs, as "deferred."

We can distinguish a third, much more interesting meaning, *meaning C*, which entails an understanding of après-coup. Memories are understood après-coup. This aspect of Freud's thought is closest

---

26 [See the following excerpt of "Letter from Freud to Fliess, January 1, 1896" in *The Complete Letters* page 160:
"According to this view, the perceptual processes would *eo ipso* [by their very nature] involve consciousness and would only produce their further psych[ic] effects after becoming conscious. The ψ processes themselves would be unconscious and would only après-coup [*nachträglich*] acquire a secondary, artificial consciousness through being linked with processes of discharge and perception (speech association). . . . It is much easier today to understand the rule of defense, which does not apply to perceptions but only to ψ processes. The fact that secondary consciousness lags behind makes it possible to give a simple description of the processes of neuroses." (Translation modified.)

Gesammelte Werke, 18S:479: "*Demnach würden die Wahrnehmungsvorgänge eo ipso Bewußtsein involvieren und erst nach dem Bewußtwerden ihre weiteren psychischen Wirkungen üben, die ψ Vorgänge wären an und für sich unbewußt und würden ein sekundäres, artifizielles Bewußtsein erst nachträglich erhalten, indem sie mit Abfuhr- und Wahrnehmungsvorgänge verknüpft werden (Sprachassoziation). . . . Die Abwehrregel, die für Wahrnehmungen nicht gilt, sondern bloß für ψ Vorgänge, versteht man heute viel leichter. Das Nachhinken des sekundären Bewußtseins gestattet, die Neurosenvorgänge einfach zu beschreiben.*"]

to what can be called *retroactivity*, a meaning that seems to reverse the arrow of time since the meaning of an event at time number one does not appear—or is not given to the event—until time number two. We will see a few examples of this *nachträglich*. Notice that I said *seems* to reverse the arrow of time, as I don't want rush into saying, nor push Freud into saying, what he does not in fact say. In several passages, this way of understanding après-coup, of understanding *nachträglich*, could indeed be well translated by "retroactive" and this retroactive meaning is also present in Freud's everyday language. I have identified a few instances from his most informal language, in the letters to Fliess, for example when he writes such sentences as: it was only après-coup that I realized a period[27] appeared in just such an illness in one of my intimates.

APRÈS-COUP BEFORE 1900: THE CASE OF ELIZABETH VON R.

First let's follow the texts from 1895 until just before the *Traumdeutung*. Identifying instances of après-coup is a complicated matter: sometimes it is the word, sometimes the idea. Furthermore, we know both that the idea is difficult to grasp and that the word is sometimes used in a completely banal way. The first reference to après-coup is in the case of Elizabeth von R. in *Studies on Hysteria*, already mentioned by Strachey as the first appearance of "deferred action." To speak of the chronology, I would point out that although *Studies on Hysteria* was published in 1895, it was written well before that date and reflects a collaboration between Freud and Breuer. From the correspondence, it seems that the histories had been completed in May–June of 1894. So it was in the middle of 1894 that *nachträglich* appeared for the first time in a context that is important for our purposes. In the case of Elizabeth von R., there are issues related to nursing an invalid. This, as

27 The periods of Fliess are periods of twenty-eight or twenty-three days. Freud is in the midst of a discussion of Fliess's theory of masculine and feminine periods, and the passage is part of that discussion. [This may be a paraphrase by Laplanche; in any case, the source in the Freud-Fliess correspondence is obscure.]

you know, was a situation Freud frequently encountered in his cases of hysteria: a person exhausted by spending hours with an invalid, even an invalid who is dying, sometimes a father, etc.[28]

In cases of those nursing an invalid, Freud is led to interpret in terms of Breuer's notion of "retention hysteria." This is to say that during the time of caring for the relative, the affects of the nurse are stored up, their expression is blocked, and so they are not abreacted; the nurse cannot spare time to indulge in sadness or other feelings, including the possibility of feeling love or even joy. The caretaker doesn't have the time, and it is not convenient to give in to affects or their expression, which is an essential integrating part of affects. Thus, the affects are stored up, retained: *Retentionshysterie* is the term employed by both Freud and Breuer.

This frame of explication is indeed marked by Breuer's way of thinking. There is kind of stasis conceived as a stasis of energy. Something is locked up, cannot be freed, and will not be freed until later when the work of caring for the invalid is over, for example if the invalid dies. Here, for the first time, Freud employs the term *nachträgliche Erledigung,* which we translated as "settlement après-coup" (*liquidation après-coup*[29]). At first glance, "settlement" seems to be a purely economic explanation in the Breuero-Freudian manner of the time: an excess of energy must find normal paths of discharge. In fact, the passage is much richer than that, and because as I've told you it was badly translated, to give you an idea, I will read a little bit translating as I go. It is on page 229 of *Gesammelte Werke*:

---

28 [At this point in the French text, Laplanche writes: "You will find these issues on pages 128–129 of the [first] French edition, and on pages 228–229 of the *Gesammelte Werke* [on pages 162–163 of *The Standard Edition.*] The French translation is extremely bad. The more one rereads it, the worse it appears. Happily, in a few years, you will have a good translation. While you wait, read the German, and then go back to the translations. You should not skip the translations if, as I am trying to explain, translation is a moment in the life of a work, a moment of the après-coup of a work."]

29 [The German word *Erledigung* can be translated as "settlement" or "completion," the French *liquidation* as "settlement" or "payment" or "elimination."]

> We also occasionally come across this same fact of the traumas accumulated during sick-nursing being settled with subsequently [*nachträglichen Erledigung*], where we get no general impression of illness but where the mechanism of hysteria is nevertheless retained. Thus I am acquainted with a highly gifted lady who suffers from slight nervous states and whose whole character bears evidence of hysteria, though she has never had to seek medical help or been unable to carry on her duties. She has already nursed to the end three or four of those whom she loved. Each time she reached a state of complete exhaustion, but she did not fall ill after these efforts, after fulfilling these tragic tasks. But, shortly after the death of each one, there would begin in her a work of reproduction {*die Reproduktionsarbeit*} which once more brought up before her eyes the scenes of the illness and the death. Every day she would go through each impression once more, would weep over it and console herself—at her leisure, one might say. This process of settling with [*Erledigung*] her affects was dovetailed into her everyday tasks without the two activities interfering with each other.
>
> In addition to these "tears that look backward" [*nachholenden Träne*] with which she made up arrears and which followed close upon the fatal termination of the illness, this lady celebrated annual festivals of remembrance. . . .[30]

Further on, Freud speaks of the work of memory, *Errinerungsarbeit,* and a few lines before in a passage that I didn't read out loud, he speaks explicitly of mourning. (I have already underlined the term "work of reproduction.")

30 [*SE* 2:162. Quotation extended. Translation modified.]

You see how rich the passage becomes. While at first it seemed there was only a question of emptying out affects, a tank needing to be emptied, it becomes much more interesting when one introduces notions that are as central to an interpretation of Freud as the notion of "mourning" and the "work of memory." The term "the work of mourning" is not yet there, but the idea is certainly present.

Since I said that in addition to following the ideas I would also *follow the words*, now I turn to the term "*nachträglich*," which arrived in this way and is, as Strachey notes, its first occurrence.

A few lines further on, we have the eloquent expression *nachholende Träne*, "tears that look backward" [*larmes qui vont chercher en arriere*]. This word is a combination of *nach* (of *nachträglich*) and the verb *holen*. There is also *einholen*, which means to go searching in the sense of "to recapture" [*rattraper*]. German dictionaries offer phrases such as "to make up for après-coup," "to redo," "to recover something that has been neglected" as synonyms for the verb *nachholen*. In Freud, *nachholen* could well have undergone a conceptual elaboration resembling that of *nachträglich*. For *nachholen*, the dictionary even gives equivalents that include the important notion of work, *Arbeit nacharbeiten*, to rework, to work après-coup, and *sich (etwas) nachträglich erarbeiten*, to acquire something après-coup by working.

APRÈS-COUP BEFORE 1900: *PROJECT FOR A SCIENTIFIC PSYCHOLOGY* (1895)

The next stage is the *Project for a Scientific Psychology* of 1895. One could say that between May-June of 1894 and the end of 1895 there was a long syncope, a long period of latency, all the more important because during that syncope the writing of the final chapters of *Studies on Hysteria* was begun—the cases and their write-ups had been finished long before—and what was important above all was that Freud gave Breuer the task of composing the chapter on "theoretical" issues while keeping most of the clinical chapters and the chapter on

"The Psychotherapy of Hysteria" for himself. I will take this opportunity to say that questions raised by Breuer's thought have never really been *"durcharbeitet,"* worked through, and we have been left with false approximations, as in the Anglophone literature, or with accurate but fragmentary information such as I myself can give. The fact that Breuer's thinking and Freud's thinking were completely different means that Breuer's thought is worthy of attention in itself. That Freud gave the chapter on theory to Breuer does not mean that Freud agreed with Breuer. Just because Freud later suggested that his thinking coincided with Breuer's doesn't mean that is true. In fact, his leaving the theoretical chapter to Breuer shows that, rather than discussing it word by word and step by step, he preferred to give Breuer free rein to take a different position—and that is what happened. If someone were to work on this (it would make a very good thesis), one could explore Breuer's thought as such, emphasizing the differences from Freud's thinking. There is enough information available, but the work has not yet been done.

In a certain sense, the theoretical chapter that Freud did not write for *Studies on Hysteria* is the *Project for a Scientific Psychology,* which has the same function, at least in Freud's own evolution, although we must remember that it never saw the light of day before the 1950s.[31] The *Project* was written during September and October of 1895 and was revealed along with Freud's correspondence with Fliess. Currently, the best German edition is that of the *Gesammelte Werke, Nachtragsband* (where one finds the word *Nachtrag*), a volume of texts discovered après-coup, published après-coup, and currently being translated into French. Finally, we must take a look at the German text, and I'll help you a little bit with another off-the-cuff and not very good translation. This is still our situation in 1989. The *Project* of

31 [Here the French text has *"les années 1930"* but the *Project* was first published in German in 1950 and in English translation a few years later. Perhaps Laplanche is referring to Marie Bonaparte's purchase of Freud's letters to Fliess from Fliess's widow but, in my view, it is more likely Laplanche's typo or the copy editor's error.]

September through October, sent to Fliess along with the letters, contains three parts that are useful for situating and giving the context for the ideas.

The first part has no title and appears under the heading "General Scheme" (*Allgemeiner Plan*). It is the part referred to most frequently, Freud's famous metaphsychology-metaphysiology with the description of the neuronal apparatus. Freud's heading for the second part is "Psychopathology" and in fact it is limited to a single chapter entitled "The Psychopathology of Hysteria." The third part is entitled "Attempt to Represent Normal Ψ Processes," an attempt to articulate a normal psychology concerning issues of the conscious, the unconscious, etc. What is interesting and surprising about the date of the *Project*, in which we find the first great exposition of the theory of seduction, is that the term *nachträglich* appears four times in the adverbial form. (You will see that the substantive doesn't appear until much later). Three times in the third part about normal psychology, and to use the A, B, and C labels to refer to the different meanings, always with meaning A, which is to say that in these three instances Freud uses *nachträglich* to modify the term secondary consciousness: a "later" or "secondary" consciousness, or one that comes at a second time. Here, *nachträglich* is translated as"subsequently," which is to say "afterwards" or "secondarily."

CONSCIOUSNESS IN THE *PROJECT*

I will be a little didactic so that those of you who are not "au courant" (I have not explained it this year) are not left in the dark. This "secondary consciousness" is explained by the fact that for Freud consciousness is linked to perception; all consciousness must be accompanied by perception and by an excitation of the perceptual apparatus. Thus, primary consciousness is perceptual consciousness, the consciousness of the external world (parenthetically, notice that this notion completely contradicts the idea of a human being starting out entirely shut up in himself.) For Freud, as for phenomenology, the human is conscious of something from the beginning: conscious of perception, conscious of the world.

So how do we have consciousness of our own mental processes, since it would seem that they are in themselves discharges, purely economic and mechanical processes? Freud's solution is that we are only conscious of mental processes when they are attached, in a discontinuous, syncopated fashion, to words. This is to say that from time to time a word pronounced internally is grafted onto a mental process that is difficult to describe. For example, consider Lagache's work on verbal hallucinations. In his book *Verbal Hallucinations and Speech*, he asks whether we pronounce the words we are thinking.[32] Is there thought without language, and, going further, is there thought without words that are pronounced and perceived? The idea of secondary consciousness in Freud entails [a mental process grafted onto internally pronounced words]. It is not a question of asserting that all thinking is language but rather that, from time to time during a mental process that is itself continuous (a group of conductions), a word is pronounced internally and throws a halo around itself, and by such discontinuous points of illumination—in other words, by the words that are pronounced and perceived—the group of mental processes is illuminated. This is what Freud calls *nachträgliches Bewusstsein*, consciousness après-coup. You see that we are, a priori, quite far from a theory of après-coup that implies coming and going along the arrow of time. The meaning of *nachträglich* in these three instances allows Strachey to translate using a single term, "subsequently," and permits him to dissociate the concept of *nachträglich*.

In contrast, Freud uses the term *nachträglich just one time* in the context of the second part, "The Psychopathology of Hysteria." It occurs in a passage I have commented on extensively in *Life and Death*

---

32 *Les hallucinations verbales et la parole* (Paris: Félix Alcan, 1934).

in Psychoanalysis. I hope you will read it; it's in the first section.[33] Of course, I will give you some sense of it in the next class, but I will not repeat my explanation of the famous case of Emma. I will give you a few insights from the angle of après-coup.

33 [Laplanche, *Life and Death*, 38–41.]

December 19, 1989

To demonstrate the complex movement of *approximation* of a Freudian concept, I will follow Freud's texts chronologically. As we will see, "approximation" is the right word in as much as the movement does not reach a final conclusion and leaves the domain to us, the post-Freudians, for the après-coup of this concept. It will take longer than I had expected; I have been forced to slow myself down to make these things accessible to those of you for whom they are not familiar.

Last week, I left off at the *Entwurf* of September-October 1895, called *Project for a Scientific Psychology*, in which "*nachträglich*" appears only four times: *three times* in the sense of "consciousness *après-coup*," that is to say, "secondary consciousness"—a notion I have already explained—each is translated as "subsequently" in *The Standard Edition*; and *once* in the central part, "The Psychopathology of Hysteria," translated by the English with an adverbial phrase: "by deferred action." The triple critique that one can make of these English translations is, first, that they sever the signifier *nachträglich* into two meanings. One meaning is purely temporal: "subsequently." The other is closely tied to the theory we are about to examine, the theory of trauma requiring two separate moments in time. Having divided the signifier in two and lacking an adverb, they transform the adjective into a substantive; these translations transform *nachträglich* into "deferred action" and then opt for the meaning that conforms to the arrow of time. I don't deny that an interpretation of Freud following the arrow of time may be plausible, but nonetheless it entails a rupture in the continuity and closes off choices for a signifier that, in spite of everything, is open: *nachträglich* and thus "après-coup."

The most interesting appearance of *nachträglich,* the most pertinent to the theory of après-coup, is in the case of Emma in the central part of the *Project* entitled "The Psychopathology of Hysteria," which I asked you to read. The French translation in *The Origins of Psychoanalysis* does not have too many mistakes, and you can read my long commentary in *Life and Death in Psychoanalysis*. Today, I will only underline some points. I don't want to repeat that commentary, which goes on for about twenty pages. Some think that the Emma in question is Emma Eckstein, but that is controversial and not important for our purpose.

What is revealed by this vignette, this fragment of Emma's analysis? Of course, from one angle we have the theory of seduction; however, the term "seduction" is not used, while the term "assault" is, and we shouldn't be in too much of a rush. It is 1895 and the theory of seduction still has a future before it. Here the theory in question is a theory of *repression as pathogenic defense* in the sense that the theory shows how and why the ego works in this defense. Freud tells us there are normal defenses against painful ideas and perceptions, so we need to know why, in certain cases, the ego doesn't use these defenses but instead uses primary processes, displacements, or, to reprise the image I used in *Life and Death in Psychoanalysis*, "full-throttle" displacements—not stepwise displacements but complete displacements of psychic energy. Above all, this vignette reveals an essential theory, which might be called the *theory of trauma in two times*. With trauma, we again find the problem of time, our guiding thread. Indeed, the idea of "in two times" clearly confronts us with the problem of time and with a proposition that may seem paradoxical: the creation of one trauma requires at least two. Freud expresses this in a less paradoxical fashion: "A memory only becomes a trauma après-coup [*nachträglich*]." This is the only place in this text where the term *nachträglich* occurs.

To orient you briefly: in the case of Emma, there is a relationship between two scenes, and everything is in the interplay of these scenes; both take place in a shop. The problem of time even appears in Freud's numbering of the scenes because the scene that comes second chronologically is numbered I, and the previous scene is numbered II. Thus, Scene II, which occurs before Scene I, is the scene of sexual assault, a more-or-less obscene and sexual gesture toward the little girl (I will let you read details); in contrast, the second scene ("Scene I"), which also takes place in a shop, may be called "innocent" but has associative connections with the preceding scene. Everything plays out in the associative links between the two scenes: I and II. Scene I comes later. Of course, the analysis—the anamnesis—goes upward from I to II, as the prefix 'ana-' indicates." Analysis also means "to climb back up" [toward the source]. Analysis is nothing other than *Auflösung,* which is to say "destroying," "dissolving" by moving something back, or leading something back to its primary elements; the German *"auf"* is the Greek *"ana"* (ἀνά). Thus, the analysis—the anamnesis—leads time back in memory, *but is that enough to invert the arrow of time*? Clearly the issue is complex.

I just spoke of connections between two scenes. In reality, that is not an adequate phrase for what Freud describes, and the disparity points to his astuteness. There is a little diagram in the text, which I suggest you examine carefully.

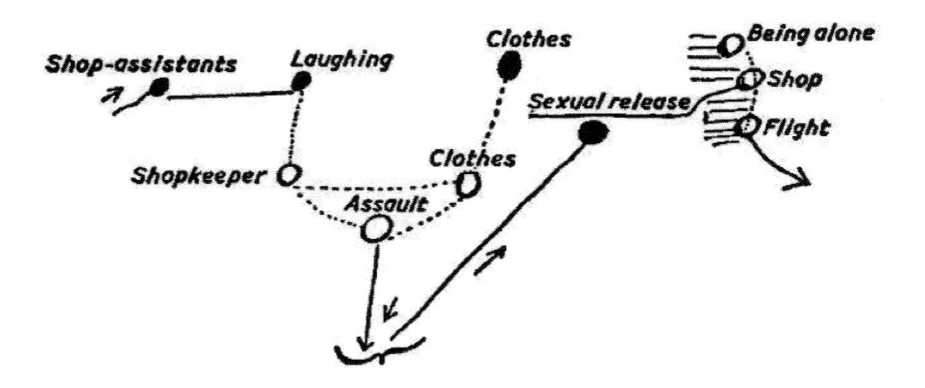

The connections are between a scene and the *memory* of another scene, between the later scene, Scene I, and the memory of Scene II, or, because here the meanings of the terms are quite close, one could say between Scene I and the "signifiers" of Scene II because Freud in fact mentions the discrete elements of Scene II—not a global scenario, but a set of elements separated from each other.

We can redescribe what happens in the following way (which is not exactly what you will find in the text, and again, I suggest you look at what is there): you have a scene, Scene I, and links are established between elements of Scene I and what I will call Scene II′ (the memories of Scene II). The links are associative by definition. Scene II itself is in the past; it no longer exists. Only the memory of Scene II is present, the associative links that Emma creates are between I and II′, and, to go quickly, here you have what Freud calls "unbinding" (*Entbindung*). But unbinding of what? Of energy, of pleasure, of unpleasure? In any case, there is an explosive unbinding of affects and energy, which are probably sexual.

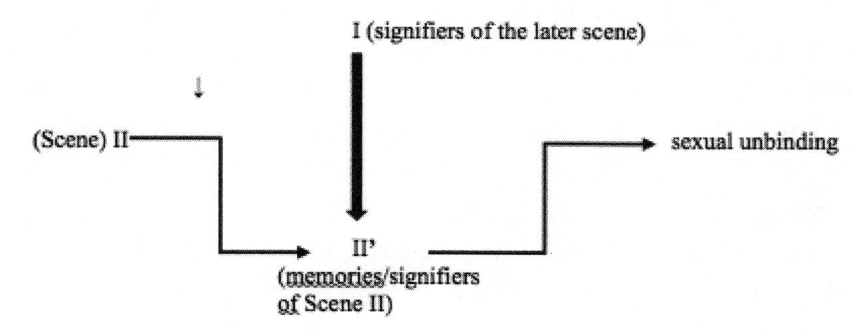

I have emphasized certain aspects of this theory as Freud understood it at the time; the economic aspect and the term "sexual unbinding" show what is in question: the economic conflict plays out in the opposition between secondary process, the binding of energy, and primary process, unbinding.

The earlier scene (Scene II) is premature in the sense that the child is not ready to be sexually stimulated. Freud speaks of "presexual sexual excitation,"[34] which is sexual on the side of the adult and presexual or nonsexual on the side of the child who receives it. The later scene is not sexual; it is innocuous. A "simple" bit of teasing in a shop awakens II′, the memory of Scene II, which is reactivated in

34 [See Letter from Freud to Fliess, October 15, 1895. The Complete Letters. 144.]

the form of an unbinding. Why? Why does II′ provoke an unbinding of energy—let us call it a sexual excitation? Why does the memory, when it is reactivated, provoke a sexual excitation that the event itself did not provoke? Well, the major precondition for this is the superposition of two temporal chain of events, where one chain stands out against, is superimposed upon, another chain. Last time I introduced the notion of syncopation; I could also speak of counterpoint. In reality, this sequence of events is thrown into relief against the background of another sequence, also a temporal sequence but one whose rhythm is set by biology. In other words, between the two times, *puberty* has occurred. Thus, a process of biological maturation results in the manifestation of the memory of a scene (II′) within a mind and a body that are different from the mind and body that were present for Scene II itself. As a consequence, the recalling of the memory triggers a physiological reaction, triggers a discharge (because for Freud all of this translates into bodily reactions), an unbinding (*Entbindung*) that is also an "emission of sexual products," perhaps hormones. Here of course things are not yet precisely defined; all of this is not yet synthesized: there is both a somatic excitation and, at the same time, capacities acquired in the interval come into play, capacities for a new understanding of what had happened during Scene II. In other terms, a little girl who has reached puberty understands après-coup the sexual meaning of the gestures in Scene II.

TRAUMA[35] = APRÈS-COUP

I will read you two major passages:

35 [The trauma in question here is not trauma in general but precisely psychic trauma as Freud has understood it since at least a year earlier in the "Neuropsychoses of Defense" in which he defines psychic trauma as "an occurrence of incompatibility in ideational life." That is to say, in psychic trauma as opposed to other kinds of trauma, ideas qua ideas are causal and at the origin of the trauma. Also see Laplanche's answer to the second question, just below.]

> Here we have the case of a memory arousing an affect that it did not arouse as an experience, because in the meantime the changes of puberty had made possible a different understanding of what was remembered.

Freud continues (and this is where the term *nachträglich* appears):

> Now this case is typical of repression in hysteria. We invariably find that a repressed memory has only become a trauma "après-coup." {There *nachträglich* is undeniably emphasized.} The cause of this state of things is the retardation of puberty as compared with the rest of the individual's development.[36]

And also this passage:

> The significance of one of the determinants that we have put forward and that were furnished by clinical experience would thus seem to be confirmed. The retardation of puberty {implicitly, Freud is referring to humans} makes possible posthumous primary processes.[37]

The term "posthumous" appears here more frequently than "après-coup," but in the end it has a neighboring significance. Nevertheless, it is not elevated to the rank of a concept. So in this instance, what's going on with *nachträglich*? A priori, it is something like a delayed action.

***

Question from the audience: Must the earlier scene remain repressed?

Reply: No, at first the earlier scene is not repressed. It is inscribed without being repressed. Between the earlier and later scene it remains

36 *SE* 1:356 [translation modified Strachey has "by *deferred action*" rather than après-coup].
37 *SE* 1:359 [translation modified].

inscribed. Repression occurs only during the later scene. Pathogenic repression is precisely the process that happens at the later time—at least in the general schema. In truth, many links are missing, making it difficult to say that there isn't a part of the earlier scene that is repressed before the later scene. At the time he drafted the *Project*, Freud only had an extremely simple underlying sequence at his disposal: prepubertal/postpubertal. In 1895, the "sexual stages" amounted to no more than that.

Question from the audience: Here, what does "traumatic" mean?

Reply: Scene II, the earlier scene, becomes traumatic only when the memory of it (II') traumatizes. The memory of it traumatizes because it provokes *more excitation* than the scene itself and also because it *comes from inside*. This is an aspect I have not brought up this year because I don't want to get bogged down in what I have discussed before, but I do want to point out that this "coming from the inside" is the reason Freud calls this process a *proton pseudos*.[38] The *proton pseudos* is not an assertion that Emma is a liar; it is the fact that objectivity is lying to her. Within her experience, something ends up lying to her, misleading her. Memory can be stronger than a scene as it was lived, which is the opposite of everything one would think. The effects of a memory should be weaker than those of the lived scene. The second aspect of this deception concerns the ego. Because the ego has developed between the two scenes, it is attacked from an unexpected direction. It is ready to defend itself against an attack coming from the outside, but here it is attacked from the inside, from a memory. Thus we arrive at trauma in two steps, which means that, because of the nature of the second step, all psychic trauma is *self-traumatization, internal traumatization*. That is to say, it is the residual memories of an earlier scene that have a traumatic function.

38 [Freud is referring to Aristotle's logic, in which the first or primary premise of a proof or demonstration is the "*proton*." If the "*proton*" is false—"*pseudos*"—then the conclusion will be false.]

A STAGE OF FREUDIAN THOUGHT THAT MUST NOT BE FORGOTTEN

The idea of a "deferred action," the English translation, is completely plausible in itself; I mean to say that the memory of the scene does have a deferred action. A preexisting condition—that is possession of the first scene—is added to a second condition (or even to several later conditions), which is both to say that between the two scenes puberty has occurred and that, by chance, another scene has appeared which has associative links to the memory of the first scene. What's more, it is important to see there is nothing magic here, because for Freud it is not the first scene that acts; it is the memory of the first scene. Clearly, in this text, there is a complex interplay that Freud has not perfectly mastered, but there is nothing that moves a priori in the direction that inverts the arrow of time. We could say that the interplay of a "too early" and a "too late" —*a too early of the sexual scene and a too late of puberty*—is not sufficient to produce a retroactive effect. How could it be otherwise in a text that, given Freud's major influences, is deterministic, even mechanistic; a text in which his aim is to give an account of the process of repression in terms of "neurones and quantity," as he says in the first sentence of this *Project*:

> The intention is to furnish a psychology that shall be a natural science: that is, to represent psychical processes as quantitatively determinate states of specifiable material particles, thus making those processes perspicuous and free from contradiction. Two principal ideas are involved: (1) What distinguishes activity from rest is to be regarded as Q, subject to the general laws of motion. (2) The neurones are to be taken as the material particles.[39]

39 *SE* 1:295.

We are not at the end of his evolution, and it is not the right moment to map out what is missing but rather only to hint at it. The theory of seduction will be deepened and completed; its closest eclipse is still a long way ahead of us—about two years further on.

LATER USES OF THE TERM

With help from a computer, I have created an inventory of the word in Freud's letters to Fliess. The four occurrences of *nachträglich* from the beginning of 1896 add nothing particularly new. Nevertheless, I will pick out one that is interesting because it is completely "colloquial," i.e. in line with everyday usage. Here is the phrase, from a letter in which Freud reacts to rereading Taine:[40] "The oldest ideas are really the most useful ones, as I am finding out après-coup."[41] Here it is truly an après-coup of *retrospection*. If you like, it is *"rückgreifen,"* diving into the past, going back where one has been. To recall Taine and to be able to say, après-coup, "It's not so bad after all" clearly leaves no question of retroactivity.

THE LETTER OF DECEMBER 6, 1896

Now we arrive at the next stage, which comes more than a year after the *Project*: the famous letter of December 6, 1896. A new edition of the Freud-Fliess correspondence due to Jeffrey Mason has been published by Fischer under the title *Briefe an Wilhelm Fliess*. There is an English translation, also the work of Masson. As for the French translation, it is in labor but not yet born, probably because of the difficulties it presents.[42] This letter, which I have often discussed and

40 [Hippolyte Taine (1828–1893), an influential French critic and historian who promoted historicism and sociological positivism.]
41 Freud, "Letter from Freud to Fliess, February 13, 1896," in *Complete Letters*, 172. [Translation modified; Masson has: "The oldest ideas are really the most useful ones, as I am finding out belatedly."]
42 *Lettres à Wilhelm Fliess* (Paris: PUF, 2006).

will soon take up again, is inseparable from a slightly earlier letter, that of May 30. A long time had passed since the *Project*. Some periods in the correspondence are prolific; others less so. To orient us, I will quote the beginning of the December 6 letter, which will recreate the atmosphere:

> As you know, I am working on the assumption that our psychic mechanism has come into being by a process of stratification: the material present in the form of memory traces being subjected from time to time to a *rearrangement* in accordance with fresh circumstances—to a *rewriting*. {"Rearrangement" is *Umordnung* and "rewriting" is *Umschrift*.} Thus what is essentially new about my theory is the thesis that memory is present not once but several times over, that it is laid down in various kinds of signs.[43]

And you will immediately see that between these signs, from one rewriting to the next in the sequence, there is a process of translation.

Although I don't want to go into detail in terms of the general architecture of Freudian thought, I want to point out the following: the first part of the *Project for a Scientific Psychology*—the "General Scheme"—is a kind of abstract psychology, a neuronal psychology; the second part is a theory of the neuroses in terms of their clinical history, the case of Emma provides an example. Thus clinical history only appears in the presentation of the theory of the neuroses. Here one could say there is a complete inversion of perspective: it is *clinical theory, the theory of après-coup, that becomes the general frame for a psychology, for a theory of psychic apparatus*. In the "General

43 Masson has "retranscription" where I have "rewriting," but the German is *Umschrift*." [Masson's translation has also been modified in this respect and also in that the German Zeichen is rendered as "signs" here, while Masson has "indications." ("Indications" might work if understood in the sense of "indexes.") Laplanche has "*signes*."]

Scheme" of the *Project,* repression was a pathological phenomenon, but in the second part, which addresses psychopathology, repression becomes a quasi-normal phenomenon (although Freud doesn't go so far as to say so explicitly); it becomes a phenomenon which is characteristic of the passage from one stage to another. Inversely, one could say that *the clinical theory* of the second part structures the nonclinical aspect, the aspect of abstract psychological functioning, of the first part. In other words, there is something within each of the parts that functions according to the model of the first part, but the succession of the phases [in the development of the individual] is structured according to the second part. I hope all that is clear to you.[44]

What more is there to say? First, the schema of two times that we have just seen, the prepuberty/postpuberty model, is generalized in the sense that, from here on, there are not only two times but N times (though N is limited to three or four according to the number of systems one accepts). Even more importantly, the passage from one time to another is characterized as *translation.* Freud uses the word for "rewriting" and "rearrangement," but, at another moment, he clearly defines the process as translation. What is repressed is only repressed at the moment of translation from one system to another that comes later in time, and it is, to use Freud's

44 [Laplanche's hope suggests that he suspects his lecture has been less than completely clear. A translation of his thinking might run: "In the *Project,* the meaning of repression achieves clarity only in so far as it follows the model of après-coup, a model for establishing meaning, a model for which the case of Emma is exemplary," or "The meaning of repression in the first part of the *Project* becomes clear après-coup, in the second part: repression is a two-step process in which each step follows the model of neuronal functioning elaborated in the first part of the *Project,*" or "It is only après-coup, only in the combination of the first and the second part of the *Project,* that Freud (implicitly) recognizes repression as a normal and universal aspect of mental functioning," or "Although the case of Emma is a case of pathology, it provides an example of the functioning of a mental process that is not limited to pathological states but is universally present in humans."]

words, the *Versagung der Übersetzung*, the "refusal to translate,"[45] repression. In this way, repression is refusal. Here is the exact phrase: "A failure of translation—this is what is known clinically as 'repression.'" That which is not translated as it goes from one stage to the next is repressed.

Now for the sequences. A moment ago I pointed out that in "Psychology for Neurologists" [the *Project*[46]] Freud already found it necessary to present the memory process, the processes taking place between scenes, as emerging in relief against a sequence that is itself temporal. The sequence is indispensable because there can be a translation only to the extent that for each period there is something comparable to a language or a code. Here is another passage from the letter of December 6:

> I should like to emphasize the fact that the successive registrations represent the psychic achievement of successive epochs of life. At the boundary between two such epochs a translation of the psychic material must take place. I explain the peculiarities of the psychoneuroses by supposing that this translation has not taken place in the case of some of the material, which has certain consequences.[47]

45 [Alternatively and perhaps more precisely this could be rendered as "refusal of a translation" or "refusal of *the* translation"—and indeed, Laplanche renders it in French as "*Le refusement de la traduction*"; however, these two options suggest that a specific translation has been made and then rejected, refused admission to system II, e.g., to the conscious/preconscious system as it exists after puberty. While this is possible, the choice of "refusal to translate" leaves open the possibility that no specific translation—or translations—has been "refused."]

46 Freud did not use a title in the original manuscript; the use of *Project* was an addition coined by the editors of *The Origins of Psychoanalysis*. In his letters to Fliess, Freud calls it "Psychology for Neurologists."

47 Freud, *Complete Letters*, 208.

Thus, languages[48] are absolutely necessary, and the periods are to be defined by codes.[49]

SOME CONFUSIONS ABOUT THE STRATA…

In fact, when you do get into the details, this distinction is completely ambiguous—and I say "ambiguous" in order not to say "completely confused." Several layers are superimposed in this sequence of inscriptions. First there is an ordering according to types of intellectual or conceptual functioning. In this way, the first epoch is characterized by a certain form of association of ideas, association by simultaneity; the second form of association of ideas is characterized by causality; the third, by linkage with words, etc. Thus one sequence could be called "formal" and is based on the assumption that humans develop by going from simultaneity to the principle of causality and then from the principle of causality to linkage with words. Then, another sequence is completely superimposed on the prior sequence, which makes things rather confusing for Freud's readers: this next sequence is a sequence based on *location* in the psychic apparatus in relation to the potential for consciousness, thus a "*topographic*" ordering. Finally, there is a sequence concerned with sexuality and with the possibility of pleasure and unpleasure linked to sexuality, a sequence one could call "*clinical*" or "*historical*."[50]

Clearly this sort of superposition of sequences is extremely embarrassing because it leads to diagrams that are impossible to accept—except perhaps as a reflection of the creative ferment bub-

48 [Here "languages" is used in a broad sense which would include not only languages like French and English but also the language of the street, the language of childhood, Shakespearian language, etc.]
49 [See Laplanche, "Failures of Translation," in *Freud and the* Sexual, trans. Jonathan House and Nicholas Ray (New York: The Unconscious in Translation, 2011), 115–131.]
50 ["Historical" is used in the sense of anamnesis, in the sense of an individual's clinical history.]

bling up in Freud at this time. For example, it ends up locating the appearance of the notion of causality between the ages of four and eight years, and even locates the appearance of language—or at least of the function of words—in the period between eight and fourteen years old, etc. This is why the first editors refused to publish the whole thing for fear of giving an impression of Freud as eccentric and unreliable; but this complexity covers Freud's attempt to provide a kind of infrastructure explaining what precedes it and what, at one point, he calls a simple "superstructure."

This search for an infrastructure will proceed in two directions. Both are biological of course, but there is a special form of "biology," Fliessian biology, for which the entire infrastructure is an interplay of *periods* that Fliess claimed to find everywhere. There are periods of twenty-eight days and twenty-three days; the period of twenty-eight days is the feminine period (which may be understandable), but as for the period of twenty-three days, the masculine period, no one has yet explained to me how Fliess arrived at this number. There is probably a Jewish cabalistic source, but I admit my ignorance. In any case, this is the Fliessian infrastructure. Many have considered it crazy, and it is in fact stunning to see the kind of complex calculations that Freud indulged in to find a relation to the numbers twenty-eight and twenty-three for this or that neurotic phenomenon.

...BUT THEN THE APPEARANCE OF EROGENOUS ZONES

But behind that Fliessian infrastructure another type of infrastructure is budding, a bodily sequence: the idea of "abandoned erogenous zones." (This idea will without a doubt get mixed in with twenty-eight and twenty-three, numbers which are themselves are thought to be characterized by substances of anxiety and sexuality.) What suddenly emerges is sexual unlinking (let's say "sexual discharge") in connection with zones of the body called "erogenous," but when, later, these zones are abandoned, the discharge produces anxiety.

As the editors rightly point out, this is the first appearance of the notion of erogenous zones and thus of the notion of sexual stages, which clearly will replace Fliessian periods in what we have called "infrastructure." What's more, Freud says that we will find "in this differentiation and limitation, progress in culture, and moral as well as individual development."[51] This highlights not only the idea of a sequence of erogenous zones that appear and are then abandoned—an idea that we will find again a few years later—but also the idea that it not only is an evolution of the individual (which is a limitation) but also is related to cultural progress, something on the order of the species, of phylogenesis.

After these complexities, I hold on to one simple idea: après-coup can only occur on the basis of a really existing periodization conceived as entailing different types of language, different codes. I will come back to this point later but I will nevertheless say something about it now. You can see that the idea of a different code being at work in each different epoch is not at all the same as the idea of determination by the infrastructure, an idea that is present elsewhere. The idea of infrastructure could be used to mean that all evolution is nothing but the evolution of that base, but there is a competing idea: the evolution of the base, possibly biological evolution, only furnishes the framework against which a process emerges that is not itself determined by the framework.

TRANSLATION: ITS DIFFERENT DIMENSIONS AND ITS RICHNESS

It is in this way that the idea of translation (*Übersetzung*), which Freud had already proposed in the letter of May 30,[52] does not do away with but takes over from the purely economic point of view of the *Project*

51 Freud, *Complete Letters*, 212.
52 [A letter that, as Laplanche points out above (page 49), is "inseparable" from the letter of December 6, 1896.]

for a Scientific Psychology. There are even passages that show that it is possible to give an economic interpretation of the need to translate, meaning the need to translate itself must be explained in physicalist terms. To go further into Freud's idea, this need has something to do with the tendency toward a "quantitative equalization."[53] It must be possible to derive the tendency to translate from the tendency of the neuronal apparatus to equalize quantities of excitation within itself.

The idea of translation, to which I give great importance, offers a clear way to account for idea of après-coup. Every translation can be conceived as a double movement, a "going backward toward what is to be translated" as well as a "going forward" in the sense of going forward to what will become explicit in a different form. Neither of these two movements, however, is more determining than the other. Each includes an already determined potential or demand and a potential or demand for creativity. Let's take the aspect of "going forward": the fact of *being translated into* more and more elaborated forms amounts to "going forward" beyond a primitive or crude form; it presumes that what came first was limited or impoverished and that it goes on to be enriched by interpretation. Consider manuscripts of ancient religious music, such as hymns or songs or chants, for example medieval Gregorian chants or Christmas carols, and notice the extremely rudimentary way they are transmitted to us; the extremely crude notation will obviously be translated and enriched by later harmonies, which will at the same time be transformed into more sophisticated forms. And yet, "going forward" could be conceived as the development of something already present that determines all future translations. Similarly, the "going backward" of the translator or the interpreter could be conceived as "retroactive interpretation" ("retroactively fantasized," a term we will certainly come back to), an interpretation enriching an ambiguous and impoverished past. If the past is reduced to a few traces, we can make of it what we like! But the

53 [A concept close to the notion of homeostasis.]

opposite is true when a translator goes back to a text, where the translator is always searching for additional richness, for an additional "not-yet-translated" [*non-encore-traduit*]. In Freud's model, every translation leaves out a part of what was there "to be translated" and so transforms that untranslated part into the repressed. It is the same for the translator (in the sense of a professional translator), who usually considers previous translations; he translates Freud while taking into account Strachey's work and other existing translations, going through these preceding translations, reintegrating what has dropped out and what has been, one could say, "repressed." Thus the second sense, "going backward," does not mean a purely arbitrary endowment or an entirely voluntarist interpretation of the past, but rather an attempt to collect from the past, from the earlier text, even its "pre-text" (I may have a chance to speak more about this pre-text), to collect everything that could have been allowed to drop out.

The letter of December 6 does take up the question of a first "*to-be-translated*" [*un premier "à traduire"*]. In a sequence of translations, either one goes back indefinitely, and thus necessarily arbitrarily, or else one accepts that there is a "a first to-be-translated."[54] For Freud, this first to-be-translated is what he designates as the *Wahrnehmungszeichen*, the sign/index of perception. There is a major problem contained in the meaning of this "*Zeichen*," which is either "sign" or "index"—an alternative which sums up all its ambiguity. Does it have the nature of a scene, of a memory, of a trace? Is it richer (a sign) or poorer (an index) than that into which it will be translated? Now that I have raised this question I will leave it open, as I have often offered meditations on its meaning.

What about the word *nachträglich* in the letter of December 6? As I mentioned, it occurs only once and in a way that is not central for the theory of translation. It appears as a modifier of secondary

54 [For an approach to this issue in the domain of visual perception, see the work of Zenon Pylyshyn, e.g., *Seeing and Visualizing: It's Not What You Think* (Cambridge, MA: MIT Press, 2003).]

consciousness. We have already seen this usage, consciousness of a mental process that is consciousness linked to a word: it is secondary and, Freud adds, *"etwas der Zeit nach nachträgliches,"* "something après-coup in time." The English translated it as "subsequent in time." It's obvious that "retroactive" wouldn't work—this is not a retroactive consciousness—nor would "deferred" work in English. You see how much the idea of *"nachträglich,"* which is central in this text, and the idea of the après-coup of translation, are separated from the use of the word which is, as if by a trick of the signifier, utterly marginal. The word *"nachträglich"* appears as if in the corner of a painting, marginal in relation to the central process, which itself is an important description of the idea of après-coup.

I will go on a little longer.

FOUR MAJOR LANDMARKS

After this letter of December 1896, in the months of April and May 1897, there are four uses of *"nachträglich"* that are absolutely essential. These texts are the letters of April 6th and of May 2nd, manuscript L (attached to the letter of May 2), and the letter of May 16th. Four texts in which *nachträglich* suddenly emerges in tight connection with *"hören,"* "to hear" or, more precisely, "to hear said," "to hear to be said."[55] The four passages say the same thing and I will read each of them to you. In each case they concern the formation of "fantasies" on the basis of experiences, and each time Freud's explanation uses the same words: everything takes place in the relationship between what is "heard" and what is "understood." Here is the first instance, in letter of April 6th:

> What I have in mind are hysterical fantasies, which regularly, as I see it, go back to things that children

55 [To fully illustrate the possible connotations of the French would require at least three valences: "I've heard it said that..." (evoking the notion of hearsay); "Is there anything one doesn't hear!" and "The things one must hear!"]

> overhear at an early age and understand only après-coup {SE: understood later}.[56]

The letter of May 2nd says the same thing:

> The fantasies stem from things that have been *heard* but understood après-coup {SE: understood subsequently}, and all their material is of course genuine.[57]

Manuscript L, which is attached to the letter of May 2nd reads:

> For fantasies are psychic facades produced in order to bar access to these memories. Fantasies simultaneously serve the tendency toward refining the memories, toward sublimating them. They are manufactured by means of things that are heard, and utilized après-coup {SE: made use of subsequently}.[58]

And finally the letter of May 16th that concerns the auditory hallucinations of paranoia, but a comparison is made with hysteria:

> The fantasies derive, as in hysteria, from what has been heard and understood après-coup [Masson has 'subsequently'].[59]

Here we must grasp the fact that "hearing" involves two registers and thus two possible oppositions. First there is "hearing" in relation to "seeing" and thus the possible opposition of two "senses" or "sensoriums": hearing and vision. In my opinion, there is an opposition that is much more important and perhaps more fundamental: that between "hearing" and "understanding." And we cannot ignore the fact that in German "*hören*" is not only "to hear," but it privileges

56 Freud, *Complete Letters*, 234. [Translation modified.]
57 Freud, *Complete Letters*, 239. [Translation modified.]
58 Freud, *Complete Letters*, 240. [Translation modified.]
59 Freud, *Complete Letters*, 243. [Translation modified.]

the notion of "to hear to be said," "*sagen hören*." I did not quote the whole passage from the first letter, the letter of April 6th, but I will read it to you now:

> What I have in mind are hysterical fantasies, which, as I see it, regularly go back to things that children overhear at an early age and understand only après-coup. The age at which they take in information of this kind is, strangely enough, from six to seven months on!

Beyond the opposition between hearing and vision that of course is present, the pertinent opposition is the opposition between "to hear to be said" and "to understand"; this, in my opinion, is a major indication of the first, the original "to-be-translated."

January 9, 1990

HEARD AND HEARD TO BE SAID

In following the guide wire of "*nachträglich*," of "après-coup," I return to where I ended last time: the four more or less similar versions of this locution: "what is heard (*gehört*) and understood après-coup." What I want to stress is that in German "*hören*" is often "to hear said" and not only "to hear." Sometimes what dominates the meaning of the phrase is the notion of "to be said" in the sense of signifying something. In our translations, we sometimes come upon a passage in which the author refers to what he has written above with the phrase "*wir haben vorher gehört*," which we do not translate as "we have heard above" but rather, in everyday speech, as "we have seen above." Indeed, as this is a question of *reading* a text, hearing is in no way privileged in relation to seeing.

Now I'd like to go to the heart of the problem with as much clarity as possible. In German, as in French, the verbs "to hear," "to see," "to touch," "to smell," etc., refer to what we call the "senses" or the "sensoria." To these, Freud sometimes seems to add (notably for the infant) the notion of "to live," "to feel by living": this is the famous *Erlebnis*, for which Mme Hawelka (in her translation of the *Journal of the Rat Man*) invented a good term—close to Portuguese—"*vivance*."[60]

The perceptions of the sensoria (the data of the senses) are not necessarily messages, especially if they arise from inanimate nature. The transposition of data from one sensory modality to another is uncertain, to say the least: is a musical "la" more blue than yellow? Remember Rimbaud's sonnet "Voyelles," in which we are pushed to establish bridges of meaning, latent and invisible, between vowels and colors. The domain of *sensoria* must be contrasted with the domain of *messages*. Every sensory modality is capable of conveying messages and even of being vested with a comprehensive code for

60 [Approximately "lived experience."]

messages. Of course, we are accustomed to thinking of verbal messages as coming from what is heard. (This is why, as we pointed out, it is easy to conflate "to hear" with "to hear said.") With a striking laziness of thought, we suppose that the visual can only give us a copy in written form of what is heard. But in fact there are purely visual codes that totally avoid the intermediary of spoken language—semiotic codes—and it is not unimaginable that every sensory modality could be the basis of specific codes.

In the letters we are studying, Freud advances in a specific direction: not going from one sensory modality to another—from hearing to seeing, for example—but *from a sensory modality, whichever one it may be, to its being "understood."* So we are barely stretching the point when we say that what is "perceived" or "sensed" in infancy carries within it something that must be "understood" après-coup. The "seen," the "heard," and even the "lived" each carry latent messages in themselves, messages that at a second moment—*nachträglich*—the subject must try to translate. They are not pure, inert sensory material, they are not simply "noise"; rather they contain *a demand to be translated*. Thus meaning is not purely retroactive: it is a response to a prior, latent attempt at communication. In the human being, the *hören* is not only a pure "to hear"; it is often a "to hear to be said" (*sagen hören*), and the "to hear to be said" is, in turn, a "to-be-translated," even a primal "to-be-translated."

THE BIRTH OF A CONCEPT AND OF A TERM: NACHTRÄGLICHKEIT

Having clarified this point, let's turn to the *genesis of a concept* in Freud's thought: the genesis of "*Nachträglichkeit*." Those of you who don't speak German must put a few "barbarian" words in your mouths. It's not very difficult. We'll start with *nachträglich*, used as an adjective and an adverb, and with the substantive derived from it: *Nachträglichkeit* (with a capital letter, which is the mark of a substantive). German has the capacity to forge substantives thanks to a certain number of suffixes: *-heit*, *-keit*, *-ung*, etc. Notice, however, that this power is not always used. And indeed, *Nachträglichkeit* is not listed in German lexicons; it is Freud's creation but nonetheless perfectly correct in its genesis.

On the other hand, the question of the birth of a concept is difficult to separate from another issue, namely "homonyms," or more precisely, from a double problem: *homonymy* on one hand and on the other hand the way the concept survives the *test by translation*. I will try to be both brief and clear, and I also refer you to passages in *Traduire Freud* that are devoted to this question. By "homonymy," we mean the fact that a single signifier may convey different signifieds. The linguist Charles Bally rightly distinguishes between homonymy and polysemy. For my purposes and to refine things a bit, I distinguish three possibilities by subdividing Bally's polysemy into two

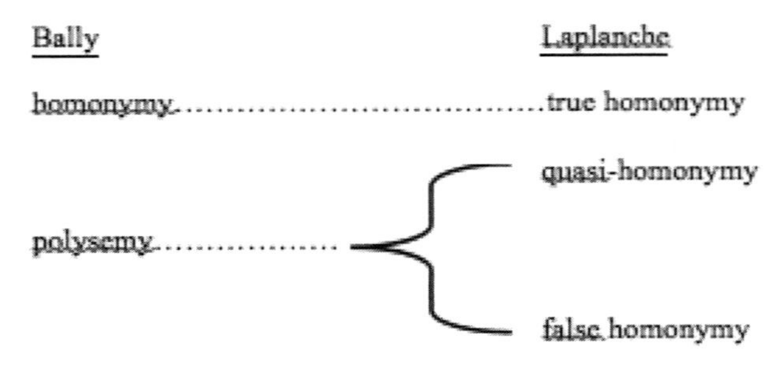

We will go quickly. What is most important is what is most ambiguous: quasi-homonymy and, above all, false homonymy. With true homonymy, there is no confusion between two terms that are identical but carry completely different meanings. The two words often have:

- distinct etymologies
- different headings in the dictionaries.[61]

61 [One example in English is "bark" (sound made by a dog; etymology Old English) and "bark" (covering of a tree; etymology Old Norse) and "bark" (sailing vessel; etymology Provençal).]

Two examples:

- *étalon (monétaire)*
- *étalon (cheval)*[62]

and

- *pompe* (*cérémonial*: etymology Greek)
- *pompe* (*appareil servant à déplacer les liquides*: etymology Latin)[63]

I just said that there can be no confusion . . . at least consciously. But . . . the unconscious plays with these homonyms in dreams and in puns. In this way the "communicants" who used to be required to *"renoncer à Satan, à ses pompes et a ses œuvres"* ["renounce Satan, his pomps and his works"[64]] quickly turned the phrase into derision by changing it to *"Je renonce à Satan, à ses pompes et à ses tuyaux"* ["I renounce Satan, his pumps and hoses"].

In any case, as true homonymy is specific to an individual language, it is strictly untranslatable; witticisms and wordplay such as puns, based on homonymy, cannot be transposed into another language. On the other hand, for quasi-homonymy and false homonymy, the linguistic knowledge of the speaker plays a part, and translation is a test or a touchstone.

In *quasi-homonyny,* we have *the same word* but with clearly distinct meanings, which in dictionaries have subheadings easily spotted by the speaker. Let's go back to the word *pompes*. In addition

62 [In French, one meaning of *étalon* is "standard" in the sense of a unit of measurement, as in the "gold standard"; metaphorically it can be used in the same way that "yardstick" is used metaphorically to mean a standard of measuring something. A second meaning of *étalon* is "stallion," a "stud horse," and, if employed in reference to a man, it can also mean "stud" just as "stallion" can in English.]

63 [In French, one meaning of *pompe* is "ceremony." This meaning is quite similar to that of the English word "pomp," for which the *OED* gives: "splendid display or celebration, a magnificent show"—as in the phrase "pomp and circumstance." Another meaning in French is "pump" as in pumps used for water, such as the pumps and hoses used by firefighters.]

64 [The usual version in English, e.g., in the baptismal vows, is "Renounce Satan, his works and his pomps."]

to the true homophone—*pompes* meaning splendid ceremony—we find another meaning: *pompes* meaning "shoes" [*chaussures*]. The pumps of the firefighter and those of the cobbler have more than one point in common: the same etymology and derivation of meaning—the old-fashioned perforated shoes pump water in and out. What's more, in the dictionary the two meanings are listed under the same heading but in a given context there is no confusion: "Go get my *pompes*," says the gentleman to his valet; "Go get the *pompes*," the captain orders the firemen.

Nevertheless, these almost-homonyms retain traces of their connections to which the translator must be sensitive, at times seeking to retain some ambiguity. For instance, in reading the French word "*homme*" [man], the German translator will easily choose between *Mann* (a male human) and *Mensch* (a human being). And yet there will be gray areas that will call for deeper reflection: Should "*le grand homme*" [the great man / the big man] be rendered as "*der grosse Mensch*," as it should be, or "*der grosse Mann*," as Freud wrote in *Der Mann Moses*?[65] Does the phrase "God created man in his image" invoke a male-centric legend?

Finally, and even more important, we have "false homonymy." Here the transposition from one language to another is indispensable for detecting the homonymy. The French speaker sees a single meaning in the word *femme* [woman], while for each occurrence of *femme*, the German translator must choose between *Weib* (wife) and *Frau* (woman): two completely distinct terms that can in no way be considered to be "synonyms." The inverse can be demonstrated with the German word *Bedeutung*, whose sense oscillates between "*signification*" [meaning] and "*importance*" [importance, size, extent, standing, etc.] and oscillates in such a way that the correct translation is often undecidable—to such an extent that the translators of *OCF.P*[66] chose to

65 *GW* 16:214ff.
66 [The French translation of the complete psychological works of Freud.]

render it with the modern term "*significativité*" [significance. as used in the phrase "statistical significance"], which harbors both nuances. Thus, there is a kind of diffraction from one language to another, and there are differences when several languages are involved:

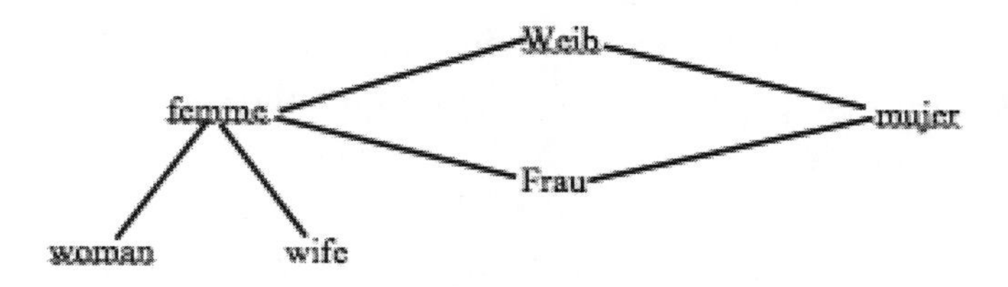

REMARKS OF A TRANSLATOR

I have four comments on all this. First: the boundaries between quasi-homonymies and false homonymies are not as clear as I have drawn them. Second: false homonymy is not at all sterile; it is not a simple artifact. I would even say, and here I am referring to one of the central formulas of *Traduire Freud,* (which we borrowed from Antoine Berman) that false homonymy is the very model of the "test by the foreign." As we will see with "*nachträglich,*" but as is true for many other examples, the analysis of a false homonymy conducted by the translator—conducted through a test by the foreign—is a sort of diffraction that, like a crystal diffracting light, spreads out meanings and possible usages; this analysis by translation returns to the language of origin, diversifying and enriching it.

My third comment: the veneration of this or that language is not reasonable; in fact, it is ridiculous. I am thinking particularly of the veneration of sacrosanct German, full of all its "richness," at times supremely concrete and at other times highly philosophical, etc. Sometimes German is admired for its depth and its polysemy when it condenses things into a single word. One says: "What richness in a single word! It is this, but it is also that!" But then, inversely, it is revered for the multiplicity of its nuances when it makes use of several words, that is, when it makes use of more terms than does French. In one case we say, "One cannot really translate the richness of this term, which has many meanings," and in the other case, "French is impoverished because German has ten words and we only have three." What I have tried to show is that the relation between languages reverses itself at every moment—for example, the French word "*homme*" is more polysemic and vaguer than the German while for "*Bedeutung*" it is the reverse.

Finally, my fourth point concerns the importance of "the test by the foreign" for the linguistic question of homonymy, sometimes as a simple test, sometimes as a test of a meaning, and sometimes as a true cultural experiment. The "test by the foreign" is translation, and on this subject, I would suggest you read a recent article by one of the team of translators of the *OCF.P*, Jeanine Altounian, which appeared recently in the *Revue française de psychanalyse*: "Humour et exil dans l'écriture freudienne" ["Humor and Exile in Freudian Writing"]. To my way of thinking, the emphasis on exile is only one of the dimensions of the test by the foreign, that of loss. Loss necessarily has its counterpart, because exile in a foreign language is not only loss but also fruitfulness. The whole dialectic of German thought from Hölderlin to Hegel (and how many others!) insists on the fact that *it is at the extreme of the foreign* that the *Eigene*, "one's own," comes closer. As I have spoken of Hölderlin, I would like to read you a few lines from his poem "Mnemosyne" (Mnemosyne is the goddess of memory):

> *Ein Zeichen sind wir, deutungslos,*
> *Schmerzlos sind wir und haben fast*
> *Die Sprache in der Ferne verloren.*

> We are a sign, without interpretation,
> Without pain we are an have nearly
> Lost language in foreign lands.[67]

67 [Laplanche's translation is: *Nous sommes un signe, sans interprétation, / sans douleur nous sommes et avons presque / perdu le langage à l'étranger.*]

Hölderlin, great translator and great schizophrenic. It is the "nearly" in the "nearly lost" that is important. It marks a point of no return and a point of a possible return, of a possible translation. For translation is both test and return, loss and refinding. This is also what is at issue in schizophrenia, but for the moment I will not take up that question.

HOMONYMY: CRYSTALLIZATION OF A CONCEPT

Why have I led you on this detour—both too long and too short—on the forms of homonymy? Because quasi-homonymy and false homonymy enrich the path of the concept's creation, of the concept's crystallization. Here what will occupy us is the path by which the concept and the substantive *Nachträglichkeit* emerged, beginning from the possible polysemy of *nachträglich*. Concretely, the translation of Freud has had a double effect, a double test by the foreign. English translators opted for a diffraction of translations; in the French translations, there was first a diffraction and then a return to a single word. The English translator is led to treat each use of *nachträglich* as belonging to clearly different meanings. Thus, he explodes the meaning into:

- afterwards in time: *later, subsequently*
- delayed, having a deferred effect: the famous "*deferred action*"
- retroactive

For French translators, not so much for Lacan as for those who followed his lead, the question of whether *nachträglich* has a unity of meaning was resolved by adopting the term "après-coup." But before Lacan, French translators had, like the English, chosen the quick and easy solution: a multiplicity of meanings "according to the context"—which is to say abandoning the signifier.

So, how did Freud move (or, more simply, did he move) from a term used in a vague way, and in any case as an adjectival or adverbial modifier (*nachträglich*), to the formulation of the concept *Nachträglichkeit*? The evolution is profoundly paradoxical and will reward your sustained attention.

THE PARADOXICAL EVOLUTION OF A CONCEPT

We left Freud in April–May of 1897, in the full flowering of the theory of seduction and, notably, in a profusion of theorizing about the origin and the structure of fantasizing. Yet the term après-coup (adjective and adverb), one of the prime movers of the theory, completely fades away until, on November 14, 1897, it reappears, finally, in the form of the *substantive*. But take note! In the meantime, between May and November, the theory of seduction itself has been "abandoned." I am referring to the famous letter of September 21, 1897, which I am in the habit of calling "the letter of the equinox," because it was written on the autumnal equinox, the end of summertime and the beginning of wintertime. I am inserting the letter, which I have carefully retranslated, as the there are many difficulties:

> September 21, 1897
>
> Dear Wilhelm,
>
> Here I am again, since yesterday morning refreshed, cheerful, impoverished, at present without work, and having settled in again, I am writing to you first.
>
> And now I want to confide in you immediately the great secret that has been slowly dawning on me in the last few months. I no longer believe in my *neurotica*.[68] This is probably not intelligible without

68 *Meine neurotica*. Given the form of the German sentence, one cannot decide if the Latin word *neurotica* is the singular (feminine) or the plural (neuter). A number of arguments suggest that it should be seen as a plural. In letter 119, Freud employs the expression *in neuroticis* (i.e., in the dative plural), which in English might be rendered as "in matters of the neurosis" or "in the domain of the neurosis." Furthermore, when Freud uses a Latin word in the context of a German sentence, he declines it: *meine libido gegen matrem . . . sie nudam zu sehen* (letter 141). Therefore, if *neurotica* was intended to be in the singular, he should have written: "*an meine Neuroticam.*" Finally, a collection of poems by Felix Dörmann had been published in 1891 and then was banned for immorality; it was entitled *Neurotica*, clearly a neuter plural, as is shown by this passage by Karl Kraus in *La littérature démolie*, 1896: "[First] the *Neurotica* were confiscated, followed by the *Sensations* and then the *Risée*."

an explanation; after all, you yourself found credible what I was able to tell you. So I will begin historically [and tell you] where the reasons for disbelief came from. The continual disappointment in my efforts to bring a single analysis to a real conclusion; the running away of people who for a period of time had been most gripped [by analysis]; the absence of the complete successes on which I had counted; the possibility of explaining to myself the partial successes in other ways, in the usual fashion—this was the first group. Then the surprise that in all cases the father, not excluding my own, had to be accused of being perverse—the realization of the unexpected frequency of hysteria, with precisely the same conditions prevailing in each case, whereas surely such widespread perversions against children are not very probable. The [incidence] of perversion would have to be immeasurably more frequent than the [resulting] hysteria because the illness, after all, occurs only where there has been an accumulation of events and there is a contributory factor that weakens the defense. Then, third, the certain insight that there are no indications of reality in the unconscious so that one cannot distinguish between truth and fiction that has been cathected with affect. (Accordingly, there would remain the solution that the sexual fantasy invariably seizes upon the theme of the parents.) Fourth, the consideration that in the most deep-reaching psychosis the unconscious memory does not break through so that the secret of childhood experiences is not disclosed even in the most confused delirium. If one thus sees that the unconscious never overcomes the resistance of the conscious, the expectation that in treatment the opposite is bound to happen, to the point where the unconscious is completely tamed by the conscious, also diminishes.

I was so far influenced [by this] that I was ready to give up two things: the complete resolution of a neurosis and the certain knowledge of its etiology in childhood. Now I have no idea of where I stand because I have not succeeded in gaining a theoretical understanding of repression and its interplay of forces. It seems once again arguable that only later experiences give the impetus to fantasies, which [then] hark back to childhood, and with this the factor of a hereditary disposition regains a sphere of influence from which I had made it my task to dislodge it—in the interest of illuminating neurosis.

If I were depressed, confused, exhausted, such doubts would surely have to be interpreted as signs of weakness. Since I am in an opposite state, I must recognize them as the result of honest and vigorous intellectual work and must be proud that after going so deep I am still capable of such criticism. Can it be that this doubt merely represents an episode in the advance toward further insight?

It is strange too that no feeling of shame appeared—for which, after all, there could well be occasion. Of course I shall not tell it in Dan, nor speak of it in Askelon, in the land of the Philistines,[69] but in your eyes and my own, I have more the feeling of a victory than a defeat (which is surely not right).

How nice that your letter has arrived just now!

69 An allusion to 2 Sam. 1:20: "Tell it not in Gath, publish it not in the streets of Askelon; lest the daughters of the Philistines rejoice, lest the daughters of the uncircumcised triumph."

It induces me to advance a proposal with which I had intended to close. If during this lazy period I were to go to the Northwest Station on Saturday evening, I could be with you at noon on Sunday and then travel back the next night. Can you clear that day for an idyll for the two of us, interrupted by an idyll for three and three and a half [of us]? That is what I wanted to ask. Or do you have a dear guest in the house or something urgent to do elsewhere? Or, if I have to leave for home the same evening, which would then not be worthwhile, do the same conditions obtain if I go straight to the Northwest Station on Friday evening and stay with you one and a half days? I mean this week, of course.

Now to continue my letter. I vary Hamlet's saying, "To be in readiness":[70] to be cheerful is everything! I could indeed feel quite discontent. The expectation of eternal fame was so beautiful, as was that of certain wealth, complete independence, travels, and lifting the children above the severe worries that robbed me of my youth. Everything depended upon whether or not hysteria would come out right. Now I can once again remain quiet and modest, go on worrying and saving. A little story from my collection occurs to me: "Rebecca, take off your [bridal] gown; you are no longer a fiancée."[71] In spite of all this, I am in very good spirits and content that you feel a need to see me again similar to mine to see you.

---

70 Shakespeare, *Hamlet*, act V, scene 2. In actuality: "*The readiness is all.*"

71 [Masson's translation is modified here.] Freud uses the word *Kalle*, a Yiddish word meaning "fiancée." This story of Rebecca could be an allusion to the second wife of Jacob Freud, Rebecca. Cf. Vladimir Granoff, *Filiations* (Paris : Minuit, 1975): 320–323, and Marie Balmary, *L'homme aux statues*, (Paris: Grasset, 1979): 67–69.

There remains one small anxiety. What can I still understand of your matters? I am certainly incapable of critically evaluating them; I shall hardly be in a position to comprehend them; and the doubt that then sets in is not the product of intellectual work, like my doubt about my own matters, but is the result of mental inadequacy. It is easier for you; you can survey everything I bring and criticize it vigorously.

I have to add one more thing. In this collapse of everything valuable, the psychological alone has remained untouched. The dream [book] stands entirely secure, and my beginnings of the metapsychological work have only grown in my estimation. It is a pity that one cannot make a living, for instance, on dream interpretation!

Martha came back with me to Vienna. Minna and the children are staying in the country another week. They have all been exceedingly well.

My pupil, Dr. Gattel, is something of a disappointment. Very gifted and clever, he must nevertheless, owing to his own nervousness and several unfavorable character traits, be classified as unpalatable.

How all of you are and whatever else is happening between heaven and earth, I hope—anticipating your reply—to hear soon in person.

Cordially your Sigm.[72]

---

72 From the point of view of translation alone, a single word in this letter could lead to a misinterpretation: "*diskutierbar*," which has led some to render it in French with the word "*discutable*." But "*discutable*" has a meaning that is purely negative: "*contestable*" ["questionable" or "doubtful"]. If Freud had wanted to say "*contestable*" or "*discutable*," he would have used another term, *enfechtbar*, for example. Here, "*diskutierbar*," which is rarely used in German, must be understood in the positive sense of "worthy of being discussed," which I have translated with the word "*envisageable*," which completely changes the meaning of the sentence. [In agreement with Laplanche, Masson uses "arguable."]

I don't intend to take up another full discussion of this letter but only to underline a few points:

1. This letter constitutes a heartbreaking reevaluation of the theory of seduction. As such, it is a true attempt at "falsification" in Popper's sense of the term. The theory of seduction is refutable, as much by arguments from facts ("clinical" facts) as by general considerations (anthropological, even statistical).

2. One of his major arguments is that memory can never recover the initial event. But, the theory of seduction is inseparable from the idea of a trauma requiring two separate moments according to a schema that can be presented, in a simplified way, like this:

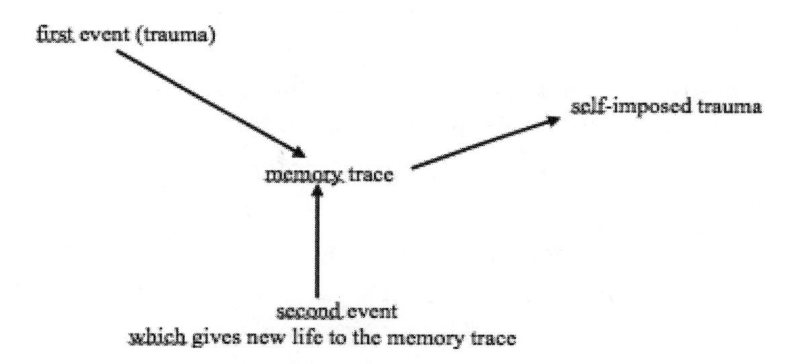

   In this sequence, the first event (the trauma) has become an unstoppable internal trauma, a trauma caused by the subject's own libido. But, from the moment that the first event gives way [becomes questionable], the whole system seems to collapse.

3. Freud's line of reasoning is approximately this:
   a) The initial event cannot be recaptured.
   b) That being the case, fantasies of early events can be attributed to the influence of later events, to a *retroactive* imagining.

c) Such a solution is not enough and will never be enough for Freud. He will always fight against the hypothesis of a pure "retro-fantasizing" that would create the past on the basis of the present.
d) Consequently, retroactive imagination must stop somewhere; this stopping point, which cannot be located in the history of the individual, must be searched for in the history of the species and in heredity, in the inheritance of dispositions. We can see how powerfully Freud's phylogenetic hypotheses are determined by the abandonment of the theory of seduction: it is absolutely necessary to find a real starting point, which can serve as the support for all later developments, for the "drives" (in Freud's sense of the term), for primal fantasies, etc. "*Im Anfang war die Tat.*" ("In the beginning was the deed.") Those are the last words of *Totem and Taboo*, which underline the reality of the murder of the prehistoric father.
e) Finally, note in the same sentence, note the conjunction of these two aspects of a new theorization: the possibility of retroactive imagining and the rehabilitation of the hereditary hypothesis; from here on, for Freud, this pair will be indissociable: "It seems once again arguable that only later experiences give the impetus to fantasies, which [then] hark back to childhood, and with this the factor of a hereditary disposition regains a sphere of influence from which I had made it my task to dislodge it—in the interest of illuminating neurosis."

4. We must again emphasize: the theory of seduction did not die with the letter of the equinox:
   a) In Freud's own approach to patients, we continue to find the search for a prototypical episode of seduction in the individual's history. This quest, which is retraced in Jac-

qaueline Lanouzière's book *Histoire secrète de la séduction,*[73] is pursued even further as a general hypothesis in clinical investigations. The most important instance of this quest is the passage in *New Introductory Lectures,* which became well-known, in which the mother appears as the principal seducer:

> Here, however, fantasy touches the ground of reality, for it was really the mother who by her activities caring for the child's bodily hygiene inevitably stimulated, and perhaps even roused for the first time, pleasurable sensations in her genitals.[74]

However, for all that, Freud does not restore the *theory* of seduction as an axis of metapsychology.

b) In a passage such as the one just cited, it is important to notice what is lacking that would permit a renaissance of the "theory of seduction" in a generalized form.
   - It lacks the aspect of a *message*: the maternal action is reduced to the performance of caretaking without evoking any kind of *address* by the mother to the child.
   - It lacks any mention of the mother's *fantasies* or, simply, her *sexuality,* which is inevitably aroused in this relationship.
   - It lacks many other elements necessary for Freudian thought to return to the path leading toward a generalization of the theory of seduction from the bifurcation presented by the letter of the equinox. I would add that, in the analytic situation itself, the detailed search for memory traces of archaic events can not be teased

73 *Histoire secrète de la séduction sous le règne de Freud,* Voix nouvelles en psychanalyse, no. 36 (Vendôme: PUF, 1991): 651.
74 [*SE* 22:120. Translation modified.]

> apart from restitution of, revelation of the *adult message*—which may be dispersed in a multitude of fragments that, in themselves, were insignificant events—a revelation in which of course transference plays the major role.

RESUMPTION OF THE PROGRESSION OF APRÈS-COUP: THE "*EXPERIMENTA CRUCIS*"

We must accept the idea that *the history of the theory of seduction is not completely parallel to the history of the concept of après-coup*. Now, I will return to that history of après-coup starting with the letter of October 3–4, 1897. The letter is important because it shows the functioning, within Freud's self-analysis, of a nondialectical, unresolvable opposition between the search for a first cause and the hypothesis of pure retroactivity. Freud is in the throes of his self-analysis. He recounts the history of his nanny—his "instructor in sexuality," even his "author in sexual matters," as he puts it, his "*Urheberin*" [female creator]—and especially the anecdote in which she washed him, he thought, in water reddened by her menstrual blood. You see that he is obviously still within the structure of seduction and see how much that structure comes and goes after the so-called "abandonment of the theory of seduction." Having recounted the story of the red water, Freud ends the letter as follows:

> A harsh critic might say of all this that it was retrogressively fantasied instead of progressively determined. The *experimenta crucis* must decide against him. The reddish water would indeed seem to be of that kind. Where do all patients get the horrible perverse details that often are as remote from their experience as from their knowledge?[75]

75 [*Complete Letters*, page 270.]

In brief, he points out that one could argue that what is involved is retroactive imagining, but it is Freud the determinist who responds to such a "harsh critic" that this would be to proceed in the direction opposite to the arrow of time: that it would be imagination. It is important to notice that, even at the very moment of the "revision of the theory of seduction," Freud never abandons the idea of "*nach vorne bedingt*," the idea of the past conditioning the present. Freud never yields on this point—though the alternative to which, in the end, Freud submits is insufficient as I have shown, for Freud, there must either be determinism by the past or else retroactive illusion.

In the last lines, Freud, the good positivist, refers to Bacon's "*experimenta crucis*" as a decisive argument against the critique he invokes, against the idea of retroactive fantasy; for Freud, the red water of the bath does seem to be something of this kind, which is to say an "*experimentum crucis*": "Where do all patients get the horrible perverse details...? How could I have invented that history of red water if it were not truly something that really happened?" Is his argument valid or not? I leave the question open.

From the point view of our journey, I want to emphasize that between *nachträglich* as "understood après-coup," which I discussed above, and the *Nachträglichkeit* at which I am now arriving—the formation of the substantive and of the concept—there were two letters of major importance in which the word did not appear. These two letters are indispensable for understanding the evolution, with its syncopated rhythm, between the word and the thing. The thing sometimes appeared more often, but then the word did not appear at all; and sometimes, as you will see, the word appears at a point where it does not have the full meaning it could well have had at the height of the theory of seduction.

In our next class, I will spend a good deal of time on the letter of November 14, 1897. Today, I will simply open the discussion. In that letter, the term "*Nachträglichkeit*" occurs five times and the adjective or adverb "*nachträglich*" twice. In L*a naissance de la psychanalyse,* the translation is scandalous. I will give you the specific translations. (The translation is by Anne Berman but, *mea culpa*, I continue to publish this text for want of a new translation. In fact, it is possible that I was the copy editor of later editions.) So here they are: the first occurrence of "*Nachträglichkeit*" is rendered as "après-coup": "*par la voie de l'après-coup*"; the second occurrence is rendered as "*effet après-coup*" [the après-coup effect], which is not too bad. This leads to "*l'effet d'après-coup*" [the effect of après-coup], and then, suddenly, we find "*action différée,*" which simply shows that Anne Berman translates the English "deferred action" as "*action différée.*" Her translation relies more on the English than on the German. And following these, there are two occurrences of the adverb *nachträglich*, one of which is translated as "*ensuite*" [then, next] and the other as "*plus tard*" [later].

I do not claim that translating "*Nachträglichkeit*" is easy. We have hesitated, and are still hesitating, about simply saying "après-coup" as the substantive in French, but that would not do justice to the suffix "*-keit,*" because, after all, Freud could equally well have written "*das Nachträgliche*" and not "*die Nachträglichkeit.*" Even though it is not so bad, "*l'effet d'après-coup*" [the effect of après-coup] is quite annoying because there are also certain texts with "*nachträgliche Wirkung*" [après-coup effect], and thus, confusion is possible. I don't use "*l'effet après-coup*" [the après-coup effect], but I do willingly use "*l'effet d'après-coup*" [the effect *of* après-coup] or even perhaps "*le phénomène d'après-coup*" [the phenomenon of après-coup]. We would have to find the most neutral word possible to render the "*-keit*" in French, which doesn't have a suffix that can simply be added to transform an adjective into a substantive. "*Beau*" certainly gives us "*beauté,*" but one can't say "*après-coup-ité.*" English could do it easily by adding "-ness" to "afterwards," yielding "afterwardsness."

Next time I will go into the content of the letter and thus take account of the uses of the term "*Nachträglichkeit.*"

January 16, 1990

Those who are familiar with my thought tell me that I am going too slowly. Perhaps others find I am going too quickly. I don't know. I am going along as best I can, going into detail: it is a sort of recapitulation. I am not only expressing new thoughts. In part I am saying things about après-coup I have said before but trying to express them more clearly and so, by the end, to provide a point of view I dare to call innovative.

THE APPEARANCE OF THE SUBSTANTIVE

Today I will move on to the letter of November 14, 1897, in which the substantive, "*Nachträglichkeit*," appears for the first time. Like letters at certain other moments in the development of his thought, Freud begins this letter humorously with a horoscope:

> "It was on November 12, 1897; the sun was precisely in the eastern quarter; Mercury and Venus were in conjunction—." No, birth announcements no longer start like that.

There is a very learned note by Kris who suggests that this is probably a reminiscence of the way Vasari, the famous biographer of painters of the Quattrocento, began his biography of Michelangelo: with a horoscope. Thus, under the signs of this horoscope, we have the announcement of an event—indeed, of an advent, a birth:

> After the frightful labor pains of the last few weeks, I gave birth to a new piece of knowledge.

This is labor and delivery. And it is not the only time Freud marked a moment in the development of his thought in this manner. You know the famous story of the marble tablet:

> Do you suppose that someday one will read on a marble tablet on this house: "Here, on July 24, 1895, the secret of the dream revealed itself to Dr. Sigm. Freud."[76]

Moreover, in the end, the marble tablet is there. So this is an event, an advent, and at the same time it is a recapitulation since, he says, "I have a presentiment of such events a good while beforehand." Thus there was a presentiment of all that. But these ideas are recapitulated at a specific time, the period of his self-analysis. Moreover, he ends the letter on the self-analysis, saying: "True self-analysis is impossible; otherwise there would be no [neurotic] illness." This is a major insight but one he doesn't explore; *as I see it, analysis cannot occur except in relation to the other because the little human being has emerged as sexual—and as neurotic—in a primordial relation with the other*. Event plus recapitulation: for me, that evokes time in the form of a "spiral," because "spiral time" is also the time of après-coup. A "spiral time" is made up of recapitulation and an event, because each turn of the spiral takes into account the previous turn; every turn is at the same time both a *recapitulation* of X spirals and an *event* at point X. Each point finds itself situated on a vertical passing through another point on another turn. And every turn of the spiral is enriched in its movement by the collection of spiral turnings that preceded it.

Thus, event plus recapitulation describes both après-coup and "spiral time." You know that Kris wrote a whole series of notes on the first edition of the letters to Fliess. Kris indicates that one could describe this passage as work by the preconscious that prepares for the advent of the conscious. If you like. I think that the notion of après-coup may be more productive than that. There is another way of putting things. What is the major issue in this letter? What does the advent refer to? I would say it concerns the theory of normal repression.[77]

76 [Letter to Fliess of June 12, 1900.]
77 [Letter to Fliess of June 12, 1900.]

> Strangely enough, I have a presentiment of such events a good while beforehand. For instance, I wrote to you once in the summer that I was going to find the source of normal sexual repression (morality, shame, and so forth) and then for a long time failed to find it. Before the vacation trip I told you that the most important patient for me was myself; and then, after I came back from vacation, my self-analysis, of which there was at the time no sign, suddenly started. A few weeks ago came my wish that repression might be replaced by my knowledge of the essential thing lying behind it; and that is what I am concerned with now. I have often had a suspicion that something organic plays a part in repression.

For this whole period, all the way up to *Three Essays* and long after, normal repression is linked to what is called "reaction formation" and "sublimation" (the two were not clearly distinguished). Normal repression is repression common to everyone that is linked to mental formations such as "morality, shame, and so forth," which are *not pathological.*

It is important to underline that there is something new here—the existence of normal repression—since, as you recall, the letter of the equinox explored pathological repression and the etiology of the neuroses. The unconscious was implicitly considered pathological, and it was precisely the failure to eliminate that unconscious, to make it conscious, that marked the failure of the theory of seduction and the failure of the search for first scenes. In the letter of the equinox, which is said to be an abandonment of the theory of seduction, we can clearly see that the abandonment is not exactly an abandonment of the theory of seduction, since the letter's theme is the failure of the theory of *pathological repression,* which, in the last instance, is enigmatic. Thus, from my point of view, the movement to the question of *normal repression* in the letter of November 14 marks progress. In *New Foundations,* I said that one of the causes of the failure of Freud's "theory of seduction" was precisely his conception of repression as a purely pathological process and thus thinking of the unconscious as something that had to be completely and permanently abolished. Of course, he didn't stick with that in what followed.

In one sense, there may be progress—progress toward a generalization—but immediately afterwards comes the idea that normal repression cannot be linked to the contingency of the event.

> A few weeks ago came my wish that repression might be replaced by my knowledge of the essential thing lying behind it; and that is what I am concerned with now.

So this movement toward understanding repression is, as you can see, also a movement toward replacing the theory of seduction with something more fundamental. This development is quite ambiguous, but the next sentence makes clear what is fundamental: it is the organic. Freud writes: "I have often had a suspicion that something organic plays a part in repression." In any case, what enters the scene here is the biological, the organic, and at the same time, the phylogenetic. Kris, in a note that is accurate although inadequate, writes that at this point Freud does not yet distinguish clearly between three different meanings of the word "repression." I will read Kris's note and comment on it as I read it:

> In this letter Freud does not yet distinguish clearly between the three meanings of the word "repression" {I think Freud does distinguish them clearly, but that's not important here}: (i) the psychological mechanism of repression; (ii) the processes which take place in the course of the child's development toward maturity {thus the second level is that of infantile biological

> evolution} by means of which cathexis is withdrawn from certain zones of the body; and (iii) alteration in the apparatus, which takes place in the course of the development of the species {which corresponds to Freud's later conception of "organic repression" (*organische Verdrängung*)}.[78]

Along with Kris, we will distinguish three levels. First the psychological level, which I will call level I. The second level, II, is the level of the organic or the level of the biological individual, especially the child—the level of individual development. Finally, there is level III, the level of the species, a phylogenetic level. Notice that Freud says he has had a presentiment for quite a while which prefigured this development, since as far back as the letter of December 6, 1896—the letter in which Freud describes the mental apparatus in terms of translation (this was in at the height of the theory of seduction). In that letter we find this sentence: "Furthermore, behind this lies the idea of abandoned erotogenic zones." Thus behind psychological repression there is the idea of an evolution, the evolution of libidinal stages and the successive abandonment and replacement of erogenous zones.

This notion, which seems to have originated in Freud's presentiments of the summer of 1897, has an important future. It will be found in the theory of stages that will endure in Freudian thought in *Three Essays* (at least in the editions after the first edition of 1905) and also in the idea of organic repression, which, along with Kris, I situate at the third level. We will see what is at issue. For now, I will simply point to references, a partial list, given in *The Standard Edition,* volume 21, pages 60–61, in the editor's introductory note to *Civilization and its Discontents.* It is a very late text in which Freud puts the term "organic repression" in quotation marks. This clearly shows that Freud is alluding to something he has already said. It is very difficult

78 [Freud, *Origins of Psychoanalysis* (New York: Basic Books, 1954): 230.]

to find where he mentioned it. It does not appear to be in the letters to Fliess. I found one occurrence in a text, not indicated in *The Standard Edition,* that marks all of this out.[79] The term "organic repression" is found in the 1905 text entitled "My Views on the Part Played by Sexuality in the Aetiology of the Neuroses." One could say a lot about this text: in brief, it is written in full retreat; it is one of the texts that most strongly backs away from the theory of seduction. It holds that the etiology of sexuality is purely and simply biological.

Let's go back to the letter of November 14, 1897. I won't translate it as you can read it in *La naissance de la psychanalyse*. Even if it is not very well translated, it is adequate for a first reading. At level III, the phylogenetic level, it describes something that Freud considers extremely important and that he will continue to believe and approve of as late as *Civilization and its Discontents*. It concerns the evolution in animals from walking on four legs, nose to the ground, to an upright posture, a development he correlates with abandonment or diminution of the role of smell in sexuality (sniffing the sexual organs of the other) and equally with the abandonment of smell tied to anality. Sniffing in animals is as much anal as genital. It is in that passage (and only there) that "organic repression" is described. Let's not forget the importance of the nose and of olfaction in the history of psychoanalysis, from Fliess to the *Wolf Man,* etc., etc. In the history of psychoanalysis, the nose is a long chapter. For animals, the nose smells strongly exciting odors. And let's not forget German expressions such

79 [The Standard Edition has this, "I think it is worth emphasizing the fact that, whatever modifications my views on the aetiology of the psychoneuroses have passed through, there are two positions which I have never repudiated or abandoned—the importance of sexuality and of infantilism. Apart from this, accidental influences have been replaced by constitutional factors and 'defence' in the purely psychological sense has been replaced by organic 'sexual repression'." *SE* 7:277-278 emphasis added. See also: *"Ich halte es der Hervorhebung wert, daß meine Anschauungen über die Ätiologie der Psychoneurosen bei allen Wandlungen doch zwei Gesichtspunkte nie verleugnet oder verlassen haben, die Schätzung der Sexualität und des Infantilismus. Sonst sind an die Stelle akzidenteller Einflüsse konstitutionelle Momente, für die rein psychologisch gemeinte "Abwehr" ist* ***die organische "Sexualverdrängung"*** *eingetreten."* GS 5:157]

as *"Er trägt die Nase hoch"* (he carries his nose high), which is to say that "he turns up his nose, he regards himself as something particularly noble" [Masson].[80] The notion can even be found in expressions like that. Here, I would emphasize that in the phylogenetic sequence going from animal (with four legs) to man (who stands on two) there is a single change and thus only two "stages": the anal stage (which is the olfactory stage) and then the genital stage. "Organic repression" comes down to that.

THE ORGANIC STAGES OF SEXUALITY

At level II, the level of the maturation of the individual, this letter describes all the elements of what will become the classic sequence of stages: not only is the phylogenetic movement from anal to genital but also the buccopharyngeal (*Mund-Rachengegend*) zone.[81] Thus, in II we find the oral stage identified as a region, the oral region identified as an abandoned region, and we also find not only the genital regions but also women's genital sexuality subdivided into two substages: a phallic stage (which is not named "phallic") under the dominance of clitoral sexuality and a stage which is properly genital. So for women there are four stages, and for men only three, since for men the phallic stage is considered the final stage. All this will be slightly refined in what follows, much later texts, but as you can see everything is already identified.

Finally, in level I, we see the play of repression described in both its normal and pathological aspects. One could say that normal repression is precisely the repression that goes hand in hand with the sequence of stages. In girls, normal repression (from the mental point of view) occurs when there is abandonment (from the biological point of view) of the oral, anal, and phallic sexualities. The normal result of this repression is the formation of morality, shame (or modesty), com-

80 In French, one says: *"Il porte la tête haute"* [He carries his head high].
81 *Der Rachen*—the throat or mouth—seems to have no etymological relationship with *die Rache*, vengeance.

passion, etc. This is repression on the psychological level (to follow Kris, let's use this term provisionally as a first approximation), and it is here that après-coup functions and here that "*Nachträglichkeit*" appears. There is no doubt that this is the first time the term appears as a *substantive*. Let's underline two points: founding repression on the organic, on the evolution of zones in the child, does not mean abandoning the idea that psychic trauma requires two moments in time; but, from another angle, it may be to drop something essential from the theory of seduction. That is more or less the line of thought I will develop.

What is the relationship among levels I, II, and III? Going back to III, the oldest and most fundamental level, there is the completely dazzling passage about anality that shows that, for Freud, something runs through all the three levels. Phylogenesis, biological ontogenesis, and psychological genesis are concentrated in the *repression of anality*. I will read you this astonishing passage in which Freud truly speaks as a psychoanalyst, beyond psychology:

> To put it crudely {which is to say "a simplification," but it is also crude in the other sense of the word}, the memory actually stinks just as in the present the object stinks; and in the same manner as we turn away our olfactory sense organ (the head and nose) in disgust, the preconscious and the organ of sense that is consciousness turn away from the memory. This is repression {the word is underlined by Freud.}[82]

You see why I cannot hold onto a single line of thought, why I cannot simply cover all that is interesting in this or that text; you see that what we have here could quite reasonably be called an anthropomorphism or a radical realisticomorphism of the psychic apparatus. The model of repression used here is not an abstract model; it is not a "psychological"

---

82 [Letter from Freud to Fliess, November 14, 1897, in *Complete Letters*, 278–282. Translation modified.]

model. Here, the psychological is an exact copy of a concrete, physical movement to such an extent that the memory actually "stinks" and the "preconscious" actually turns away from the stink.

THE MODEL OF ANALITY

Another important point is that the major object of repression in this passage, perhaps the very model of the repressed, is anality. To my knowledge, this has never been clearly put up for discussion. Which is to say that this point has been left out of all the different vulgarizations of psychoanalysis in different ways in the popular media and even scholarly articles; in short, you won't find much about anality anywhere. It remains the great repressed of psychoanalysis; anality is the great repressed of the pure. All the rest, the blablabla, the papa, the mama, that's fine. But when Salvador Dalí said in a televised discussion: "The train station in Perpignan is a shithole [*trou du cul*]," everybody nearly fainted, including the interviewer and the philosopher he was conversing with. Salvador was dramatically anal, and he had the audacity—in a truly Freudian way—to discombobulate his interlocutors, those right-thinking conformists of sexual propriety. In any case, Freud doesn't beat about the bush: the model for repression, and perhaps the principle object of repression, is anality; and it is also *your* principle object of repression!

After this concreteness, I will return to more abstract matters. Consider the relationships between levels I, II, and III, which I have distinguished following Kris. The relation between III and II is the relation between phylogenesis and ontogenesis. You've heard of Haeckel's law, according to which "ontogeny recapitulates phylogeny," which he proposed in his 1868 book *The History of Creation* [*Natürliche Schöpfungsgeschichte*]. Haeckel was a Darwinian, and the idea was probably pointed out to Freud by a man named Baldwin, himself a post-Darwinian.[83]

---

83 See letter of November 5, 1897, in which this Baldwin is mentioned.

A PARENTHESIS ON INHERITANCE OF ACQUIRED CHARACTERISTICS

The mention of the post-Darwinians permits me to insert a small marginal comment on the question of inheritance of the acquired. The neo-Darwinists speak of inheritance of the acquired. It is usually said, with a kind of mental laziness, that the difference between Darwin and Lamarck is that Lamarck accepts inheritance of the acquired and Darwin does not, but this is not true. Both Darwin and Lamarck accept inheritance of acquired traits, which, moreover, is more of a genetic than an evolutionary theory. Both agree on the existence of inheritance of acquired traits; the difference between the two lies in the *mode of acquisition*. For Lamarck, it is function and adaptation to the environment that are determining: if one adapts to the cold by covering oneself, then little by little one has more fur on one's back; we could say that adaptation is the mode of acquisition but not of inheritance. As you know, it is the opposite for Darwin and the neo-Darwinists: what's new occurs by random mutation followed by selection. But in both cases, once the trait has been acquired, both Darwin and Lamarck agree that the inheritance of the acquired follows the laws of genetics.

All this is to say that Haeckel's law is as true for a Darwinian as for a Lamarckian. Since I am digressing on the question of the inheritance of the acquired—a problem that, with the introduction of phylogenesis, is constantly present for Freud—part of the question would be to ask *what is and what could be inherited*: organs, behaviors, fantasies, scenarios, etc.?

DIFFICULTIES OF PHYLOGENESIS

In the letter we are considering, what Freud seems to consider as acquired is a *sequence of dominant organs*, one after the other, or else, perhaps, a sequence of fantasies—primal fantasies. Therefore, to examine the question of phylogenesis in psychoanalysis, one has to identify not only the mode of acquisition in inheritance but also the question of what can be considered inheritable. Yet here, Haeckel's law goes much further: it says not only that the individual reproduces what has been acquired by the species but that the individual *recapitulates* the development of the species. The genesis of one recapitulates the genesis of the other. What is inherited in Haeckel's law is not only this or that capacity; it is the history of its evolution. In other words, if living entities passed through a stage that could be called "aquatic" before passing through a stage on land, then the human individual—and this is an embryological speculation—passes through an aquatic stage before passing into a life in the air. It's a simple example. What Freud is alleging here is a reproduction in the evolution of the individual, in his individual sexuality, of the evolution of the species: this is to say that the sexual zones of childhood are abandoned in the same way that each zone has been abandoned in the history of the species.

As I pointed out just above, at level III there is a generalization of something that *Freud only shows for one evolutionary development*, which is to say the development that goes from *the anal to the genital*. The same is true in *Civilization and its Discontents*. The only evolutionary sequence that is supposed to be reproduced in the sequence of sexual stages of childhood is the evolution from anal to genital. It seems fair to say (there is absolutely nothing about this in the letter) that a movement from "orality" to "anality" is not plausible. It would be hard to imagine the existence of "oral" animals before "anal" animals; and although Freud clung fiercely to the idea and made it central to his later article on "infantile genital organization," it is even harder to conceive of a phylogenetic development from a phallic stage to a genital one. This idea was based on the notion that at a certain time there was only one sex, the masculine sex (the phallic stage), and that in women the development of a genital stage began with a castration. Thus, at first there would have been a single sex, a masculine sex; then the male remained phallic, and the woman abandoned the phallic (notably clitoral excitation) to move on to her definitive genital sexuality. As to this putative transition—for a long time I have had the opportunity to say this, most clearly in my book *Problématiques II: Castration*[84]—this idea of the development of two sexes from a single male sex, if one were to take it for anything other than what it is, namely an "*infantile sexual theory*," would be completely contradicted by science and particularly by what is known about embryonic sexual differentiation. This is to say that if there is something that should be considered unisexual with a physiological potential from bisexuality, it is a *female* unisexuality. In other words, if the embryonic or infantile organization is isolated from all masculinizing hormonal influences, it will develop in a female direction. Clearly this removes all realistic value from the idea of a biological development of a phallic stage culminating in a genital stage. From a biological point of view, it is the opposite that happens. I will quote a very simple passage from the biologist Kreisler:

> Masculinization is an active phenomenon which requires the presence of a functional testicle. Feminization is a passive phenomenon that does not require the presence of a functioning ovary. The experimental castration of male embryos leads to a feminine internal morphology.

Thus, the natural development of the organism removed from hormonal stimulation is feminine development; one could say that masculinizing development grafts itself onto this feminine organism. Far from castration, as Freud would have it, the biological reality is more of an addition.

I will conclude this point by saying that we are in the presence of one of many avatars of Freud's tendency found, within phylogen-

84 Paris: PUF, 1980, and, before that, published in the journal *Psychanalyse à l'université*.

esis, a missing piece of reality, something he needs in order to explain the genesis of the unconscious. I have pointed to others: in addition to a phylogenesis of stages, there is a phylogenesis of primal fantasies. We will come back that.

THE QUESTION OF STAGES OF SEXUALITY

This failure of the attempt to found ontogenesis on phylogenesis does not necessarily invalidate the sequence I have called Sequence II, the "sequence of stages" from infantile sexuality up to puberty and adulthood. However, the failure to find a phylogenetic foundation weakens that ontogenic sequence of stages; it calls into question of the notion that the sequence of stages has a purely biological cause (and also, as we will see, raises the question of whether there is any need to resort to that sort of explanation at all). For context, remember that Freud frequently oscillates on the question of stages: if one consults his *Project for a Scientific Psychology* of 1895, in the end the only biological stage in which après-coup emerges, the only biological stage in relation to which the movement of après-coup is defined, is puberty. Which is to say that a stimulus—a seduction, any event X—has a different effect after puberty as compared to before puberty; the whole story is played out between the prepubertal and the postpubertal. From the biological point of view (given the evident effects of hormones), puberty is an undeniable boundary. On the other hand, if there are other, prepubertal biological pressures they are not evident. A second step in the evolution of Freud's thinking about stages is marked by letter of November 14, 1897, in which the whole sequence of stages is prefigured—I spoke of them a moment ago: *oral, anal, genital I*, and *genital II*.

Now let's turn to *Three Essays*—but we must specify that we are speaking of only the first edition, the edition of 1905, and not of the later ones as these contain many additions, most notably the addition of 'stages.'" The *Three Essays on the Theory of Sexuality* of 1905 is a return to the *Project* in that there is only one critical biological point: puberty. The very structure of *Three Essays* demonstrates this. The entire last essay is entitled "The Transformations of Puberty." In the second essay, entitled "Infantile Sexuality," sexuality is not described as a linked sequence of stages but rather as polymorphous sexuality without organization; anal and oral sexual activities exist side by side without organization and without sequence. In 1905 there is a return, a kind of repetition, a spiral: a return to the opposition specified in the *Project*: prepubertal versus postpubertal. It is only gradually (in 1915, 1920, etc.) in different articles and different reworkings of *Three Essays*, that the prepubertal period is again subdivided into stages or organizations. Moreover, the first organization to be described is the anal organization, in "The Disposition to Obsessional Neurosis" of 1913, in which the idea that there are organizations *before* those of puberty is presented the first time. Only later will Freud present the idea of an oral organization, a phallic organization, an infantile genital organization, etc.

NACHTRÄGLICHKEIT IN THE LETTER OF NOVEMBER 14, 1897

Having followed me throught this series of didactic digressions on heredity of the acquired and on the idea of a sequence of sexual stages, you may be wondering: What's happened to après-coup? What about "*Nachträglichkeit*"? There is nothing better to do at this point than to read the passage in which the term appears four times within ten lines (and then a few more times in what follows). I ask that you pay close attention as I am both translating from the German and adding a few comments:

> An unbinding[85] of sexuality {"an unbinding of sexuality" is a term that has existed since the *Project* and even before}, as you know, I have in mind a kind of secretion

85 [In Freud: *Entbindung*; Laplanche renders it: *déliaison*; Masson renders it: "release."]

{It is precisely a hormonal secretion} which is rightly felt as the internal state of the libido. {Thus, here libido is the perception of this hormonal secretion.} The unbinding of sexuality comes about in three ways, not only through a peripheral stimulus of the sexual organs {the first way of producing a sexual excitation, external stimulation of the organs} or through the internal excitations arising from those organs {which is to say that those organs can be excited internally and biologically}, but unbinding of sexuality may also be produced by representations, that is by memory traces, and therefore also by the path of après-coup. {*Nachträglichkeit* is this third mode of sexual excitation. There are two modes that work by themselves: the organs being excited by physical action from outside and action from inside the individual; additionally, there is a third mode of excitation by *representations*.} You are already familiar with this line of thought. If a child's genitals have been irritated by someone, years afterwards by après-coup {*Nachträglichkeit*} the memory of this will produce an unbinding of sexuality far stronger than at the initial occurrence, because the apparatus that initiates and determines the quantity of secretion has grown in the meantime. {This is the old reasoning about "après-coup": normally, compared to the event itself, a memory of an event only produces a weak effect. It is only in the case of sexuality that a memory has stronger effects than the event itself because, in the time between happening and recalling, the organism holding the memory has evolved and can react more powerfully.} Thus a non-neurotic après-coup {*Nachträglichkeit*} may occur normally, and this generates compulsion. . . . But an

> après-coup {*Nachträglichkeit*} of this kind can also occur in connection with memories of the excitation of the *abandoned* sexual zones. In which case the outcome is not an unbinding of libido but a sensation of unpleasure analogous to disgust.[86]

I will not discuss the mechanisms of all that; what is essential is that Freud maintains—even emphasizes—the idea of après-coup, which thus becomes a concept, based on the evolution and the sequence of erotogenic zones and on their being or not being abandoned.

APPEARANCE OF THE CONCEPT, REGRESSION OF THE SEMANTIC CONTENT

We can see that après-coup as a concept, as *Nachträglichkeit*—for which I still see no French equivalent other than "après-coup"—comes at the moment when the theory of seduction is weakening. Even in this last passage, a number of negative elements point to this weakening. Above all, après-coup is reduced to purely a play of quantities, which is to say that the difference between the effect of the event and the effect of the memory of the event is a purely quantitative difference due to the fact that, in the interval, the apparatus has become capable of reacting more strongly. It is a game that appears mechanistic—we could call it an engineer's model of après-coup. It would not be difficult to imagine a machine created in the manner of Leonardo da Vinci, a model which clearly, in spite of the term après-coup, would in no way contradict the determinism so dear to Freud: in no case is the "arrow of time" inverted. Here, not only is the arrow of time not inverted but, as a result, the idea we encountered a short time before, the idea of "understood après-coup," of "heard to be said and understood après-coup" (*gehört und nachträglich verstanden*), this idea has gone missing. What arrives "après-coup" is no longer an "*understood*

86 [Freud, *Complete Letters*, 279-280 translation modified.]

après-coup"; it is simply a stronger reaction.

I don't want to say that there is nothing in this letter but negative elements. I have emphasized the extremely ambiguous but nevertheless important element: the introduction of a biological sequence. In this text, repression and après-coup can only be conceptualized on the basis of a sequence, a temporal ladder, of zones and types of sexuality. Sequence I (individual psychobiology) can only be conceived as cut out from and emerging against the background of Sequence II (the biology of the species). So, I'd say this: to begin with, there are several ways to conceive of Sequence II (of course, I am speaking for myself). It is not necessary to conceptualize it purely biologically. The sequence oral, anal, genital can have many determinants other than those of biological maturation. It can be understood on a level that is much more interpersonal, even anthropological. The precession of orality can be understood not on the basis of an internal maturational sequence but rather as a consequence of the fact that the first motherly care is feeding; the problem of excretions will come quickly after—very early, but secondarily.

Above all, what I want to emphasize is the relation of Sequence I to Sequence II. One could characterize it as "cut out from the base," "emerging from the foundation." The sequence of psychological repression is founded on an organic evolution. Term by term, all this can be understood as coming from a narrow determinism. In this period of Freud's thought, the schema he uses is not far from the opposition "substructure/superstructure." In fact, Freud uses these terms (without, however, referring to Marx). One example is in the letter of December 6, 1896: after having described repression, he writes: "So much for the superstructure; now let's go to the substructure."[87] Remember, at that time, the substructure was constituted by Flies-

87 Both Kris and Masson avoid the terms "substructure" and "base," perhaps protecting Freud from a seeming allusion to Marx. Both render the sentence as follows: "So much for the superstructure. Now for an attempt to set it on its organic foundations."

sian "periods," a *so-called* biological bedrock that, in reality, came from fantasy. So, the relation between Sequence I and Sequence II could be conceived as strictly determined and above all as a term-for-term correspondence. You can see where all this could lead: to express this correspondence, one could say that fantasies are the expression or the blossoming of the drive while the drive, in its turn, has its origin in the biological organism.

THE BIOLOGIZING CONCEPTION OF DRIVE: THE KLEINIANS

Fantasy as the blossoming of drive, drive as the blossoming of an organic sequence: this is precisely the conception of the Kleinians. We can refer to a classic article by Susan Isaacs (in which the idea of après-coup is completely absent, as is true for Kleinian thought in general): "The Nature and Function of Phantasy" (1948,) which was included in *Developments in Psychoanalysis* (1952).[88] I will quote a few lines:

> Unconscious phantasies are primarily about bodies, and represent instinctual aims toward objects. These phantasies are, in the first instance, the psychic representatives of libidinal and destructive instincts.

One could certainly call this conception Freudian; although, happily, there are other ideas to be gleaned from Freud. Fantasies as psychic representatives of drives, drives as representatives of biological processes! Whether one calls this a mechanism or even understands it as what Spinoza calls an echo, what is important is the term-to-term correspondence. And it is here that I try to contrast this as a conception with another way of conceiving the play of repression "on the

88 Susan Isaacs, "The Nature and Function of Phantasy," *International Journal of Psychoanalysis* 29 (1948): 73–97; also published in *Developments in Psychoanalysis*, eds. Melanie Klein, Paula Heimann, Susan Isaacs, and Joan Riviere (London: Hogarth Press, 1952).

base of an underlying sequence." The essential difference is conceiving the underlying sequence not as a term for term translation into the psychological sequence but as a sequence in which each sequential stage furnishes a collection of signifiers, a language or a code. You can clearly see that the notion of translation can be invoked in both cases: for the Kleinians, it is present in the idea of representation, one could say that oral fantasies are the translation of oral biological processes. There is certainly a term-for-term correspondence; but as for the libido, understood precisely as that hormonal discharge, can it make its way into a mental translation? The Kleinian conception does not completely reject the notion of translation but conceives of it in a very limited fashion. The other conception is the one I advance and that is sometimes present in Freud. For instance, it underlies the conception of the December 6 letter in which Sequence II, the sequence of the base—whatever its nature may be, either biological or maybe (and this is my view) biocultural—furnishes a sequence of languages. And this is very different because *a language cannot be translated*; a language is what permits translation; it is "what one translates into."

January 23, 1990

The letter of November 14, 1897, which I have discussed for so long, led me to rework, yet again, the notion of translation. I proposed the superimposition of two sequences. First the sequence of events ordered by time, the sequence of sexual stages which Freud considers to be biological. I'd prefer to speak of a sequence of situations between the adult and the infant, stages of childrearing. Then there is another level, the level of fantasy, which may be the level of the drive. I also contrasted two conceptions of the "translation" between those two levels: (1) a term-by-term conception of translation. This is what Susan Isaacs proposes: a fantasy in which "phantasies" are "mental translations" of biological transformations, vital processes. Oral processes, anal processes, etc., translate themselves into "phantasies;" (2) another conception emerges, a conception of a "to-be-translated" presented to the child, which the child will translate using what one could call, metaphorically, a succession of languages—of codes presented to the child in a succession; I leave open the question of whether this succession is purely "biological" or perhaps "anthropological" or "bioanthropological."

To be even clearer: Susan Isaacs, like many others, invokes a well-known passage from Freud's 1925 paper "Negation" in which Freud speaks about language. It is a text whose purpose and value lie in its philosophical contribution to the notion of negation and to its psychoanalytic foundation. Translated completely erroneously as "*dénégation*" [which is closer to 'denial' than to 'negation] by many, including by myself and Pontalis, "*Verneinung*" is negation [*négation*] both in the logical and in the psychological sense of the term. I will read from Freud:

> The function of judgment is concerned in the main with two sorts of decisions. It affirms or disaffirms the possession by a thing of a particular attribute;

> and it asserts or disputes that a presentation has an existence in reality.[89]

Here Freud takes up what have classically been considered two functions of judgment: judgment of attribution on one hand and judgment of existence on the other. What is novel in Freud's approach (but not unique in philosophy) is his placement of judgments of attribution before judgments of existence. Before deciding if a thing exists, first it is necessary to decide what it is, whether it is *good or bad*. Here it is the first issue, the judgment of attribution, that is in question. Closing this parenthesis, I continue reading from "Negation."

> The attribute to be decided about may originally have been good or bad, useful or harmful. Expressed in the language of the oldest drive, the oral drives,[90] it would be translated as: "I should like to eat this," or "I should like to spit it out"; and, pushing the translation further: "I want this inside me and that outside."

I won't go into the details of the notion of primal introjection in Freud. What interests me here is that Freud says "the language of the oral drive." Here's how Susan Isaacs uses this text:

> What Freud picturesquely calls here "the language of the oral impulse," he elsewhere calls the "mental expression" of an instinct, i.e., the phantasies which are the psychic representatives of a bodily aim.[91]

There is a radical confusion in what Susan Isaacs writes. Freud does not say that oral fantasy is the translation of the oral drive. He says that there is something to be translated, a primal to-be-translated,

89 [*SE* 19:236–237.Translation modified.]
90 [Translation modified. Strachey has "the language of the oldest—the oral—instinctual impulses."]
91 Isaacs, "The Nature and Function of Phantasy." Isaacs, following Strachey, here and elsewhere uses 'urge' and 'instinct' rather than 'drive' to translated '*trieb*'.

originally the "good or bad," which is then translated into a language. You can see that Freud does not assimilate the drive to an expression of a bodily urge but rather to a language in which something must be expressed. As to this "something"—nothing prevents it from being on the order of a "message" addressed to the child.

Now I will finish my comments on this letter in which, for the first time, Freud introduces *Nachträglichkeit* as a concept. In the same letter there is the introduction of an underlying sequence, an underlying biological sequence, which is to say a succession of biological stages in which one stage "represses" the previous stage, or in which stages are successively abandoned—an abandonment that, I remind you, is itself born from a phylogenetic abandonment of successive forms of sexuality (and there we are in the midst of florid Freudian speculation). I have pointed out that the introduction of an underlying sequence is not necessarily negative, but only if one preserves the idea (which here, in my view, Freud does not preserve) of a fundamental "to-be-translated," which is precisely the idea of a translation of a message from the other. And yet, *it is at the moment when the theory of seduction is fading away, the very moment when the translational theory of repression that we see in the letter of December 6 disappears, that* "Nachträglichkeit" *appears as a concept*. Clearly this is a particularly interesting effect of syncope that will lead us to other après-coups of après-coup.

C. F. MEYER: *GUSTAV ADOLF'S PAGE*

Now I will take up two later occurrences that are essential both for the Freudian concept of "*Nachträglichkeit*" and for our own discussion. One, in the letter of June 9, 1898, is "literary." This example clearly shows that Freud and Fliess regularly discussed "Nachträglichkeit" because we see it in Freud's comments on a novel he is reading by Conrad Ferdinand Meyer (well-known at the time, somewhat forgotten now).[92] In the following letter [June 20, 1898], Freud analyzes a novel by Meyer titled *Die Richterin*.[93] As noted by those who have commented on the "letters to Fliess," it is the first "application" of psychoanalysis to literature. Yet in the earlier letter, of June 9, Freud was already reading Conrad Ferdinand Meyer, and the novel in question was *Gustav Adolf's Page*." I will summarize the story very briefly: It takes place during the Thirty Years' War. Gustavus Adolphus, king of Sweden, father of Christina, is attempting to conquer Germany in the name of the Reformation, fighting against the Catholics and their allies in the Holy Empire. Gustavus, a major and romantic figure in the novel, is recruiting a page. Being a page is not an easy job. These are not pages in court but pages who serve as aides-de-camp to soldiers and suffer all the uncertainties of war; the previous three or four of Gustavus's pages have all been killed in battle. The king has set his sights on the son of a bourgeois family he knows well. The father and the son understand this proposition to be disastrous, knowing that if they accept they would be sending the boy to his death, and yet, of course, they can not refuse the great honor. Now it happens that in the family there is not only a son but also a daughter, and this daughter, Gürtel, has been in love with Gustavus since her childhood, so much so that she proposes to go in her brother's place. The brother is quickly made to disappear by sending him away on a trip, and Gürtel is disguised as a boy.

As was common at the time, when someone was recruited into the army, someone else could take his place. Disguised as a page, Gürtel spent several months with Gustavus, and the reader is witness to this companionship. Gustavus suspects nothing; he doesn't know he has a girl next to him; and, at a moment when she risks being revealed to be a girl, rather than being accused of being a traitor to him, she flees. In the novel, both of them die. He is killed by treason,

92 C. F. Meyer was quite well-known at the time, but these days one doesn't even find him listed in a dictionary of particularly good works, which is rather puzzling.
93 *Die Richterin (The Judge)* (1885).

and she is killed defending him. It ends in a macabre scene in which both are brought into a church and one hears the beautiful funerary chanting for the two of them.

Why is Freud interested in this? I will pass quickly over this story of transvestitism, which might be amusing to analyze at length, but here is what Freud says:

> I am reading C. F. Meyer with great pleasure. In *Gustav Adolf's Page* I found the idea of *Nachträglichkeit* twice: in the famous passage you discovered, the one with the slumbering kiss, and in the episode involving the Jesuit who insinuates himself as little Christine's teacher.

Freud continues, leaving his account of the novel: "In Innsbruck they actually show the chapel where she converted to Catholicism!" I will give the second example mentioned by Freud, which lies outside the letter. In the novel, the little Christina, the future Christina of Sweden, future correspondent of Descartes, is given a teacher who is, of course, a Protestant. But one day the little Christina is discovered in a corner in the midst of saying her rosary. Horror! The teacher is revealed to be a Jesuit disguised as a Protestant in order to—it is necessary to say it clearly—seduce the little girl into Catholicism; and where Freud sees après-coup is when the teacher is chased away. (Gustavus, who could have cut off his head, is lenient, satisfied by sending him away.) Nothing more is said. Where is the *Nachträglichkeit*? Is the idea that, après-coup, the little Christina converted to Catholicism? If so, it is an extremely dubious example of après-coup.

The much more interesting example is the one Fliess pointed out, the slumbering kiss, the 'kiss that goes to sleep'; the circumstance is as follows. Little Gürtel has fled Gustavus because she could be accused—wrongly—and the king could suspect her of betrayal. No one suspects that she is a girl; however, suspected of treason, she is desperate and flees, wandering on horseback into Gustavus's army where she encounters a colonel. Now this colonel, who knew the girl's father, recognizes her—first by her bearing and then by a scar she has had since childhood, caused by a fall from a horse. He recognizes her and greets her with the words "my poor little girl." He doesn't chastise her but says this: "It's very dangerous, my child. If you had been discovered by Gustavus, he would have said, 'Away! You idiot!' to scold you and a second later would have thought about something else. But if the queen had unmasked you, what a scandal! And as for me, this is what I say: 'One shouldn't give kisses to children. The kiss goes to sleep then reignites itself when the lips grow and swell. There is the "slumbering kiss." Place a kiss on a baby's lips and there the kiss sleeps, only to catch fire later when the lips have grown and swollen. The officer explains it:

> "This is true and will remain true. One day the king took you from my arms, my little goddaughter; he pressed you to his heart and covered you with kisses, and this resonated because you were a bold and pretty child." The page no longer remembered the kiss, but it resonated in her violent blushing.

Freud probably did not discuss this example, but one can easily see in what sense he took it and also see what is lacking in his conception. The scene of the "slumbering kiss" takes place in two moments. The first is the inscription of an excitation on the lips of the child. This inscription will remain asleep until the oral erogenous zone is woken up by pubertal or prepubertal processes—"when the lips grew and became swollen." At this point, the trace of the kiss is reinvested from the inside and with a much stronger excitation completely overwhelms the precocious infantile excitation the kiss had initially produced. As the model proposed in the *Project* indicates, the excitation is: 1) much more intense and 2) arises from the interior, the direction from which the subject does not expect to be "attacked." Thus, the absence of preparation, and the effect of surprise, which will trigger the pathological process of repression. There we really have the model of a "time bomb" [*bombe à retardement*], which the English translators have rendered with the phrase "deferred action." The action consists of a quasi-mechanical unwinding that can neither be thwarted nor enter into a dialectic with the past-to-present, which is to say with the "arrow of time."

Forgotten are the suggestions of a reverse movement, or, to put it precisely, there is no hint of something that was originally "heard to be said" and later "understood après-coup." To the extent that Freud limits the former to a *process of impersonal excitation*, he cannot escape this forgetting. Conceived "mechanically," the original kiss is not open to reinterpretation or to translation après-coup. What happens is simply that the memory of an excitation is amplified by puberty, but what starts as a purely somatic excitation remains a purely somatic excitation. What is a solipsistic excitation of a subject remains a solipsistic excitation. Staying solely with the story of the young Gürtel in its successive phases, one is stuck in a circle. The element missing from the classic Freudian interpretation is the intersubjective aspect of the event. The adult other, Gustavus Adolphus, implants an excitation by kissing the child on the lips; the kiss is a message to be deciphered, an enigmatic message, which is itself impregnated with the adult's unconscious sexuality. In this way a dialectic with a double meaning (according to the direction of time) will be established between the survival of the message, its reawakening, and then its translation, when it is reinvested and strengthened at puberty.

A second major example punctuates the distance between the letters to Fliess and the publication of the *Wolf Man*. It is a passage from *The Interpretation of Dreams* that comes in the long elaboration of associations to and considerations about the dream called the "dream of dumplings" (the "meatballs" that Freud's mother was preparing). Here is the passage that is important for our purposes:

> Love and hunger, I reflected, meet at a woman's breast {*Frauenbrust*}. A young man who was a great admirer of feminine beauty was talking once—so the story went—of the good-looking wet nurse who had suckled him when he was a baby: "I'm sorry," he remarked, "that I didn't make a better use of my opportunity." I was in the habit of quoting this anecdote to explain the factor of après-coup {*Nachträglichkeit*} in the mechanism of the psychoneuroses.[94]

Here, with the focus on a woman's breast, there is a quite complicated interplay between infantile oral sexuality, linked to nursing, and adult oral sexual play with the breast. I have commented on this text many times. Here I would like to underline several points. To begin with, one could consider it to be a story about one and the same person, first as a nursling and then as a young adult. It is the same person who sees himself at a very early age and who regrets missing out on what was a sexual opportunity. Freud does not choose between the two ages of a single person; he presents them as simultaneous. One could say he leaves the direction of the arrow of time indeterminate. There are two symmetrical assertions he could have proposed: "This is how the pleasure-taking in nursing precociously determines the sexuality of adults" or "This is how a young adult retroactively puts himself back in and injects sexuality into an infantile situation, which in itself is absolutely innocent." In fact, the concept of *Nachträglichkeit* leaves the choice between the two directions completely open.

Here, as in the case of the "page," we can't help but notice that something is missing, and that what is missing reveals that, in spite of everything, the symmetry of the two arrows of time is artificial. What is missing arises from the fact that Freud, in a solipsistic fashion, situates the entire process in *one and the same* person, the

94 *GW* 2:211; SE 4:204–205.

baby / adult masculine subject. It is the same subject who had been the child who, as an adult, contemplates that child. In addition, the infantile experience that is evoked is one of pure and simple enjoyment, without any representational content, which for us is to say *without a message*. This is because the person who is missing from Freud's little demonstration, missing from the action and from the interaction, is quite simply *the wet nurse*. Even if she is physically present, she is absent as an interlocutor, as a subject sending a message in the direction of the child. In a limiting case of Freud's conception, *she could be replaced by a* [non-living] *physical source*, comfortable and voluptuous, emitting some marvelous liquid, or by a fruit with an extraordinary taste but which doesn't talk. So, in the stories of Gürtel and of this young man, the "great admirer of feminine beauty," all the dramatis personae are at Freud's disposal, and they number three, not two: the subject as a baby, the subject at the age of sexual maturity, and a third person, an actor with a whole role: Gustavus Adolphus or the wet nurse. In our understanding, the whole process has its origin in this adult other, because his or her gesture is indissociably a sexual and nonsexual message, a message that will sleep for years and then be awoken and will demand "understanding après-coup," which is to say a translation.

Yet in his description of après-coup, Freud completely ignores this third actor, who is truly the motor of the whole process. From then on, he is reduced to speculating about the history of a sole and unique person, alternating, unable to decide between a determinism arising from a supposedly biological infantile sexuality and a sort of "retroactive" interpretation, opening the door to all the hermeneutic derivatives of "meaning attribution" or "resignification."[95]

95 See "Interpretation between Determinism and Hermeneutics," [translated by Philip Slotkin in *Essays on Otherness*, ed. John Fletcher (New York: Routledge, 1999), 138–165; and translated by Luke Thurston in *The Unfinished Copernican Revolution*, (New York: The Unconscious in Translation, forthcoming)]

ON "SCREEN MEMORIES"

To conclude for today, I will refer to a text, from the same period, in which, quite surprisingly, the word *nachträglich* does not appear. It is the 1899 article entitled "Screen Memories" ["Des souvenirs-couverture"] ("Über Deckerinnerungen"),[96] which studies the problem raised by banal memories from childhood that, in spite of their trivial character, for unknown reasons are vividly preserved in memory. The article can be approached in two ways: One concerns Freud's biography, because the memory he used for his example is, in reality, one of Freud's own. For such considerations, I recommend Didier Anzieu's work on *Freud's Self-Analysis*,[97] where Freud's analysis of this memory is extensively retraced. This biographical point of view will not be our concern; our interest will be in the theory that Freud is trying to elaborate, particularly its relation to the "arrow of time." Freud's theoretical conclusion, which occupies one or two pages, is quite strange. As these memories are anodyne, Freud first demonstrates that, in reality, they are defensive—thus the term "screen" (*couverture*). These are memories that "screen," that "cover the truth," the anodyne hiding the sexual; in addition, there is a complex relationship between the sexual and the nonsexual and also between the past, childhood, and different epochs of life. Here is a short passage from Freud's conclusion:

> One may describe a screen memory as either 'retrogressive' or 'anticipatory,' depending on which of these two temporal relations is established between the screening and the screened.[98]

96 [In the *OCF.P*, the title is "Des souvenirs-couverture," and Laplanche notes, in parentheses, that the title in previous French translations was "Souvenirs écrans."]
97 Didier Anzieu, *Freud's Self-Analysis* (Madison, CT: International Universities Press, 1986), 404–412.
98 *SE* 3:320. Translation modified.

"Retrogressive" means the screen memory is covering a prior event, and "anticipatory" means the memory is covering a subsequent event. An interesting conclusion. "Retrogressive" is Strachey's rendering of "*Rücklaüfig*." The term "*nachträglich*" is not used, but it could have been. Yet what's most interesting is that this text scotomizes, cuts out, the infantile sexuality of the narrator (which is to say of Freud), putting sexuality only in the adolescent and the adult. It is striking because it is done completely knowingly. We know that in his "self-analysis" Freud understood perfectly well the sexual nature of these childhood scenes—Anzieu shows it clearly. Yet here is a scene that is analyzed but utterly cut off from the aspect of infantile sexuality and that permits a completely biased theoretical conclusion. We know to what extent Freud camouflaged his childhood. We know that his dreams, in the *Interpretation of Dreams*, have most of their sexual aspect amputated. Yet in this article, in which Freud proposes show a "camouflage" or a "cover," it is precisely that which is camouflaged—infantile sexuality—that is absent. What Freud does in this text, in using the idea of a camouflaged sexuality, necessarily leads to errors in everything one might extract, especially with respect to après-coup, from Freud's theory of screen memories.

Take a look at this text and the commentary by Anzieu. The relationship with the sexual *in childhood* is easy to find, if only in the idea of tearing off a petal or pulling off a branch, which, moreover, Freud reads as a reference to masturbation. The common German expression "to pull oneself off," a euphemism for masturbation, can be found hidden in the way Freud tells the story of his childhood: he says, "At three years old, there was a catastrophe in the industrial branch of my father's business." And of course, it is the same word for the "industrial branch" and the "branch" one pulls off.

I will conclude with a few words on this text: despite being rich in personal clinical experience, its underlying conception of time would seem a failure. The juxtaposition of 'retrogressive screen-memories' and 'anticipatory screen memories' allows Freud to avoid grappling with the problem—more pressing here than elsewhere—of the doubled direction of time.

Next time I will speak to you about the *Wolf Man*, which will be the last reference point for *nachträglich*. Its is there that we will find the only major reappearance of *Nachträglichkeit* after the two texts I already cited and notably after the *Traumdeutung*. It is yet another blossoming of the concept of *Nachträglichkeit*. My first approach is to ask you to read it, because if I have to summarize and comment on the whole text, it would take us five or six classes. It is an extremely complex text, which has been used and commented on from all directions. An excellent book that was published recently could help you; it's a book by Mahony entitled *Cries of the Wolf Man*.[99] Particularly helpful is chapter four, "The Expository Nature of *From the History of an Infantile Neurosis*." Mahony shows how Freud's exposition reflects all the complexity of *nachträglich* because, while taking account of the chronology, it is always, and on many levels, squarely within après-coup. Of course the whole history of the Wolf Man is within après-coup just as the history of any human being is, but Freud's account itself is within après-coup, as can be seen in its title, *From the History of an Infantile Neurosis*, since it is from an adult illness— not from memories of childhood— that he claims to reconstitute an infantile neurosis as a clinical reality.

The *nachträglich* of the Wolfman's story is incessantly interrupted by the account of the treatment and what treatment brings to the story as *Nachtrag*, which is to say as addenda. The *Nachtragsband* of a work is a volume après-coup, a volume of additions. In the *Wolf Man*, there is even a chapter entitled "*Nachtrag*," which, lacking a better alternative, we have translated as "*supplement*" [supplement] but which is really a "supplement après-coup." What's more, there is the play of frequent injections one could compare to "flashbacks"

99 Patrick J. Mahony, *Cries of the Wolf Man* (New York: International Universities Press, 1984).

in movies. Above all, the final *nachträglich* in the *Wolf Man* is that of Freud's own thought. There is the return *nachträglich* of the "old trauma theory of the neuroses, which . . . suddenly regained its importance"[100] (exactly like Gürtel's slumbering kiss), and, in addition, reappearance of the debate with Jung, a debate which precisely concerns the question of "retro"—retroactive fantasy or "retro-fantasizing" ("*Zurückphantasieren*"). Finally, when the text, composed in 1914, was published four years later in 1918, it included the two *Nachträge* that were written after Freud's 1917 *Introductory Lectures on Psycho-Analysis*. Yet these two pieces of "après-coup," which accompanied the first publication of the main text, profoundly and fundamentally called into question the thesis that the main text had initially proposed.

I will discuss the *Wolf Man* without making a step-by-step commentary, trying, rather, to extract only what emerges from this last resurgence of *nachträglich*. I will also stress the fundamental reasons that lead to the conflict between Freud and Jung about the terms *Nachträglichkeit* and *Zurückphantasieren*, terms that one might consider, a priori, to be neighbors, and which a certain kind of modern hermeneutics has no difficulty assimilating these terms into a "constructivist" vision of human history in which the key word is "resignification." Freud obstinately opposes Jung and, finally, fails to find the grounds to really refute Jung's theory, a theory that is "pregnant" with a hermeneutic yet to come.

100 *SE* 17:95. [Translation modified.]

January 30, 1990

We have arrived at the *Wolf Man*, a text that constitutes the major resurgence of après-coup. Although it does not close my own development of the concept, it does mark the end of the concept's journey in Freud's work. I have pointed out how complex this resurgence was. I urge you to read the whole text, *From the History of an Infantile Neurosis*, known as the *Wolf Man*. In that book, the adjective or adverb *nachträglich* appears some fifteen times, and the substantive, *Nachträglichkeit*, at least twice. There are also other terms that pose a problem for the translator such as *Nachwirkung* and *nachträgliche Wirkung*.

TEMPORALITY IN CASE REPORTS

Even in its rhetoric, the mode of exposition of the *Wolf Man* is entangled with temporality. Of course this is an instance of a general problem with presenting psychoanalytic cases: having to deal with both the chronology of the case and the chronology of the analysis. But the problem is much more complex than is typical. There is, indeed, a linear chronology in the precise dates given by Freud—a chronological reference, recalled many times in the text and summarized in a note added to the end: 'I remind you that... at for years, etc.'—but in no way does this chronological sequence constitute the guiding thread of the presentation. There are many instances of backtracking, which are themselves complex—sometimes they consist of what could be called 'total' returns to the past and sometimes of partial returns, returns that, to borrow a term from film, could be called 'flashbacks'; but these returns are not simply [returns] to memories, to scenes simply remembered; they are returns to past understandings. Additionally, and most importantly, there are the *Nachträge*. I pointed out above that *Nachträge*, which can be translated as "supplements," means "additions made après-coup."

The most important of these are the two *Nachträge,* dating from 1917-1918, that are clearly separated from the composition of the main text, drafted in 1914. They are extremely important for the concept of après-coup itself because during this après-coup of 1914 to 1917 the whole question of après-coup was upended. Finally, there are also the notes added in 1923. For an examination of this intrication of the rhetoric with the case, I refer you to Patrick Mahony's book, *Cries of the Wolf Man.* "Cries" here could means "shouts" or "tears" of the Wolf Man, and, as I mentioned last time, one chapter is entitled "The Expository Nature of *From the History of an Infantile Neurosis.*" Like others who had studied Freud from this point of view, Mahony establishes a close relation between the case itself and the way Freud presents it.

Yet another après-coup, a third if you will, is the one that led to the Wolf Man himself being reanalyzed again and again, by multiple analysts. To imitate the title of a famous surrealist painting, he was "cut up, by his psychoanalysts even" [*il a été "mise en coupe, par ses psychanalystes même"*].[101] After Freud, he was reanalyzed by Ruth Mack Brunswick, then seen yet again by others; he was interviewed; he kept a journal; from beginning to end, his fate was entangled with psychoanalysis to such an extent that in the preface to one of two important books on him, Michel Schneider wrote that he had become not only *"L'Homme aux loups"* ["The Wolf Man"—or, more

101 [The witticism here cannot be translated, as its effect relies substantially on a play of sound (and, as a further translational difficulty, "mise en coupe" suggests both "being sliced up" and "being under the thumb of"). Laplanche is referring to *La mariée mise à nu par ses célibataires, même (The Bride Stripped Bare by Her Bachelors, Even)* by Marcel Duchamp, whose approach to his own work—and to creativity generally—is arguably a variation on the notion of après-coup, at least in such comments of Duchamp's as "I believe that the artist doesn't know what he does. I attach even more importance to the spectator than to the artist" and "The creative act is not performed by the artist alone; the spectator brings the work in contact with the external world by deciphering and interpreting its inner qualifications and thus adds his contribution to the creative act." And, if you like, by the epitaph he chose for his grave: *"D'ailleurs, c'est toujours les autres qui meurent."*]

literally, "The Man of the Wolves"] but also *"L'Homme aux analystes"* ["The Man of the Analysts"]. The two books are *The Wolf-Man by the Wolf-Man*[102] by Muriel Gardiner and *The Wolf-Man: Conversations with Freud's Patient Sixty Years Later*[103] by Karin Obholzer.

LIMITING OURSELVES TO THE PROBLEM OF APRÈS-COUP

I have no intention of contributing to this "cutting up" or remaking the Wolf Man. I have asked that, if possible, you read Freud's text. What interests me is après-coup in Freud's thought and theoretical practice, which includes his way of presenting a case like this one; that in itself is sufficient for our investigation of après-coup because, there again, one can distinguish different aspects. There is the après-coup of the resurgence between 1914–1917; the après-coup of something that dates from about twenty years earlier, the years from 1895–1900. All of a sudden [*tout d'un coup*], there is an après-coup of après-coup in Freud: a crucial debate in this text about reality and fantasy, and thus about the "reality" of childhood memories, a debate that is situated entirely in the après-coup since it is an intervention by Jung that leads Freud to rediscuss his own theses. Finally, in my view, there is another après-coup: the aporia of Freud's après-coup, an aporia from which I, Jean Laplanche, will propose an exit. In other words, if you prefer, the question is: In this text, what makes Freud run? What makes him turn around and around, makes him fail, or makes him go to this or that expedient explanation, this or that deus ex machina (e.g. "primal fantasies")? In the end, what is it that, outlined by its absence, motivates the obstinacy and explains the failure of the Freudian pursuit of the reality of the original scene?

---

102 New York: Basic Books, 1971 and *L'homme aux loups par ses psychanalystes et par lui-même* (Paris: Gallimard, 1981).

103 *Gespräche mit dem Wolfsmann: Eine Psychoanalyse und die Folgen* (Hamburg: Rowohlt, 1980).

THREE SIMPLE CHRONOLOGICAL LANDMARKS

Assuming you have read and that you more or less remember the text, I will content myself with the chronological apparatus, which I'd call minimal, that is found in note of 1923 that Freud added to the end of the text. Although minimal, I won't go over it in detail but will only extract two or three dates simply to specify the ideas.

I. At the age of one and a half, there is the "primal scene" (whatever reality one attributes to it);
II. at the age of four years, Christmas Day (which is the birthday of the subject) or the night of Christmas, there is the famous dream with the wolves, which is at the origin of the activation of his infantile neurosis, his phobia;
III. finally, twenty years later, from twenty-four to twenty-eight years old (1910–1914), there is the analysis with Freud.

Hold on to these three milestones. Whatever our philosophy of time, these three dates must be placed on a hierarchy: the hierarchy of cosmological time, the hierarchy of days and nights, of the number of years.

So, between dates I and II, between one and a half years old and four years old, a whole series of episodes take place, scenes that do not involve the parents so much as other important characters: first there is the Wolf Man's sister; then the governess, Nanya—let's call her "Nounou"—then the English governess; and finally Grusha, the little nursemaid. This series of scenes contains diverse elements: some sexual, some repressive. That's what Freud uncovers about the Wolf Man's life in the first period between the ages one and a half and four years. After the Wolf Man turns four, the infantile neurosis is launched, first in the form of a phobia—specifically a phobia of wolves and more generally of animals—which progressively assumes the form of an obsessional neurosis and thus involves obsessional defense mechanisms. Finally, there is the third period: the analysis. Freud places this marking out of three times under the rubric of après-coup, of *Nachträglichkeit*. [Here is the text of the footnote in which he speaks of it directly:

> We might perhaps best do justice to this statement of the patient's by supposing that the object of his observation was in the first instance a coitus in the normal position, which cannot fail to produce the impression of being a sadistic act, and that only after this was the position altered, so that he had an opportunity for making other observations and judgments. This hypothesis, however, was not confirmed with certainty, and moreover does not seem to me indispensable. We must not forget the actual situation which lies behind the abbreviated description given in the text: the patient under analysis, at an age of over twenty-five years, was putting the impressions and impulses of his fourth year into words which he would never have found at that time. If we fail to notice this, it may easily seem comic and incredible that a child of four should be capable of such technical judgments and learned notions. This is simply another instance of après-coup. At the age of one and a half the child receives an impression to which he is unable to react adequately, unable to comprehend; he grasps this impression only when it is revived in him at the age of four; and only twenty years later, during the analysis, is he able to apprehend with his conscious mental processes what was then going on in him. The patient justifiably disregards the three periods of time, and puts his present ego into the situation which is so long past. And in this we follow him, since with correct self-observation and interpretation the effect must be the same as though the distance between the second and third periods of time could be neglected. Moreover,

we have no other means of describing the events of the second period.[104]]

In this passage, Freud points out that there is not only one après-coup in this story—the one between one and a half years and four years—but a second après-coup, a second effect of *Nachträglichkeit,* in the analysis, two decades later, when the subject can grasp by a conscious thought process what was happening in him in the first après-coup. That first après-coup entails, in the form of the dream, a comprehension and elaboration of the primal scene; the second après-coup, in the analysis, puts all that into words. Yet Freud adds that in the end we can ignore the second après-coup. We can, he says, "neglect" the distance between the second and third periods of time, the second *nachträglich* being only a putting into words of what the dream had already understood.

This was already noted by Lacan in the text I cited at the beginning of this course.[105] In short, Freud collapses the second après-coup into the first, which is to say that in the end he considers the après-coup of the analysis as negligible. He justifies this point of view by the "objectivity" of what has been unearthed by the analysis. Clearly this is to eliminate a large part of the Jungian objection from the start, the objection according to which all the psychoanalytic stories of childhood are merely invented in the analysis, that they are "retroactive fantasizing" (*Zurückphantasieren*).

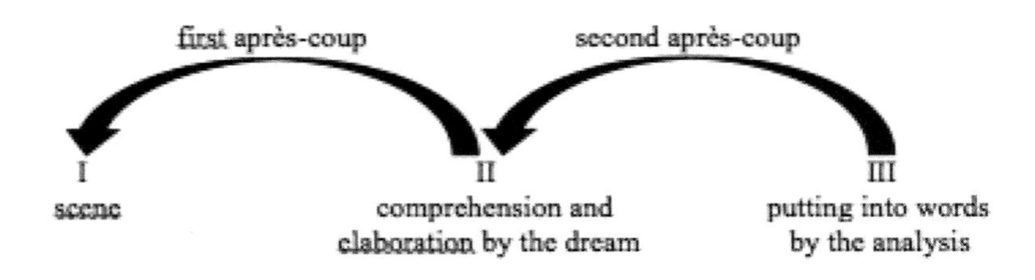

104 *SE* 17:45. [Translation modified. In the French text Laplanche puts this quotation in a footnote.]
105 Lacan's "Report from Rome."

BETWEEN FREUD AND JUNG

A rivalry is established between the Jungian *Zurückphantasieren* and the Freudian *nachträglich*. There is a discussion that is often difficult to follow. Freud wants to distinguish his position from retroactive fantasizing, but his argumentation is not always up to the task, to the extent that he sometimes admits that certain things are retroactive fantasies, which is to say purely and simply imagined at a later time for what one could call "the needs of the cause."[106] After all, how could one better summarize the Jungian thesis than with these words: "a reconstruction of an imaginary past to meet the needs of some present concerns"?

Let's return to what Freud affirms, namely that one can ignore the second *Nachträglichkeit*, the one that happens during the analysis. The major justification is that, in the case of the Wolf Man, we are not only confronted with memories of infantile scenes, always subject to doubts about their reality; we are in the presence of an *infantile neurosis*. The title itself alludes to this: "From the History of an Infantile Neurosis." The analysis of the Wolf Man leads not to the infantile origins of his adult neurosis but to his infantile neurosis that preceded it which is documented not only by the subject but also by family history. We know that from four years to about ten years old, the Wolf Man was affected by a serious neurosis, which was profoundly disabling and which there is no reason to suppose could possibly be a retroactive fantasy. Moreover, it would lead nowhere to consider the neurosis as imagined a posteriori. Whatever merit this argument may have, it is also used to support the notion that the time between four years old and twenty-four years old can be flattened out, telescoped, thus eliminating the problem of the après-coup in the analysis, a problem that, as far as I know, Freud never directly confronted.

---

106 ["*Les besoins de la cause*." One might wonder if in using this phrase to underline problems in Freud's thinking Laplanche, consciously or otherwise, is alluding to la Cause freudienne, which Jacques Lacan had founded in 1980, a year before his death, to replace l'École freudienne de Paris.]

RECONSTRUCTION OF THE PRIMAL SCENE

Once Freud has closed the parenthesis that he himself had opened, all the action of après-coup takes place between the times I have labeled I and II, between one and a half and four years old. The event at one and a half, the observation of parental coitus, is called the "time of the primal scene," whatever questions Freud may raise from time to time about the reality of the scene. The observation of parental coitus, of the "primal scene," is entirely a construction of the analysis. It is not remembered; at no point does it emerge directly as a memory. Many years later, the fact that it was not remembered was confirmed by the Wolf Man himself in an interview with Karin Obholzer. The very idea of a construction prefigures an article written much later which Freud entitled "Constructions in Analysis."[107] Yet from the perspective of realism, Freud underlined, over and over again, that what he called a construction was in fact a *reconstruction*.

How is the primal scene (re)constructed? It is entirely reconstructed on the basis of a dream, the famous dream of wolves in a tree, the dream image sketched by the Wolf Man himself. Of course, the text of the dream is not a construction of the analysis. It was recounted; and the Wolf Man had always remembered it.

So we have the dream of a four-year-old, which occurred precisely on the Christmas of his fourth year and which was recounted to Freud; on the basis of this dream, we have a construction après-coup, in a retrograde direction, which concerns the journey from II to I and which is a model of analytic construction. Every one of the dream's elements is examined in a meticulous way, no doubt going beyond the rule of "free association," since there is often an aspect of directed associations. In fact, Freud undertakes a systematic investigation of the elements of the account of the dream one by one. On the basis of these associations, chains of associations that frequently confirm one another, we arrive at a series of final elements which are presented to the Wolf Man for verification.

---

107 *SE* 23:257–269.

THE FREUDIAN METHOD

As you know, a long time before, in his correspondence with Fliess, Freud had made a sketch of this approach to the intersection of associations.[108]

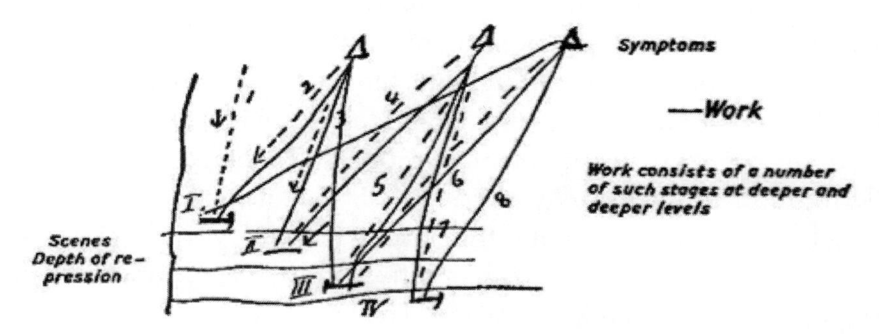

This approach is not a term-for-term translation, which would be a simplistic word-for-word reading. Each element of the manifest content can lead to several terms in the latent content and vice versa. Here, "elements" must be understood in the broadest sense: not only the words or the ideas, but also the stylistic elements, the bodily effects, transitory elements, etc.

Thus, starting from all these dream elements, associative lines take off and cross at a certain number of points, which Freud usually calls "nodal points." It is by linking up these points of intersection that one arrives at the latent content or, as in the present case, at the content of the reconstructed scene. This approach is summarized in a footnote:

> Now that we have succeeded in making a synthesis of the dream, I will try to give a comprehensive account of the relations between the manifest content of the dream and the latent dream-thoughts.[109]

108 "Draft M," *SE* 1:251.
109 *SE* 17:42.

And in this way we arrive at the latent content, which is nothing but the "primal scene" in all its details.

When he presents these details to the patient for verification, Freud sometimes accepts a historical verification in the sense that he doesn't bother to ask the Wolf Man to associate or dig in his memory for particular elements in his history. But, in principle, it is not a verification by history or by the family—all the more so as the family was far away. For Freud, what is essential is a verification by results. That is to say, each element proposed to the patient finds its verification in its productiveness. If it falls flat, it simply is not verified. On the other hand, if it is the starting point of new associations, if it proves to be fruitful either in terms of these associations or in some other way, then it is verified. This is what Freud calls verification, and it is a position that he held consistently, notably in the text on "constructions" in which he criticizes himself with a feigned reproach for presuming: "Heads I win, tails you lose."[110] The true response according to Freud would be: "I win when my interpretation leads to further developments." The fecundity of a hypothesis is its only verification. Among the elements he relies on are not only the Wolf Man's verbal associations—or, as we say, "the material he brings"—but also, at times, the appearance of transitory symptoms. It is in this way that, according to Freud, intestinal symptoms verify the whole part of the primal scene, which is anal, intestinal. On the other hand, Freud says, in effect, "I tried to suggest to the Wolf Man that this detail came from a threat of castration on the part of his father. I tried to suggest it, but it fell flat. In this case, I never had verification of a threat of castration coming from the father, so I was forced to suppose that the threat of castration came from elsewhere." You see that *for Freud, there are noes and not only yeses in psychoanalysis,* but they are noes of a specific form: the absence of reaction, the fact that no associative line arises.

---

110 "Constructions in Analysis," *SE* 23:257.

The whole theoretical debate, which I will get to shortly, is concerned with the nature of the reality to attribute to this construction of the "primal scene." Is it veridical, factual? Was there a scene like this that actually took place? Is it pure imagination? Or is it something between the two? But here I insist on pointing out, if only parenthetically, that while the debate is based on that scene—which is certainly of central importance—Freud finds other scenes that, in the end, are *remembered*. Notably, the "scene with Grusha," the little maid whom he saw washing the tiled floor with her bare buttocks sticking out, a vision that excited him. Now, this scene was remembered *following some analytic work*, which Freud takes as support for asserting:

> The scene with Grusha, the part it played in the analysis, and the effects that followed from it in the patient's life can most naturally and completely be explained if we consider that the primal scene, which may in other cases be a phantasy, was a reality in the present case.[111]

THE RETURN OF THE THEORY OF TRAUMA

Before taking up the debate between "factual reality" and "imagination," I want to underline that in this text there is the reappearance—in the après-coup—of two major terms, terms reemerging after a latency of fifteen to twenty years: "trauma" and "seduction." I've said that the *Wolf Man* places itself in the après-coup of 1895. Freud himself says this explicitly. I quote:

> The old trauma theory of the neuroses, which was after all built up upon impressions gained from psychoanalytic practice, suddenly regained its importance.[112]

---

111 *SE* 17:96. [Translation modified.]
112 *SE* 17:95. [Translation modified.]

After a period in which the question of psychic trauma had been, if not completely abandoned or refuted, at least completely overlooked, here it is again recovering all of its validity in a flash. This is a veritable revival for Freud. I want to stress that the theory of trauma is not vague or banal common sense. I have said, and repeated often enough, the theory of psychic trauma is not a theory that the neuroses are caused by important and shocking events. It is the theory that psychic trauma always requires two separate moments in time. There can be no psychic trauma without these two moments of time, and the need for *at least* two times does not mean there may not be more than two. One cannot speak of an event that, in itself, would be psychically traumatizing unless it echoes a past event or until it finds its echo in a future event. You can see that *"the old trauma theory" is inseparable from après-coup*. The psychic trauma is not within either of the two moments although it constitutes itself as psychic trauma at the second moment.

THE DREAM AS TRAUMA . . .

Well then, what was the little Wolf Man's psychic trauma? Freud tells us that the second moment, the time when a psychic trauma is constituted as such, was not an event but a dream. Utterly extraordinary! Here is the rebirth of the theory of psychic trauma, but the moment in which the trauma comes into existence is not an external event. It is a dream motivated by Christmas, expecting presents, the tree, etc. This psychic trauma is so powerful that it announces the appearance of the infantile neurosis, the phobia. Before the dream, there was all the sexual abnormality, mainly sadomasochistic, that Freud places under the rubric of "perversity," but suddenly at four years old, after this dream, the neurosis appears. Here is the passage at the end of chapter III, introducing chapter IV which is entitled "The Dream and the Primal Scene":

> The date of this transformation can be stated with certainty; it was immediately before his fourth birthday. Taking this as a fixed point, we are able to divide the period of his childhood with which we are concerned into two phases: a first phase of naughtiness and perversity from his seduction at the age of three and a quarter up to his fourth birthday, and a longer subsequent phase in which the signs of neurosis predominated.[113]

A passage like this follows Freud's model that had been firmly established since 1905, according to which "neurosis is the negative of perversion."[114] Here the Wolf Man goes from perversion to neurosis following the event that marked his fourth birthday. Freud concludes:

> But the event which makes this division possible was not an external trauma, but a dream, from which he awoke in a state of anxiety.

I emphasize the fact that the dream is said to be a "trauma," or, to be more precise, it is the second moment of what constitutes the trauma.

. . . AND AS "ANALAGOUS TO SEDUCTION"

I will now take up another passage that says the same thing but introduces another term:

> We have now carried our account down to about the time of the boy's fourth birthday, the point of time when the dream caused his observation of intercourse at the age of one and a half to have its effect après-coup. It is not possible for us completely to grasp or

113 *SE* 17:28.
114 *SE* 7:231 (*Three Essays*) and 7:277 ("My Views").

> adequately to describe what now ensued. The activation of the image {the scene of parental coitus}, which he was now able to understand, thanks to the advances in his intellectual development, acted not only like a fresh event, but like a new trauma, like a foreign intervention analogous to the seduction.[115]

Here you see the dream activates the old image, inscribed since the age of one and a half, which begins to be understood; indeed it is precisely the dream which plays the role of understanding. This activation resembles, for Freud, both a trauma and equally a foreign intervention analogous to seduction. The dream is a foreign intervention *coming from the inside*! One could also say that this dream constitutes an "understanding après-coup of the scene" or an "elaboration of the scene." In chapter IV, "The Dream and the Primal Scene," there is a precious footnote:

> I mean that he understood it at the time of the dream when he was four years old, not at the time of the observation. He received the impressions when he was one and a half; his understanding of them was après-coup, becoming possible at the time of the dream owing to his development, his sexual excitations, and his sexual researches.[116]

It seems to me that what is gained by this reasoning is a demonstration that only what comes from within can create a psychic trauma—the dream of the wolves is paradigmatic. It is the internal attack that is psychically traumatizing.

Thus, Freud has delivered a verdict. In this text he once again makes full use of the term "trauma" and, equally importantly, of the

---

115 *SE* 17:109 [Translation modified.]
116 *SE* 17:37n6. [Translation modified. In the French text, Laplanche puts this in a footnote.]

term "seduction," a term which had largely been condemned in a series of texts beginning at the moment called "the abandonment of the theory of seduction" and continuing for a long time thereafter. Here, the term "seduction," which returns from several directions, is in no way deprived of its causal power—there is a whole chapter titled "The Seduction and Its Immediate Consequences." Freud does not limit the seduction and its immediate consequences to what happened at one and a half or what happened at four years old, but includes the whole intervening period, notably the date at three years and three months when the Wolf Man was seduced by his sister, therefore seduction by another child who says: "Let's show our bottoms."[117] Freud does not go as far as he had in the past—previously, every time he came across a story of seduction by another child, he searched for a prior seduction of the other child by an adult. Here, he does not impose the task of analyzing the Wolf Man's sister on himself; he simply stays with the seduction by the sister, to which he devotes a whole chapter.

There are numerous real seductions in this case in addition to the one by the sister. But I would like to return to the central point we mentioned a few moments ago: the dream itself is "a foreign intervention analogous to the seduction." Here it is worth meditating on the meaning of the word "seduction" beyond interpretations in purely factual terms. In short, it is the dream in its relation to the primal scene that realizes the old schema of the theory of seduction. Freud, however, does not take the step of saying that *the primal scene itself*, which is to say the spectacle of parental coitus, is a form of seduction. At the time of Freud's theory of seduction, one could say that seduction was the fundamental structure, the basic structure, governing all the other structures. However, from this time on, Freud reduces seduction to being merely one structure among others. In other words, he will place seduction in a group of other archetypical scenarios, which he calls "primal fantasies." What is important here is that seduction

117 *SE* 17:20; GW 12:43: "*Wollen wir uns den Popo zeigen.*"

is no longer the general structure of all adult-child relations but has become one structure among others. From my point of view, this is a regression in Freud's thought, a regression tied to the fact that he does not grasp the *constitutive*[118] element that makes it possible for a scene to be called a seduction.

I will stop here for today. Next time I will examine the famous "fantasy-reality" relationship, which, as I have said, is what makes Freud run and does the same for plenty of others. I will not run after the "fantasy-reality" relationship. I will try to explain why we have to relativize it by introducing a third term, a term that, unhappily, is absent in Freud.

***

Question from the audience: Would Freud have said that trauma is always bound to après-coup?

Reply: I think that *psychic* trauma is always linked to après-coup. One could say that is clear for the traumas of those who are said to be "traumatized," for example, the trauma following a big earthquake or an accident. The traumas of those who have been traumatized do not become *psychic* traumas except to the extent that they have some echo with the time of early childhood. Moreover, it is on this path of après-coup and of symbolization that one can attempt to metabolize them, uncovering the tracks, however faint, leading toward early life.

Question from the audience: There is something quite modern in all this. Furthermore—I realized this in rereading the text—shouldn't what he says about the elaboration of the dream and about another form of construction be seen in relation to the importance of seduction and enigma? In this case, this paper, and even in the way it is presented, offers an enigma to the analyst.

118 See my later [2001] article "The Fundamental Anthropological Situation." [Note added to the 2006 publication of these lectures. English translation in *Freud and the* Sexual (New York: The Unconscious in Translation, 2011).]

Reply: What I may allude to next time, which I have already alluded to in speaking about the *Wolf Man,* is the competition between two models: what I call the "jigsaw puzzle" model and the model of the enigma. The "jigsaw puzzle" model is an illusion that completeness is possible, which is to say that the truth—or one could say, "the truth of the truth" —could, in principle, be found. In Freud's almost police-like investigation, there is something of the "jigsaw puzzle" model. This would mean "when the last piece is discovered, there will be nothing left to do but bring charges and put on a trial." He will have it all figured out. He will have the last piece. And that plays out in form of a jigsaw puzzle; as long as Freud does not have all the pieces of the original scene, he remains unsatisfied. The jigsaw puzzle is a kind of structure. In my opinion, the structure of the enigma is a fundamentally different structure, and that is what Freud lacks. If you like, one could say that there is a competition between a "jigsaw puzzle attitude" and an "enigma attitude."

Question from the audience: Isn't the puzzle structure a masked form, a disguised form, of the enigma structure?

Reply: I think so. Let's say that it is the way the structure of the enigma is masked for Freud. In my opinion, a "*Rätsel*" is always linked to a questioning. A jigsaw puzzle is something much more closed. Freud has an attitude that one could call, without being pejorative, objectivist, a radically scientific attitude for which one cannot reproach him. The notion that, in its very structure, something could be indeterminate is an idea he does not entertain.

Question from the audience: At the same time, the fact that he presents the dream as breaking in, as able to be traumatizing, linked to the enigma.

Reply: That is linked to the enigmatic. I completely agree with you. Let's emphasize that we are not analyzing Freud the man, but we are trying to analyze the reasons his thinking comes to a stumbling block, the reasons for the blockage about the problem of imagination versus reality, which will be the same for so many others and notably for someone like Viderman.[119] The problem for Freud will constantly remain: "Is it real or is it not real?" And yet, sometimes Freud moves forward saying, "After all, it isn't so important whether it is real or not; I will analyze it all the same." But the idea that there could be a category of reality other than the imaginary and the real—without falling into the "Symbolic" in the Lacanian sense—the idea that there could be a third term in this opposition never came into his mind.

OK, thank you.

119 [One could add to Viderman's name a list of analysts in the hermeneutic tradition more familiar to Anglophone readers, such as Ricœur, Spence, and Schafer (to a degree)—and, in a way, all who see what is knowable as limited to what is co-constructed.]

February 6, 1990

As I've already pointed out, Freud's article on the Wolf Man is itself situated in après-coup. It gives the impression of a new elaboration of the concept, but, at the same time, and even more strongly, it reveals in this elaboration a blockage or a missing piece in Freud's thinking. It is precisely this missing piece that, according to the informal expression I used above, "makes Freud run" toward unsatisfying solutions.

THE QUESTION OF SEDUCTION REMAINS UNELABORATED

Last time I underlined the reflourishing that occurs in this text: first, the theory of psychic trauma is revived, the "old trauma theory ... suddenly regained its significance"; second, seduction is revived, reappearing here in full bloom but in a place that, a priori, seems unexpected: in the dream, a dream which acts "like a foreign intervention analogous to seduction." Even if we also find seduction in the relationship with the sister, that seduction is not put on the same level—and this is of major importance—as the primal scene itself, which is to say the scene of observation of parental coitus. In brief, in the scene at the center of the investigation of the *Wolf Man*, Freud does not find seduction. In this text, seduction is conceived of as factual, as quasi-gestural, at least in the chapter on the seduction by the sister. There are "scenes of seduction"—it is of little concern whether those scenes are real or imagined—and there are scenes that in their content imply seduction, adjacent to scenes of observations of parental coitus, those, too, either real or imagined. But the idea whose absence I want to underline is that *the scene of observation of parental coitus in itself* may entail an element of seduction, an essence, a structure of seduction. To anticipate things, to recall them in a word, this element, whose absence I am stressing and the element that defines what I call "primal seduction," is the presence of an enigmatic message or an enigmatic signifier.

"*ZURÜCKPHANTASIEREN*"—RETROACTIVE FANTASIZING

"*Nachträglich,*" "après-coup," or "*Nachträglichkeit*" is everywhere in this text. It occurs at least fifteen times, and in it one finds the double movement impossible to overlook in this two-faced concept, this "Janus concept" as Mahony calls it, a concept which is "bifrontal" in its double movement, past to present and present to past. Yet one could say that in the movement of the present toward the past, in the movement of recapturing or reinterpreting the past, après-coup finds itself in a dangerous competition with a concept that never stops rubbing up against it, the concept of "retroactive fantasizing" or "*Zurückphantasieren.*" It is a concept that is often suitable and often adopted. I can't say who, Freud or Jung, was the first to speak of "retroactive fantasizing"; nevertheless, it is a concept perfectly suited to Jung while also being present in Freud. This Freud does not fail to say (it is an element of the polemic, although one of secondary importance): you speak of "retroactive fantasizing"; well, I did too. So in that respect there is nothing original in what you say; it's simply that I don't make "retroactive fantasizing" the totality of my thinking on this question.

"Retroactive fantasizing" is the construction of an imaginary past, embellished and remade on the basis of present needs. The example Freud returns to repeatedly is Livy, who rewrote, and embellished, the history of Rome from the earliest legends to the imperial period. Here is a striking passage drawn from Freud's 1925 book, *An Autobiographical Study*, which he called *Selbstdarstellung*:

> My mistake {you will see what this refers to} was of the same kind as would be made by someone who believed that the legendary story of the early kings of Rome (as told by Livy) was historical truth instead of what it is in fact—a reaction formation to the memory

> of times and circumstances that were wretched and no doubt not always glorious.[120]

What is ironic is that it is precisely in a passage on the abandonment of the theory of seduction that Freud is led, as if to bring it back, to raise the topic of "retroactive fantasizing."

One could say that Freud flirts with danger in this text in which, in spite of everything, he continues to denounce "retroactive fantasizing" even though it is at the center of his argument. After all, he is making a retrospective construction. The whole analysis of the Wolf Man is truly a "*Zurückkonstruieren,*" if you want to use the term, a 'retro-construction,' or a construction facing backward, which is to say a retroactive construction of the primal scene. As I pointed out last time, this scene was never brought back into the Wolf Man's memory but was, as it were, erected brick by brick.

LACUNA AND PUZZLE

So how is one to distinguish between the retroactive construction of the Wolf Man's primal scene and a construction à la Livy? We have to lay stress on several elements of Freud's reconstruction, the principal one being the meticulous, minutely detailed, *methodical* step-by-step process. It is a construction that has nothing to do with embellishment, with pictures drawn with a broad brush reflecting the needs of current fashion as the work of Livy is presumed to have been. What Freud does is quite different; it is a work of methodical archeology in which every element of what is constructed must be interlaced with other elements at the crossing points of numerous lines of associations. Here is the place to recall the intensity with which Freud always insisted that, before being anything else, before being a treatment, before being a theory, psychoanalysis is a method. It is the method of investigation I referred to last time. On one hand, it is a method of approach, and on the other, it

120 *SE* 20:35. [Translation modified.]

is a method of verification, and this permits me to introduce two terms that, in what follows, will present an alternative to other terms. The two terms are "lacuna" and "puzzle." The lacunar, according to Freud—and sometimes he includes it in his definition of the unconscious—has as a correlative whatever must be inserted into a context so that it is no longer lacunar, "*lückenhaft*." For a story, a dream, or a symptom to be lacunar means it is not explicable in itself, but contains holes that must be filled in. Take dreams for example—since, in reconstructing the Wolf Man's observation of the primal scene, we are starting from a dream—for Freud, all the elements of a dream are, precisely, lacunar, which is to say that they must find their concrete explanation somewhere else, beyond the manifest dream, and that another element, or several other elements, must be brought in to complete them.

I will choose two examples, two dream elements from among the many that Freud assigns himself the task of elucidating. In the dream, why are the wolves white? I don't want to repeat why. Read the book. The wolves are white for this and that reason, and in so far as this question is not answered, the analysis of the dream has not been completed. Another interesting point: a lacuna can present itself as a simple hesitation in the telling of the dream. For example, the Wolf Man says, "There were six or seven of them." Well, I remind you that Freud includes in what needs to be explained that which causes doubt or causes a lacuna and not only the elements of the manifest dream but also the dreamer's comments about the dream, even, as here, wording of comments that indicates uncertainty. The analyst must not say to himself, "Perhaps it's one or the other; he doesn't remember the dream clearly;" it is the phrase "six or seven" itself that must be explained. If, when recounting a dream, someone says, "This part of the dream is vague" or "This part of the dream is foggy," that should not lead to the notion that the memory of the dream is uncertain, but rather should be considered an element of the content of the dream, for example, an indication that something happened in the fog.

The other term I want to introduce, which is correlative to this Freudian reasoning about lacunae, is the "jigsaw puzzle." The "jigsaw puzzle" is a metaphor that Freud does not use often. Nevertheless, he deploys it in an old text written at the height of the theory of seduction, at the moment when he was hunting for the memory, hunting for the scene. In "The Aetiology of Hysteria," you will find a passage on the "jigsaw puzzle." What we have translated as "jigsaw puzzle" is the German word "*Zusammenlegbild*," "*image composé*":

> Events of this sort strengthen our impression that the patients must really have experienced what they reproduce under the compulsion of analysis as scenes from their childhood. But another and stronger proof of this is furnished by the relationship of the infantile scenes to the content of the whole of the rest of the case history.

I underline the relation of one element to the whole.

> It is exactly like putting together a child's picture-puzzle: after many attempts, we become absolutely certain in the end which piece belongs in the empty gap; for only that one piece fills out the picture and at the same time allows its irregular edges to be fitted into the edges of the other pieces in such a manner as to leave no free space and to entail no overlapping. In the same way, the contents of the infantile scenes turn out to be indispensable supplements to the associative and logical framework of the neurosis, whose insertion makes its course of development for the first time evident, or even, as we might often say, self-evident.[121]

There is a truly extraordinary rhetorical element in this passage. Freud's writing style is often mentioned; here we have a lovely,

121 *SE* 3:205.

intricate style. There is Freud's astonishment, when he finds a piece of the puzzle, at the realization that the piece must correspond to the whole in two ways: on the one hand, its jagged outline must exactly fit in the hole, fit exactly with the jagged outline of other pieces; and, in addition, its image must fit: it must complete the picture of the countryside. Thus, with the piece of the puzzle, there is suddenly this extraordinary experience: "Look! It's the chimney of the house"; and, at the same time, it is a piece that just fits there, where no other piece can fit. It is this experience that Freud seeks as the end of his quest; each lacuna must be filled in. It is this search that he already described in the texts of 1895–1897, exactly the same quest as the one found in the *Wolf Man,* since no detail of the dream can be left unexplained.

In the *Wolf Man* we have this step-by-step reconstruction of a "primal scene" depicted in its smallest details, which in itself already leads us to think of something other than a *"Zurückphantasieren,"* which would be a depiction with a broad brush where one casually creates a past in a slapdash way and not in a methodical fashion.

FREUD'S SUDDEN DOUBT, AND A NEW COMPOSITE HYPOTHESIS

And then, abruptly, when this scene had already been reconstructed down to the smallest details (I refer you to the famous footnote[122] where all of that is summarized), there are the two additions of 1917 in which Freud suddenly seems to drop the assertion of reality. But what is particularly interesting is that, while seeming to dismiss the reality of elements that are essential to the primal scene, Freud, for all that, does not drop his reasoning, nor does he criticize himself for "retroactive fantasizing." The first of these additions is found on pages 57–60 of volume 27 of *The Standard Edition*. I am obliged to cite a small fragment. Having said, "I am certain that this

122 [See Appendix 2.]

scene at the age of one and a half years old happened in precisely this way," Freud adds:

> There remains the possibility of taking yet another view of the primal scene underlying the dream—a view, moreover, which obviates to a large extent the conclusion that has been arrived at above and relieves us of many of our difficulties. But the theory which seeks to reduce scenes from infancy to the level of regressive symbols will gain nothing even by this modification; and indeed that theory seems to me to be finally disposed of by this (as it would be by any other) analysis of an infantile neurosis.[123]

In other words: I am going to suggest a possibility other than the reality of the primal scene that I have so laboriously reconstructed. Nevertheless, the theory of regressive resignification (Jung's theory) gains absolutely nothing from this suggestion. Here is how he constructs the hypothesis:

> This other view which I have in mind is that the state of affairs can be explained in the following manner. It is true that we cannot dispense with the assumption that the child observed a copulation, the sight of which gave him a conviction that castration might be more than an empty threat. Moreover, the significance which he subsequently came to attach to the postures of men and women, in connection with the development of anxiety on the one hand, and as a condition upon which his falling in love depended on the other hand, leaves us no choice but to conclude that it must have been a *coitus a tergo, more ferarum*.

123 *SE* 17:57.

So, certain elements must be considered as derived from reality: the observation of coitus and the observation of coitus *"a tergo"* (from behind). But, Freud says, the idea that it was a parental coitus can be dropped; it could well have been an animal coitus. There is some support for this: the fact that the wolves of the dream are very similar to dogs and the fact that the little boy was often taken to see his father's flocks of sheep where he saw the shepherd's dogs makes it is easy to imagine that he observed them during coitus. And—an extraordinary modification that Freud introduces casually, without giving any reason except that it is a way of beating a retreat on the question of "reality" while holding on to what is essential—this time the primal scene could be a coalescence of two elements: shortly before four years old (when the dream occurred), the observation of dogs' coitus and, at one and a half years old, because there must have been something at one and a half years, he probably saw his parents in some physical closeness that perhaps could have been simply innocuous or tender closeness rather than sexual closeness. This is the context in which *"Nachträglichkeit"* is used, one of only two times:

> It is at once obvious how greatly the demands on our credulity are reduced. We need no longer suppose that the parents copulated in the presence of their child. . . . The time period of the après-coup {*der Betrag der Nachträglichkeit*} is greatly diminished.[124]

The "time period of the après-coup" (*der Betrag der Nachträglichkeit*) is an interesting expression. When Freud creates a concept, he seems tempted to give it a quantitative signification, an "economic" signification. Here the time period of the après-coup has a temporal rather than an economic signification: the length of time separating the two moments of the après-coup is shorter and thus more plausible.

We must clearly recognize, and Freud emphasizes the point, that if we start from this conception—this time a composite concep-

124 *SE* 17:58.

tion—of the primal scene, the concern for precision and the necessity of explaining everything in detail, of completing the puzzle, is in no way diminished.

After this type of concession made to Jung about the reality of the scene of observation of parental sex, after this seeming reconciliation with "retroactive fantasizing," we are forced to enter into a discussion by Freud that is truly difficult to follow. One must read it many times. The reasoning moves in two directions.

TWO NEW LINES OF DISCUSSION . . .

Freud's *first direction* is, in spite of everything, to establish that in this case the observation of a scene of parental coitus actually occurred while conceding that such an observation may not always occur. Too many arguments are made in defense of this point, so I will mention only this one: in the second addition of 1917,[125] Freud offers as proof a quite different scene, to which I have already alluded. It is called the "scene with Grusha," in which the little maid is observed with her buttocks protruding, washing the floor. Well, according to Freud, this scene with Grusha, which is certainly actually remembered from the direct observation, is an argument that carries weight:

> Nevertheless, I cannot deny that the scene with Grusha, the part it played in the analysis, and the effects that followed from it in the patient's life can be most naturally and completely explained if we consider that the primal scene, which may in other cases be a phantasy, was a reality in the present one. After all, there is nothing impossible about it; and the hypothesis of its reality is entirely compatible with the inciting action of the observations upon animals which are indicated by the sheepdogs in the dream-picture.[126]

125 *SE* 17:95–97.
126 *SE* 17:96–97.

. . . AND THEN "PRIMAL FANTASIES"

This conclusion, which in spite of everything is called "unsatisfactory" and which is unconcerned with the reality/fantasy alternative, will open up a third and unexpected term. It is here that *another line of thought* emerges: in so far as one admits that the reconstruction does not truly get to the scene in all its details, like a cinematic recording, for Freud it nevertheless remains impossible that such a reconstruction could be created only as a function of the adult subject. To accept that would mean that all infantile sexuality could fall into an abyss, that perhaps it could simply be an adult fantasy, notably a fantasy of Freud and his patient. It is at this precise point that the third term is introduced: I call it "primal fantasies" (*Urphantasien*). This is the recourse to the atavistic, the recourse to fantasies of phylogenetic, hereditary origins, that Pontalis and I finished off. (I must remark that we first had to exhume them, because before us, no one spoke of them—that is, before *The Language of Psycho-Analysis*[127] and the article on "Primal Fantasy, Fantasies of Origin, Origins of Fantasy."[128]) It is truly and fully a Freudian concept, but, I hasten to add, the fact that we exhumed it does not mean we adhere to it. In any case, I do not adhere to it.

Because—and Freud is compelled to admit this—in the entire history of the patient, the primal scene is not present as a whole in all its details. In this sense, reality is always lacunar. And yet it is, strikingly, a major detail, that of coitus "*a tergo*," coitus "from behind," that Freud considers essential to the structure of the scene, a detail that clearly cannot be presumed to be present as a reality in every case:

> Scenes of observing sexual intercourse between parents . . . are as a matter of fact by no means rarities in the analyses of neurotic mortals. Possibly they are

127 [New York: Norton, 1973.]
128 [Laplanche, in Scarfone, *Laplanche: an introduction*.]

> no less frequent among those who are not neurotics. Possibly they are part of the regular store in the—conscious or unconscious—treasury of their memories.[129]

And it's here that the "detail" comes into play, because the "primal scene" is not a generality but a precisely detailed scenario:

> But as often as I have been able by means of analysis to bring out a scene of this sort, it has shown the same peculiarity which startled us with our present patient too: it has related to coitus *a tergo,* which alone offers the spectator a possibility of inspecting the genitals. There is surely no need any longer to doubt that what we are dealing with is only a phantasy, which is invariably aroused, perhaps, by an observation of the sexual intercourse of animals.[130]

It is on the basis of arguments of this kind that Freud moves to a universal stock of memories and then, from this, to the idea that the stock is inherited and its provenance prehistoric.

> The phylogenetically inherited schemata, . . . like the categories of philosophy, are concerned with the business of "placing" the impressions derived from actual experience. I am inclined to take the view that they are precipitates from the history of human civilization. The Oedipus complex, which comprises a child's relation to his parents, is one of them. . . . Wherever experiences fail to fit in with the hereditary schema, they become remodeled in the imagination.[131]

---

129 *SE* 17:59.
130 *SE* 17:59.
131 *SE* 17:119

. . . WHERE PHYLOGENESIS DEVOURS ITSELF

Thus, there is a hereditary schema that is not merely concerned with the "Oedipus complex" but with the way it is metabolized, notably in the observation of parental coitus. This hereditary schema even contains the observation of parental coitus and, what's more, contains it in the smallest details, as exemplified by the fact that it is a coitus in the manner of animals, from behind. When individual experiences are not sufficient, the subject fills in the lacunae in his individual history by using inherited schemata (and here we return to the term "lacuna," and also to the idea of the jigsaw puzzle).

In other words, for each of us, individual experience, childhood, is necessarily contingent, made up of a few scattered and more or less explicit memories; but in no case does the inadequacy of experience open the door to a pure and simple retroactive imagination that has no other foundation than the present. If there are holes in the experiences of childhood, there is, at the ready, a stock of primal prehistoric events, a stock of real events, which are scenes of parental coitus as observed in humanity's prehistory. You know what slips in here: all the history of the "primitive hoard," the possession of women by the "primal father," the castration or rape of the sons, etc. For these things, I refer you to two texts: *Overview of the Transference Neuroses*,[132] in which Freud elaborates this prehistoric history at length, and, again, to the article Pontalis and I wrote on primal fantasies.

A moment ago I said that just because we exhumed the notion of "primal fantasy" in Freud's work does not necessarily imply that we have adopted it for ourselves. If you look at that little text that was recently republished in a single volume,[133] you will recognize that

132 [*A Phylogenetic Fantasy: Overview of the Transference Neuroses* (Cambridge, MA: Harvard University Press, 1987).]

133 ["Primal Fantasy, Fantasies of Origins, Origins of Fantasy." In 1985, the text of this 1964 article was published with a new introduction by the authors. An English translation of the article with the 1985 addition may be found in Scarfone, *Laplanche: an introduction* (New York: The Unconscious in Translation, 2015).]

even when we wrote it we were distancing ourselves—though perhaps insufficiently—from that Freudian concept. To give you a little history, I'll tell you that in this text Pontalis and I succumbed to the temptations of structuralism, at least to some extent, even though we criticized it at other moments. It now seems apparent to me that we tried to save the notion of primal fantasies by seeing it as a way of "monetizing" a foundational primal structure: the Oedipus complex. However, such a maneuver cannot be justified historically; it would put the Oedipus complex in the starry heavens of structure (in the sense of Lévi-Strauss), making it a part of the essential needs of human beings. The Oedipus complex would then be a kind of matrix for the primal fantasies: primal scene, castration, fantasy of return to the mother's belly, and seduction; these are the ones Freud enumerates.

I have no further comments on this article. It is clear that at the same time we also said: "But there are, beside this appearance of structuralism, details within Freud's work that are not reducible to structure and that, in Freud, are put back into phylogenesis." For instance, if the coitus is a coitus *"a tergo,"* it is because our prehistoric ancestors are presumed to have proceeded in that way.

TAKING FREUD SERIOUSLY . . .

My thesis with respect to Freud—since we are in the après-coup of Freud—can be put in the following way: one must not deprive an author (one must not deprive Freud) of his limitations. This expression is a bit paradoxical; I want to say that in depriving him of his limits, one can end up making him say anything one likes and so make discussion and progress impossible. One must not refuse to take a theory seriously, even one as dubious as this one about the phylogenetic inheritance of primal fantasies. I know that in the psychoanalytic world there is a facile tendency that goes: "After all, all of this is mythology, and Myth is certainly useful in psychoanalysis." That is another question. For Freud, the theory of the reality of the horde, of these prehistoric scenarios, and of their genetic inheritance is never taken any way other than literally.

To allow a great author his limits is to allow for the possibility that those limits may be points of departure for a leap forward, for progress in his thought. What makes the issue exciting is that even when an author collides with his limits, it is not rare that the progress made in transcending them is found prefigured somewhere in a little corner of the original work. What are the limits that Freud's thought bumps up against, limits that make him run, as if in a cage, so he is caught up in a kind of repetition?

. . . IN ORDER TO CRITIQUE HIM

For Freud, the limit, whatever we go on to say about it, is essentially the opposition between fantasy and reality *in the absence of a third term*. A moment ago I said that often, in a little corner of his thought or a text, there is something that points to what is needed. Clearly, one can find the notion of "psychic reality" in Freud, and one could say this notion is the missing third term for the opposition between fantasy and reality. In fact, if you examine Freud's texts that mention psychic reality, you will find that, with the exception of a few occurrences, the term is scarcely more than the mark of an empty place for something he never truly grasped. And, in the most explicit texts—notably *Introductory Lectures on Psycho-Analysis*—"psychic reality" is reduced to the psychological reality of fantasy, i.e. to the subjective reality of fantasy.[134] This opposition, without mediation between material reality and the reality of fantasy, continues to dominate a large part of the psychoanalytic debate about the question of reality and especially about

134 For a more elaborate discussion, see the article "Psychical Reality" in *The Language of Psycho-Analysis*.

the presence or absence of reality of infantile memories.[135] Authors such as Viderman and Mahony[136] (in fact, it is true of most authors) join Freud in being bound by these two terms.

MATERIAL REALITY AND FANTASY WITHOUT A THIRD TERM?

Let's note that, in the end, in this opposition between fantasy and material reality, Freud always gives priority to material reality. It is material reality that rules fantasy, whether in the period from 1895 to 1897 or in the *Wolf Man*. Clearly, this is to prevent inversion of the arrow of time.

In the beginning, material reality was conceived of as being full, without lacunae, as the notion of "scene" certainly indicates. The final scene, the scene Freud wanted to reach in the years from 1895 to 1897 and in the *Wolf Man*, contains all its meaning within itself. Once reconstituted, whatever way one has made it hold together, there is nothing more to look for; there is nothing else to puzzle out.

As you know, there are innumerable theoretical and practical objections to this priority conferred to material reality over and against fantasy, a priority given as much by logic as by the direction of time. As long as one remains within the reality / fantasy opposition, disillusion crowds in from every side. Here we will consider two moments of disillusion that, fundamentally, are of the same order: the first is in the famous letter: "I no longer believe in my *neurotica*"; the second occurs

135Cf. the debate, which is always lively and often moved into judicial scenes in the USA, concerning memories recovered in analysis—*false/recovered memories* [in English in original]. When, because of their violent and/or sexual character, these memories may lead to legal penalties, it is sometimes the patient who takes the initiative in bring charges against the wrongdoers, and sometimes, reciprocally, it is the supposed wrongdoers who incriminate the psychotherapist for having suggested these scenes to the patient.

136 [If Laplanche's short list of examples were extended and were to include Anglophone authors, one would not omit Donald Spence or Roy Schafer.]

in the 1917–1918 additions to the *Wolf Man* and can be summarized by the declaration "I now scarcely believe in that primal scene that I gave myself so much trouble to reconstruct at great length."

It is remarkable to witness the same crisis, on the same subject, occurring a second time twenty years later. The same dogged research aiming to reconstitute the time or the scenes in the smallest detail. The same conviction, as with "the old theory of trauma," that the scene holds the secret of neurosis. Then the same doubts and the same disillusionment. In 1897, he no longer believes in his "*neurotica,*" and in 1917, in exactly the same way, he comes to doubt the primal scene he worked so hard to reconstruct.

Given all this, is the "retroactive fantasizing" of Jung true? Absolutely not, because it cannot find the necessary support within itself. To clarify the ideas, here are simplistic diagrams of three ways of conceiving of the relation between F (fantasy) and R (reality).

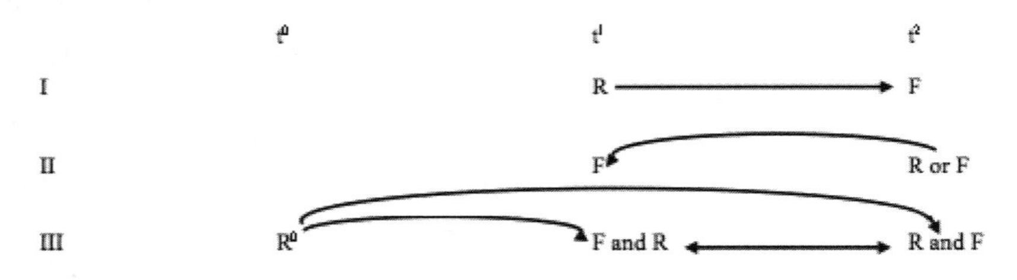

The first solution (I) puts a real infantile scene at the origin of all fantasy. This collides with the difficulty, indeed the impossibility, of reconstructing t1 with certainty. The infantile scene is irremediably "lacunar"—though I prefer the term "enigmatic" to the term "lacunar," and I will say why below—because, in itself, the scene is insufficient and because it always leaves open the possibility that lurking behind any given scene S, there is another scene S′, even more archaic, that gives S, which takes place later in time, its significance.

We can say this "realist" hypothesis is powerfully called into question at least twice: in the "letter of the equinox" of 1897 and in the additions to the *Wolf Man* of 1917 to 1918.

The second hypothesis (II) is plainly that of "retroactive fantasizing." Freud simply dismisses it. That might be a good way to go, but don't think it will die from that blow. It continues to survive in a "hermeneutic approach" that reappears in widely diverse domains and under various names: "resignification" is one of the most frequent terms. However, by extending what one might call a *socio-construction of concepts*, one will find it under the names, 'construction,' 'fabrication,' etc. One could well ask: Who is the "subject" of such an "invention"? Where does the subject obtain the materials for the invention, and the power to synthesize?

THE THIRD TERM: PREHISTORY

But for Freud, it goes differently: in 1897 and in the crisis of 1917 to 1918, he finds the same solution (III) looming. In 1897 "the factor of hereditary disposition regains its influence." In 1917 to 1918, the hypothesis is made explicit because, in the interval, *Totem and Taboo* (1912–13)[137] and its "scientific myth"[138] have opened the path. There is no longer any question of abandoning the grounding provided by the event but from here on the event will be prehistoric. The reality of seduction and of castration is present at the origin, labeled t0 in solution III. As for the murder of the father, Freud marches to the beat of *Im Anfang war die Tat*: "In the beginning was the act."[139] It is under the irrefutable, unfalsifiable tutelage of prehistory that the trivial quarrel between material reality and fantasy now plays out. From now on,

137 *SE* 13:1–161.
138 [Freud spoke of the "primal horde" as a "scientific myth" in *Group Psychology and the Analysis of the Ego* (1921): "the scientific myth of the father of the primal horde" (SE 18:135). He had first discussed the primal horde in *Totem and Taboo* (1912).]
139 *SE* 13:161.

fundamental schemata (or primal fantasies), transmitted since time immemorial, inform both our everyday actions and our contingent fantasies: whether you want it or not, you will be an "Oedipus." If you are not, you will imagine that you are, which amounts to the same thing.

February 13, 1990

We will finish today. But this "today," by a liberty I grant myself as I go over my lecture notes from 1989 and 1990, is also a today in August 2005. Probably, at bottom, little has changed since I gave this course. But the après-coup of these reflections on après-coup leads me to observe that since this course, very little has been "grasped" of what I have proposed to spring from this major concept in the psychoanalytic theory of time. In journals, colloquia, and review articles, the old "resignification," a barely modernized avatar of Jung's "retroactive fantasizing," seems to have been adopted unanimously. The sleep of very few clinicians or theoreticians has been troubled by the originality of a concept that signals an irrevocable double direction in relation to the arrow of time, an originality that had already been underlined in *The Language of Psycho-Analysis*.

So, using my words of February 13, 1990, I will again try to hammer home what arises from this Freudian development, from its aporias, and what can emerge as a *novel* contribution. Keep the schema proposed above in mind so you can hold fixed the three aporetic solutions that emerge from Freud's thought. In I, the fantasy is determined, après-coup, by the infantile scene (this is almost the *Wolf Man* solution, at least in the version of 1914); in II, we have pure "retroactive fantasizing," with which Freud never agreed; in III, we have the solution that uses phylogenetic "primal fantasies."

TWO RECOURSES TO PHYLOGENESIS

To start, we must be clear about this use of a "prehistoric" that is transmitted genetically. It is an idea that appeared twice in our journey through Freud's texts, and the two versions of the idea are profoundly different. In the letter of September 19, 1901, what Freud discusses under the heading of phylogenesis is, first of all, the evolution of living creatures in general, notably animals moving from a posture on four legs to a standing posture. Freud tries, still timidly, to establish a sequence of evolutionary *stages for living creatures* to which a sequence of *erotic stages in humans* will correspond. In fact, what is invoked before anything else is the primate's loss of olfaction and thus the loss of anal sexuality, to the profit of genitality. This type of theorizing certainly merits great caution, but nothing argues against wondering about the sexual significance of the evolution of the upright posture, the movement from primates to *Homo erectus*.

PRIMAL FANTASY OR THE SCENE OF FANTASY?

On the other hand, when it comes to "primal fantasies"—introduced, notably, in connection with the Wolf Man—Freud discusses the history of the *human being* alone, the human being since the time of the "primal man." More importantly, he also discusses what is presumed to inscribe itself: *prehistoric scenes lived* by the individual, *by an innumerable succession of individuals* so that they create an engram or a genetic inscription. This is a conception that is neither Darwinian nor Lamarkian as no role is attributed to adaptation. This conception is forcefully repeated in *Moses and Monotheism*, in which Freud does not deny that in this matter he is in opposition to scientific theory.[140]

As for the genetic transmission of scenes, scenarios, even pre-

140[Freud writes:

> On further reflection I must admit that I have behaved for a long time as though the inheritance of memory traces of the experience of our ancestors, independently of direct communication and of the influence of education by the setting of an example, were established beyond question. When I spoke of the survival of a tradition among a people or of the formation of a people's character, I had mostly in mind an inherited tradition of this kind and not one transmitted by communication. Or at least I made no distinction between the two and was not clearly aware of my audacity in neglecting to do so. My position, no doubt, is made more difficult by the present attitude of biological science, which refuses to hear of the inheritance of acquired characters by succeeding generations. I must, however, in all modesty confess that nevertheless I cannot do without this factor in biological evolution. The same thing is not in question, indeed, in the two cases: in the one it is a matter of acquired characters which are hard to grasp,

historic schemata, there is nothing in clinical practice that supports such a conception. To the contrary, this theoretical hypothesis arrives as a crutch in the *Wolf Man*, as a kind of stopgap filling in the lacunae in the reconstructed memory. We have emphasized the term "lacuna" by showing that, for Freud, the lacunae in the scene must be filled in as much as possible. This is the image of the jigsaw puzzle completed by the associative method or, if that method fails, by primal fantasies.

What's more, beyond its role as a complement, primal fantasy serves the function of restoring plausibility to the schema of après-coup, torn as it is between its progressive signification ("deferred action," the time bomb) and its regressive signification (the endowment of a new signification to an evanescent past). To stress Freud's preference for the first solution (forward movement), all that is necessary is to notice that until the *Wolf Man* and afterwards, he does not abandon his steadfast propensity favoring reconstruction of the buried past. Among other examples, you can take a look at the letter of December 21, 1899 [two years after the "abandonment of the seduction theory"], in which he speaks of the end of E.'s treatment, announcing that he has finally found "a scene from his primal period" and enthusiastically analogizing it to the archeological discovery of Troy by Schliemann:

> Buried deep beneath all his fantasies, we found a scene from his primal period (before twenty-two months)

---

in the other of memory traces of external events—something tangible, as it were. But it may well be that at bottom we cannot imagine one without the other

If we assume the survival of these memory traces in the archaic heritage, we have bridged the gulf between individual and group psychology: we can deal with peoples as we do with an individual neurotic. Granted that at the time we have no stronger evidence for the presence of memory-traces in the archaic heritage than the residual phenomena of the work of analysis which call for a phylogenetic derivation, yet this evidence seems to us strong enough to postulate that such is the fact. If it is not so, we shall not advance a step further along the path we entered on, either in analysis or in group psychology. The audacity cannot be avoided.

Moses and Monotheism SE 23:99–100 (GW 16:207).].

> which meets all the requirements and in which all the remaining puzzles converge. It is everything at the same time—sexual, innocent, natural, and the rest. I scarcely dare believe it yet. It is as if Schliemann had once more excavated Troy, which had hitherto been deemed a fable.[141]

A scene one finds or does not find, a lacunar scene that must be filled in, a scene behind which looms an infinity of other scenes—each of these possibilities punctuates Freud's journey with his patients, always with the same feverish expectation. But above all, when we look behind this empirical difficulty of finding the original scene from a "primal period," do we dare to formulate a question at once transcendental and ironic: Will we find the final scene? And if we do, so what? Must the psychoanalyst then slip into the character of the doctor in Molière's *Le Médecin malgré lui*: "And that is why your daughter is mute"?[142]

I will return to the term "lacunar," using it as an index, the finger pointing toward what troubles Freud about the scene and the memory of the scene. He conceives of the memories as *psychic realities* from which not even the smallest detail can be missing. (See Freud's exhaustive notes in the "Wolf Man.")[143]

LACUNAR REPRESENTATION OR ENIGMATIC MESSAGE?

The term "lacunar" takes us directly back to "psychic" reality. Scenes with several characters, scenes with animals, scenes that are purely material—how could I assert that, for Freud, the scenes are not also full of meaning? I must correct my phrase and affirm

141 Freud, *Complete Letters*, 391–392.
142 [The "doctor" famously says that the daughter's muteness arises from "the loss of speech."]
143 [See Appendix 2.]

that the scenes are always *events inscribed on the level of representation*: that is, they are what the subject "represents to himself" following an event that, in the last instance, is a material event. "*Lacunar representation*": this is the best expression for what Freud discovers in his search for the scene. He cannot accept the lacunae and so forces himself to fill them in using the hypothesis of phylogenetic "primal fantasies." Now it is time for us to confront that expression with a two-word phrase that is the key to the General Theory of Seduction, as well as to a new understanding of après-coup: "enigmatic message." The opposition between these two formulations, "lacunar representation" and "enigmatic message," is not the presence or absence of meaning. The idea that representations do not have meaning is utterly alien to me, nor do I think that a representation cannot change its meaning according to the attitude of the subject. To the contrary, this variability is witness to the fact that a representation is always an instance of "representing to oneself" [*se représenter*].[144] A *representation* can be meaningful, something that signifies; the difference is that a message is always a "*signifying to,*" *signifying to someone* (to a child, by an adult).

Our other term is "enigmatic." It entails taking into account the (sexual) unconscious of the sender of the message. Nowhere in Freud's writing—for example, nowhere in the *Wolf Man*—is the unconscious of the parents involved, an unconscious that could intervene in the content or in the surroundings of the "primal scene." Moreover, it follows that the same is true for the "prehistoric" primal scene and for its major protagonist, the "father of the hoard" or the "primal man." If you follow the scenarios described in the *Overview of the Transference Neuroses*, you will see that prehistoric scenes, shown from the outside—shown as realized in lived experience, in a "scene" in the theatrical sense of the word—are what become internal scenes.

144 In German, notably, we must take into account that *Vorstellung* is the substantive corresponding to *sich vorstellen*, which is something like "represent to oneself" [*se représenter*]. The verb vorstellen, in the nonreflexive form, is rarely used.

Ego, id, and superego can each be localized, alternately, in one character or another in the drama. If they can be distributed among different characters, it certainly means that for the "*Urmensch*," "the primal man," there is no possibility that his character is divided, because it is the scene that is at the origin of the division. The "*Urmensch*" has no unconscious, or to put it another way, he has no id distinct from an ego or a superego; and of course, he has no Oedipus complex and no castration complex. It would be absurd to think that primal man has a castration complex since it is the castration performed on his sons that is the origin of the "castration complex" and the "primal fantasy of castration." Freud does think that these go on to be inherited but emphasizes: "In the beginning was the act" (*Im Anfang war die Tat*).

Not only is the metapsychology of the sender of the message (essentially the unconscious of the sender) not taken into account, but the sender of the message himself, as a principal actor, is ignored: it is just as we explained in the case of Gustavus Adolphus in the story of the page and for the wet nurse in the example of the "admirer of feminine beauty." What is *transmitted along with* the kiss, or with the breast, is not taken into consideration. For Freud, neither the one nor the other is a message.

Finally, "enigmatic": the term is of central importance because the messages between adults and children are necessarily enigmatic. A reciprocal understanding, both innate and acquired, permits a self-preservative attunement, but the messages sent by the adult are "enigmatic" because "offshoots" [i.e., the untranslated residues of failed/incomplete translations] contained in the adult's unconscious creep into the message; without the adult's awareness, they insinuate themselves into the messages sent by the adult. This "enigmatic" aspect, which is intuited by the child—and is necessarily a source of uneasiness—induces the child to search out a better understanding of what is happening to him.

In the end, what are the difficulties, the incomplete aspects, that imprison Freud?

1) He is a prisoner of a mechanistic conception of the movement of time. One could say that a symptom of this conception is the English translation of "*Nachträglichkeit*" as "deferred action": postponed action, but action strictly conforming to the "arrow of time."
2) He does not uncover the notion of "message" and, a fortiori, of an enigmatic message compromised by the unconscious of the sender.
3) Finally, he does not make use of his major advance—major but temporary—which constitutes the letter of December 6, 1896, which is to say the elaboration of a "translational" theory of the process of après-coup.[145]

THE DISAPPEARANCE OF THE TRANSLATIONAL THEORY

I would say that the main reason for the disappearance of this translational theory is the absence of any notion of a "to-be-translated," because there clearly has to be a "to-be-translated" at the start for there to be translation. As we understand it, a "to-be-translated" cannot be conceived without there being, from the beginning, both an opening *for* and an opening created by the enigma of the other.

Here I will simply repeat the following: the Freudian solipsism must be fundamentally refuted. This refutation is situated at two levels: not only where I am currently situated, which is to say the openness of the subject, inasmuch as he is human, to the (sexual) enigma of the other, but also from the beginning the openness of the

145 [Elsewhere Laplanche speaks of a "translational theory of repression," and, below, of "a translational model of a theory of seduction" and "of a theory of the constitution of the human being." One could also say that the passage in the letter of December 6, 1896 provides the basis for the translational theory of psychic trauma and of the Unconscious. It is the same moment of translation après-coup, the same urge to translate, which is central to the mechanism at the origin of psychic trauma, repression, the repressed unconscious, infantile sexuality and ultimately of the human subject as a self-narrating, self-theorizing creature.]

little human, inasmuch as he is a living creature (a homeotherm), to the world of fellow creatures who provide the help necessary for him to survive. Thus, we do not start out from two closed systems of "narcissism" and "symbiosis" but, on the contrary, from a biological being open to his environment and from a little human who, from the start, is invaded by the other human, by the adult and the messages the adult sends him.[146]

For a moment, I will go back to the letter of December 6, 1896, in order to underline the enigmatic place in which the letter itself seems to hold the initial "to-be-translated." Freud places it under what he labels "WZ," *Wahrnehmungszeichen*: a sign or an indication of perception, this is the whole of the ambiguity. If one takes it as an "indication of perception," then it need not involve the interhuman world, and we are not far from the notion of "trace" or "representation." If, on the other hand, we take *Zeichen* to be "sign" (as its etymology suggests), we are not far from the idea of something that "makes a sign" in the sense of someone who makes a sign to someone else. So we could say that there is a place left open for the "to-be-translated." We have already pointed out that in the expression "heard to be said and understood après-coup" in the letter of April 6, 1897 there is something that leads us in the same direction.

Why then invoke a theory, a *translational* model of après-coup and, more generally, a *translational* model of the theory of seduction and even a *translational* model of the constitution of the human being? It is because there is no mental process that captures the double movement better than translation, the indivisible double movement of "being carried forward" and "referring back." The "being carried forward" is nothing other than what I designate as a "fundamental to-be-translated": a demand to translate the message of the other. Already present in the least complicated dialogue, this demand or exigency is at maxi-

146 [In the French text, this paragraph appears as a footnote.]

mum strength when what stands out in the message is the enigmatic aspect of the other's sexuality. Therefore the exigency to translate compels one to turn to whatever code one has on hand, even if one must invent it oneself. This is what happens with the kiss given by Gustavus Adolphus, the consequences of which go beyond the reawakening of an erogenous zone and lead directly to the page's love for the sovereign. And this is what happens when the wet nurse gives the breast (and not simply milk) as recounted in the *Traumdeutung*.

Finally, if we introduce the notion of the message of the other into the *Wolf Man*, it considerably diminishes the importance of the discussion of the "material reality" of the scene. I want to say this: what escaped Freud's notice was that an adult message can be included in the spectacle of the primal scene; indeed, the *presentation* of a parental coitus to a child is, in itself, a message. But an adult message can also result from a scene that appears completely innocuous, such as the two parents simply appearing together in front of the child and giving each other an innocent kiss. Similarly, in the story of the "coitus of dogs," after all, it is not a trivial or insignificant matter to take a child for a walk to see sheep or dogs having sex. The question "What does this adult want of me?" here becomes: "What does this adult want of me when he takes me to see that? What does he want me to understand by showing me that?"

But for the subject, the question "What does he want from me?" entails opening the whole *retroactive* movement of translation: a search for the secret of the enigmatic message, which must always more or less escape his understanding. For the human being, for each of us, this is après-coup's bidirectional movement. The progressive movement, the movement forward in time, is that of the enigmatic message originally offered by the adult to the child as something "to be translated." The retroactive, backward movement is located in the succession of attempts at a translation of the message by the receiver, while recognizing that something of the enigmatic will be left out of every translation.

APRÈS-COUP: NOT WITHIN AN INDIVIDUAL BUT BETWEEN MESSAGE AND TRANSLATION

To conclude with vigor, I will again underline that "après-coup" is a phenomenon that is not played out within the *intra*personal but within the *inter*personal. Its specificity and its ability to reverse the "arrow of time" depend on this idea and this idea alone. In an individual, après-coup does not principally depend on the successive stages of that person's life. It depends, first of all, on the *simultaneous presence* of adult and infans. The adult's enigmatic message (which itself is inhabited by the adult's own unconscious) constitutes the "*avant-coup*" of this process, introducing a disequilibrium within the receiver that, in a second moment, in the après-coup, pushes him to translate, to translations that are inevitably imperfect. That *avant-coup* is characteristic of the earliest practical messages transmitted to the child by the adult in the ineluctable frame of the "fundamental anthropological situation."

Freud's psychoanalytic method gave a new meaning to this double movement: the possibility of psychoanalytic treatment. It was necessary for Freud himself to abandon the illusion of a "great secret" that would one day be revealed, filling in the lacunae and dissolving the enigmas. The "great secret" is actually the return, always imperfect—through scenes and by the analytic method, by the associative-dissociative method—toward the elements that carry the parental enigma, but without ever filling it in.

It is also, as Freud clearly said, the resumption of a progressive movement toward approximate, and possibly temporary, syntheses that constitute the properly psychotherapeutic aspects of every treatment and in which the activity of the analysand should be predominant—even if it is at the cost of disconcerting us.

Appendix 1

Le pont Mirabeau

Sous le pont Mirabeau coule la Seine
Et nos amours
Faut-il qu'il m'en souvienne
La joie venait toujours après la peine
Vienne la nuit sonne l'heure
Les jours s'en vont je demeure

Les mains dans les mains restons face à face
Tandis que sous
Le pont de nos bras passe
Des éternels regards l'onde si lasse
Vienne la nuit sonne l'heure
Les jours s'en vont je demeure

L'amour s'en va comme cette eau courante
L'amour s'en va
Comme la vie est lente
Et comme l'Espérance est violente
Vienne la nuit sonne l'heure
Les jours s'en vont je demeure

Passent les jours et passent les semaines
Ni temps passé
Ni les amours reviennent
Sous le pont Mirabeau coule la Seine
Vienne la nuit sonne l'heure
Les jours s'en vont je demeure

Le Pont Mirabeau

Under the Pont Mirabeau flows the Seine
And our love
Must I recall again
Joy always came after pain
Come the night, ring the hour
The days go by I remain.

Hand in hand standing face to face
While our eternal gaze
Under the bridge of our arms
Passes in the weary wave
Come the night, ring the hour
The days go by I remain.

Love disappears like this running current
Love disappears
How life is slow
and how Hope is violent
Come the night, ring the hour
The days go by I remain.

Days go by and weeks go by
Neither past time
Nor love remains
Under the Pont Mirabeau flows the Seine

Come the night, ring the hour
The days go by, I remain.

Appendix 2

Now that we have succeeded in making a synthesis of the dream, I will try to give a comprehensive account of the relations between the manifest content of the dream and the latent dream-thoughts.

It was night, I was lying in my bed. The latter part of this is the beginning of the reproduction of the primal scene. "It was night" is a distortion of "I had been asleep." The remark, "I know it was winter when I had the dream, and nighttime," refers to the patient's recollection of the dream and is not part of its content. It is correct, for it was one of the nights before his birthday, that is, Christmas Day.

Suddenly the window opened of its own accord. That is to be translated: "Suddenly I woke up of my own accord," a recollection of the primal scene. The influence of the wolf story, in which the wolf leapt in through the window, is making itself felt as a modifying factor, and transforms a direct expression into a plastic one. At the same time the introduction of the window serves the purpose of providing a contemporary reference for the subsequent content of the dream. On Christmas Eve the door opens suddenly and one sees before one the tree with the presents. Here therefore the influence of the actual expectation of Christmas (which comprises the wish for sexual satisfaction) is making itself felt.

The big walnut tree. The representative of the Christmas tree, and therefore belonging to the current situation. But also the tree out of the wolf story, on which the tailor took refuge from pursuit, and under which the wolves were on the watch. Moreover, as I have often been able to satisfy myself, a high tree is a symbol of observing, of scopophilia. A person sitting on a tree can see everything that is going on below him and cannot himself be seen. Compare Boccaccio's well-known story, and similar facetiae.

The wolves. Their number: six or seven. In the wolf story there was a pack, and no number was given. The fixing of the number shows the influence of the fairy tale of "The Seven Little Goats," six of whom were eaten up. The fact that the number two in the primal scene is replaced by a larger number, which would be absurd in the primal scene, is welcomed by the resistance as a means of distortion. In the illustration to the dream the dreamer brings forward the number five, which is probably meant to correct the statement "It was night."

They were sitting on the tree. In the first place they replace the Christmas presents hanging on the tree. But they are also transposed onto the tree because that can mean that they are looking. In his grandfather's story they were posted underneath the tree. Their relation to the tree has therefore been reversed in the dream; and from this it may be concluded that there are further reversals of the latent material to be found in the content of the dream.

They were looking at him with strained attention. This feature comes entirely from the primal scene, and has got into the dream at the price of being turned completely round.

They were quite white. This feature is unessential in itself, but is strongly emphasized in the dreamer's narrative. It owes its intensity to a copious fusion of elements from all the strata of the material, and it combines unimportant details from the other sources of the dream with a fragment of the primal scene which is more significant. This last part of its determination goes back to the white of his parents' bedclothes and underclothes, and to this is added the white of the flocks of sheep, and of the sheepdogs, as an allusion to his sexual researches among animals, and the white in the fairy tale of "The Seven Little Goats," in which the mother is recognized by the white of her hand. Later on we shall see that the white clothes are also an allusion to death. {There does not seem in fact to be any further clear reference to this point. The connection is perhaps with the episode of the winding-sheet (p. 98).}

They sat there motionless. This contradicts the most striking feature of the observed scene, namely, its agitated movement, which, in virtue of the postures to which it led, constitutes the connection between the primal scene and the wolf story.

They had tails like foxes. This must be the contradiction of a conclusion which was derived from the action of the primal scene on the wolf story, and which must be recognized as the most important result of the dreamer's sexual researches: "So there really is such a thing as castration." The terror with which this conclusion was received finally broke out in the dream and brought it to an end.

The fear of being eaten up by the wolves. It seemed to the dreamer as though the motive force of this fear was not derived from the content of the dream. He said he need not have been afraid, for the wolves looked more like foxes or dogs, and they did not rush at him as though to bite him, but were very still and not at all terrible. We observe that the dream-work tries for some time to make the distressing content harmless by transforming it into its opposite. ("They aren't moving, and, only look, they have the loveliest tails!") Until at last this expedient fails, and the fear breaks out. It expresses itself by the help of the fairy tale, in which the goat-children are eaten up by the wolf-father. This part of the fairy tale may perhaps have acted as a reminder of threats made by the child's father in fun when he was playing with him; so that the fear of being eaten up by the wolf may be a reminiscence as well as a substitute by displacement.

The wishes which act as motive forces in this dream are obvious. First there are the superficial wishes of the day, that Christmas, with its presents, may already be here (a dream of impatience), and accompanying these is the deeper wish, now permanently present, for sexual satisfaction from the dreamer's father. This is immediately replaced by the wish to see once more what was then so fascinating. The mental process then proceeds on its way. Starting from the fulfillment of this last wish with the conjuring up of the primal scene, it passes on to what has now become inevitable—the repudiation of that wish and its repression.

The diffuseness and elaboration of this commentary have been forced on me by the effort to present the reader with some sort of equivalent for the convincing power of an analysis carried through by oneself; perhaps they may also serve to discourage him from asking for the publication of analyses which have stretched over several years.

[1] Footnote added 1923:

I will once more set out here the chronology of the events mentioned in this case history.

- Born on Christmas Day.
- 1½ years old: Malaria. Observation of his parents copulating; or observation of them when they were together, into which he later introduced a phantasy of them copulating.
- Just before 2½: Scene with Grusha.
- 2½: Screen memory of his parents' departure with his sister. This showed him alone with his Nanya and so disowned Grusha and his sister.
- Before 3¼: His mother's laments to the doctor.
- 3¼: Beginning of his seduction by his sister. Soon afterwards the threat of castration from his Nanya.
- 3½: The English governess. Beginning of the change in his character.
- 4: The wolf dream. Origin of the phobia.
- 4½: Influence of the Bible story. Appearance of the obsessional symptoms.
- Just before 5: Hallucination of the loss of his finger.
- 5: Departure from the first estate.
- After 6: Visit to his sick father [compulsion to breathe out].
- 8–10: Final outbreaks of the obsessional neurosis.

It will have been easy to guess from my account that the patient was a Russian. I parted from him, regarding him as cured, a few weeks before the unexpected outbreak of the Great War [1914]; and I did not see him again until the shifting chances of the war had given the Central European Powers access to South Russia. He then came to Vienna and reported that immediately after the end of the treatment he had been seized with a longing to tear himself free from my influence. After a few months' work, a piece of the transference which had not hitherto been overcome was successfully dealt with. Since then the patient has felt normal and has behaved unexceptionably, in spite of the war having robbed him of his home, his possessions, and all his family relationships. It may be that his very misery, by gratifying his sense of guilt, contributed to the consolidation of his recovery.

Time and the Other

Time and the Other

"I was in the habit," says Freud in *The Interpretation of Dreams,* "of quoting this anecdote to explain how après-coup works in the mechanism of the psychoneuroses. 'A young man who was a great admirer of feminine beauty was talking once—so the story went—of the good-looking wet-nurse who had suckled him when he was a baby: 'I'm sorry,' he remarked, 'that I didn't make a better use of my opportunity'."[1]

It's a matter of an association to the 'Three Fates' or Knödel dream,[2] introduced by the following remark: "Love and hunger... meet at a woman's breast." In this dream, Freud is explicitly concerned with sexual meanings—but nevertheless there is a point where he comes to a halt, for reasons of discretion and propriety. I will not go into the full complexity of this dream, wishing simply to take the anecdote as it functions outside that particular context: as an illustration of the concept of après-coup. There are grounds to think that this illustration, like the dream, dates from 1898—in other words from the very thick of that concept's history, which stretches from 1895 to 1917. I will not go into the detail of that complex history here, but I have followed it very carefully this year in my university teaching. To summarize two perspectives on it: Lacan locates the concept in the Wolf-man case-history, that is in 1917; but pays no attention to the

---

1 *GW* 2:211; *SE* 4 :204-205

2 Didier Anzieu discusses this dream at length in *Freud's Self-analysis,* (Madison, Connecticut: International Universities Press, 1986).

seduction theory. As if in symmetry, Georges-Arthur Goldschmidt thinks that Freud "dropped this word" after 1898![3] A simple glance at Laplanche and Pontalis would have put him right. He also sees the word as coming naturally in the flow of Freud's language; whereas in fact après-coup is an expression taken from everyday speech and converted into a noun (*Nachträglichkeit*) at a specific moment in the letters to Fliess, and which Freud himself then privileges as a technical term. Everything confirms this. The apotheosis of a concept, for Freud, was its quantification; and what could be more provocative in its scientistic ambition than a phrase like "the total amount of après-coup is thus greatly reduced."[4]

Nonetheless, in Freud après-coup is not always conceptualized at the level of significance we ourselves give the concept … après-coup. This is easily shown by the simplicity of the example he uses in the *Traumdeutung*. Let us outline, using the convenience of "the arrow of time," the past, present and future. The anecdote offers two successive scenes linked by that arrow: the child at the breast, then the adult admirer of women thinking about his beautiful nurse's breast. A theory inverting the arrow of time would be that of retroactive interpretation or retroactive imagination, which Freud called "retrospective fantasising" (Zurückphantasieren). This, after all, is the position of the young man himself, no Freudian and clueless about infant sexuality.

He simply sends himself back there: "Oh, if only I'd known! If only I'd have known how to desire, been capable of desiring!" It's practically a joke, and makes you smile. A joke is often made at the expense of someone without knowledge—here, the baby who is "unaware" of his good luck; sexuality is what is hidden from children, what they can't even anticipate. But Freud's interpretation—practically all of the texts bear witness to this—takes the opposite course: it does not invert time's arrow, it remains determinist. Strachey's English translation of *Nachträglichkeit* as "deferred action" certainly

3 G-A. Goldschmidt, *Quand Freud voit la mer*, (Paris: Buchet-Chastel, 1988), 87
4 *GW* 12:88; *SE* 17:58 [translation modified]

cements that choice, and it sticks closely enough to Freud's explicit doctrine. That doctrine, as we know, is that excitation functions "in two times:" a representation can cause much more excitation, and thus be much more traumatic, than the initial somatic irritation, but that is due to an organic maturation in the intervening period.

It is quite remarkable that the concept of après-coup appears in the context of the letter of 14th November 1897, a letter which, after the abandonment of the seduction theory, marks a powerful return of the organic. This letter, where the concept first appears, five times as the substantive *Nachträglichkeit*, immediately sets out, like a sort of programme, what will be developed over the years as a series of 'stages' linked to organic erogenous zones. Furthermore, it makes this programme itself subject to a succession of 'phylogenetic' eras, a move which as I have shown I find unacceptable.[5] This erogeneity, to be conceived of as purely physiological, organically determined and genetically predetermined, will prove too much for Freud, himself confronted by an aporia when it comes to how to *define* infantile sexuality in the wider sense he gives it. He will at least maintain the requirement to define it, preferring not to give up the word sexuality by substituting more acceptable terms like 'organ-pleasure', 'interest' and so on.[6] Truth be told, among his successors this aporia has even disappeared. Because infantile, non-genital sexuality is difficult to

5 On several occasions I have explicitly formulated my absolute opposition to the phylogenetic hypothesis in psychoanalysis, whatever form it takes: the reproduction of phylogenesis in the ontogenesis of the drive, primal fantasies which are biologically inherited, the genetic transmission of the scenarios of the horde or of Oedipus, the innateness of the id, etc. This opposition is obviously not targeted against the genetic transmission of psycho-physiological aptitudes and functions acquired in the history of the living being and of the species, which are intrinsically outside the field of psychoanalysis, even if it presupposes them. By contrast, the problem of the transmission of sexuality (in the psychoanalytic sense) and also of how it is 'bound' (the Oedipus complex) must be dealt with following the model of interhuman communication, and not that of genetics.

6 On this point, re-read chapters XX and XXI of the *Introductory Lectures on Psychoanalysis* (1916-17) as well as the articles on "Sexuality" and "Organ-pleasure" in *The Language of Psychoanalysis*.

grasp—just as in our anecdote, where alimentary function and pleasure are not distinguished from oral sexuality, with its own pleasure, zone and specific object—it was quite simply abandoned. There will be reference to orality (or anality) or to oral (or anal) object relations, but hardly ever to oral or anal *sexuality*. Who among the Kleinians ever speaks nowadays of infantile sexuality? Who is concerned with pregenital erogenous pleasure?[7] In a sense, the French groups, especially the APF, are perhaps the exception: one of the last bastions of the idea of infantile sexuality.

If I chose to start off with the anecdote about the admirer of feminine beauty, it is because it gives the simplest outline of a temporal sequence—but also because it opens onto two interpretations of *Nachträglichkeit*, equally impoverished and in the end equally desexualizing. The 'retrogressive' path, that of the so-called hermeneutical interpretation, completely dispenses with any postulation of infantile sexuality. But the 'progressive' path, that of a succession of stages, runs no less a risk of desexualization. In today's conception of object relations, the infantile stages, even when they are still termed 'sexual', are only so metaphorically or by convention. We are no longer in the presence of metamorphoses of sexuality, but of those of love and hate, rendering practically obsolete all reference to sexual pleasure, to a sexual object, and to the zones of sexual excitation.

This discussion of time proposes an elaboration of our thinking about time that takes account of the advances of psychoanalysis. To be clear, there are two advances indicated by psychoanalysis, which are situated on entirely distinct levels of thinking about time: one explicit, the other completely implicit. Concerning the latter everything, as it

7 It would be interesting to count the occurrence, in texts like those of Melanie Klein, of the terms 'sexuality' or 'erogeneity'. One would notice that they are completely disconnected from any relation to the erogenous zones: the tongue and the lips, the anus, let alone the breast, which is never conceived as the source of sexual pleasure. When one speaks of this in certain analytic milieu, one gets the surprising reply: "It is you who are denying infantile sexuality; you ignore the baby's precocious erections." The prepsychoanalytic reduction of sexuality to the genital is clearly at work.

were, remains to be done on the basis of flashes of insight or summary hints. As a preliminary clarification, I would like to introduce the following distinctions: thinking about time, whether philosophically or scientifically, is developed on four levels[8] at once sharply distinct and deeply connected. What I call level I is that of cosmological time, or let's say, the time of the world. Level II is perceptual time, that of immediate consciousness; as I will shortly stress, this is also the time of the living being. Level III is the time of memory and of planning, the temporalization of the human being. Finally, level IV is that of history, the time of human societies, or even of humanity conceived as a whole. Each thinker occupies one or several of these levels. One level is usually taken as a privileged departure-point for moving on to the others to a greater or lesser extent. Here, we can peremptorily (at times provocatively) insert some names: at level I, we can situate Aristotle. At levels I and II, with an intimate and privileged relation between them, we situate Kant. At level II, recall, we place perceptual time, and nothing allows one to say a priori that it is not the time of the animal in general. It is even more paradoxical to situate thinkers like Husserl and Saint Augustine there. I refer here to Ricoeur's analyses in *Time and Narrative* (1985). Enthroned at level III are Heidegger and existentialism, and also hermeneutics. Level IV, the time of history, implies not only temporalization like level III, but recapitulation. It's indisputable that historical societies must be defined as those for which we have the archives and not merely what is integrated into current memory or culture. There can also, of course, be a history of individual temporalization, in other words a recapitulation of the history of level III; this is precisely what we are discussing at today's conference: 'case-histories'.

---

8 During the discussion of this paper, Didier Anzieu reproached me for speaking of 'levels', preferring to this term that of 'fields'. I maintain the idea of levels, which is an explicit reference to a positivist hierarchy, just as much in the domain of reality as in that of the sciences. I see no reason to dispute the idea that life is constructed on an inanimate foundation, and the human being on life; only the relation between levels III and IV is more complex than the simple idea of superimposition would suggest.

Where is Freud on this ladder? As you know, he makes many incursions onto the historical level (IV), but his predominant location is double: his theory of time that I call explicit is situated on level II; it is a theory formulated by Freud as a psychological theory. The implicit thinking about time, implied by psychoanalysis but not developed by it, is situated on the level of the temporalization of existence, that is to say on level III.

The explicit theory, that of perceptual time, is presented in many places, but its most important presentation is in the text on the "Mystic Writing-Pad."[9] It is necessary to go back to it, because it is put forward as the Freudian theory of time, and thus as incontestable. But I wish to show precisely that it should be contested in order to elaborate a way of thinking about the time of human existence. Freud tells us that he kept this theory secret for a long time. In fact, it emerges at very precise points in his speculations, and it probably originates partly in Breuer, or at least begins in the exchange between Breuer and Freud. This way of thinking links the consciousness of time to a consciousness of the working of the perceptual apparatus which, in turn, is conceived as periodical, rhythmical, made up of flashes and interruptions. I quote:

> It is as though the unconscious stretches out feelers, through the medium of the system *Pcpt.-Cs.*, towards the external world and hastily withdraws them as soon as they have sampled the excitations coming from it. ... I further had a suspicion {Freud speaks in the past tense, as of something he has been thinking of for a very long time} that this discontinuous method of functioning of the system *Pcpt.-Cs.* lies at the bottom of the origin of the concept of time.[10]

9 *SE* 19:227-232 (1925)
10 Ibid., p. 231.

I don't want to enter into the details here, as it is not my main object; I will limit myself to five remarks on this fascinating model. First, the consciousness of time is linked to a rhythm, which in a sense counters the seemingly obvious objection that the consciousness of time is being deduced from the consciousness of an apparatus's functioning in time and thus there has been no advance, since time has been deduced from time. In a sense, Freud escapes from this objection by linking the consciousness of time, as it were, to the time of time, in other words to rhythm. Linear time must be doubled in its 'derivative' (in the mathematical sense of the term), it must be reduplicated materially as rhythm—the rhythm precisely of interruption and connection, of light and dark—in order to become consciousness of time.

My second remark is that the creature being described is present to the world from the beginning.[11] The perception of the world, far from being constituted by a *first not me*,[12] is on the contrary linked to the periodical extinction of excitation, to the periodical shutting-down that opposes the continuous action of the *not me*. In the living being, the world is constituted by a retrenchment in reaction to an excess of world that, in the case of an inanimate being, could be said to be 'perception'. The stone has an excess of world; the living being cuts off from this excess of world precisely in order to establish a time for itself. There is no perception and no memory (even immediate) without something constituting itself as a separate organism.

My third remark is that there is no reason at all to think that the model being advanced applies exclusively to the human being. The whole of the functioning described is that of a living being, albeit of the most rudimentary kind, since Freud uses as a model (*Vorbild*) of the protoplasmic animalcule. The protoplasmic animalcule is at once described realistically as itself and taken, with some modifications, as

11 This runs counter to the image of the pseudopodia Freud advances. The model of the animalcule again carries the risk of conceiving the world as constituted on the basis of a narcissistic subject.

12 [Winnicott's phrase, in English in the original.]

an example of what happens in a very complex creature. One might say there is simultaneously metaphor, a model for the living being, and metonymy in the continuity with the hierarchy of living beings. This clearly indicates that we are at level II and only at this level, the level of a psychology of perception. Moreover, with some irony, but not with *impertinence,* I place Freud side by side with Husserl and Saint Augustine.[13] They all rely upon the link between perception and a rhythm. The examples most often put forward, those found in Husserl, in Saint Augustine, and no doubt also in Bergson, are those of the perception of a sound or of a musical sequence. I could also have invoked the authority of Merleau-Ponty, who never hesitated in his *Phenomenology of Perception* and in his *Structure of Behaviour* to re-establish the continuity between phenomenological analysis in the case of human beings and observation or experimentation in the case of animals.

My fourth contention is that this theory, whose truth remains to be tested and in my opinion deserves to be, is situated in one sense outside psychoanalysis. Not one of the major concepts of theory and practice can be found there: sexuality is absent, as are repression, defense and transference. As for time III, which is that of the history of a life, a case-history or history of a sick person, it is not clear how it would benefit from this theory of perception.[14]

My last point will finally take things further. This extra-psychoanalytic theory can become anti-psychoanalytic from the moment when one seeks to super impose it onto analysis. For me, testimony to this is given by the use of the term 'unconscious' in the text quoted: "the unconscious stretches out feelers, through the medium of the system *Pcpt.-Cs.,* towards the external world." Here Freud lapses back (as he does in many places, starting with "Formulations on the Two Principles of Mental Functioning"[15] and going on to the notion

13 Cf. J. Lagrange, "Problématiques du temps: phénoménologie et psychanalyse," in *Psychanalyse à l'Université,* 1988, vol. 13, no. 52, pp. 575-607.
14 This theory is not called upon for support in any of the case-histories.
15 *SE* 12:218-226 (1911)

of the id,[16] etc.) into a conception of the human individual constructed around a primal kernel, which would be the unconscious—a necessarily innate, biological, instinctual kernel. The unconscious would thus be at the center of the individual, from where it would send out pseudopodia; the individual would resemble a Russian doll. Far from being an alien inside me, the unconscious would be my foundation, my starting-point.[17] Here, one encounters one of the many forms taken by the attempt to construct a psychology on the basis of psychoanalytic notions—with the latter thus losing all of their specificity, their extraneousness, their alienness.

Human time, the time of level III, could be said to be proper to man. To be sure, there are many things 'proper to man': *erectus, habilis, sapiens,* or rather *sapiens sapiens;* laughter is proper to man, language is proper to man. For today's elaboration I am sticking to three attributes 'proper' to man: he temporalizes himself; he has an unconscious (with the fully scandalous nature of that expression: *having* an unconscious); he has an originary relation to the enigma of the other. I wish to show the conjunction of these three essential properties.

What more suitable terrain is there for this aspect of time than that of loss, of the human being confronted with loss; to the extent that the dimension of loss is probably co-extensive with temporalization itself? Thus mourning, which is discussed by Freud well before "Mourning and Melancholia"[18] and afterwards, too. It is mentioned in *Studies in Hysteria* to indicate two elements which are directly linked to temporalization: mourning is a kind of work, the work of memory (*Erinnerungsarbeit* in the case of Elisabeth); and it

---

16 *SE* 19:12-59 (1923)

17 In the text, from the same period as this one, "Negation" (1925), it is no longer the 'unconscious' but the 'ego' which puts out these pseudopodia: an indication, in our view, of the absolute wavering of Freud's thought at the moments when he reduces the psychoanalytic to the psychological. On all of this, see Jean Laplanche, *New Foundations for Psychoanalysis,* (New York: The Unconscious in Translation, 2016.)

18 *SE* 14:243-258

is an affect with a duration (*Daueraffekt*): it has a beginning and an end, it occupies a lapse of time. So I will once again speak of Freud, not to set out his theory, but to pick out from it, both as an indication and as a lack, indeed precisely as an absence, that which is most important. After all, absence being in question, is it so surprising that the most important elements announce themselves in the theory by their *absence*?

Thus "Mourning and Melancholia" is not the only text on mourning, and it is framed by at least two other texts—*Totem and Taboo* and "On Transience." Nowadays, *Totem and Taboo* is not often read, even though Freud considered it his best book; something Jones reports, but in spite of which, without showing the least shame, he classifies that work among the "non-medical applications of psychoanalysis."[19] In general, when it is referred to, it is for the great drama of the horde, the problem of the totem and the murder of the father. The murder of the father in *Totem and Taboo* overshadows everything, including our memory of the text; notably it overshadows chapter II, which is completely autonomous[20] and whose title is "Taboo and Emotional Ambivalence." In passing, let me pick out the term 'enigma' (the enigma of the taboo)[21] from the beginning of this chapter; Freud never uses the term enigma to characterize merely minor problems needing to be resolved. The principal part of this second study is indisputably the 'taboo of the dead'. Other taboos than this, notably the 'taboo of enemies', are discussed, but it is quite remarkable to see how they are subordinated to it. The only taboo enemies are dead enemies. In other words, it is not enough to be an enemy to unleash a phobia about "laying a hand on" or touching, one must, above all, be dead.

---

19 Ernest Jones, *The Life and Work of Sigmund Freud*, part 2, volume II, chapter XIV, "The Non-medical Applications of Psychoanalysis," (London: The Hogarth Press, 1955.)

20 *Totem and Taboo* was published in a series of instalments; they are separate essays.

21 [Translated by Strachey as "the riddle of the taboo." *SE* 13:22.]

I am going to pick out some elements from this text, without going through it from beginning to end. A first interesting element is the notion of 'reserve'; the term is in French in Freud: 'something like the concept of a reserve is connected with the taboo';[22] for instance, in the sense in which the painter employs this term. *Spatial reserve*: there are, in the territory of the clan, zones one is not allowed to enter, spaces one cannot encroach upon, objects or persons one cannot touch. But it is also a temporal reserve, for there is a time of the taboo: those who have touched the dead are impure and untouchable but only for a determinate time, which moreover varies according to the honor and rank of the dead. One finds here, incidentally, something which evidently gives Freud pleasure, because of his fondness for quantification: there is a force of the taboo which is, as it were, quantitative, analogous to the forces of universal gravitation, attraction and repulsion; a force greater with a chief than with a deputy, greater with a father than with an uncle, etc. This empty space is thus not only constituted as a reserve zone, but also in time. The time of the taboo, however much it may be bound up with ritual, irresistibly evokes the time of mourning. Besides, even quite recently, mourning itself was ritualized: one 'wore mourning' for a certain precise period, longer or shorter according to one's closeness to the person one was mourning.

A further very stimulating aspect is a third kind of what Freud calls 'reserve', although he does not use the term here. This is what I would call a linguistic reserve. Here we reach the 'taboo of names'. Indeed, among the things which cannot be touched, there is the name of the dead person, which can no longer be pronounced. The best way to avoid the temptation of uttering the dead person's name is to change his name. Thus, the dead man's name is changed to take account of this prohibition, and to enable us still to speak of him. Little

22 [Strachey translates *réserve* by "something unapproachable" in *Totem and Taboo*, *SE* 13:18.]

by little, all the names that relate to him are changed: those of persons, but also those of animals (especially totemic animals), familiar objects, etc. I quote a short passage with its air of folklore:

> Indeed, among the Guaycurus in Paraguay, when a death had taken place, the chief used to change the names of every member of the tribe; and 'from that moment everybody remembered his new name just as if he had borne it all his life'. Moreover, if the name of the dead man happens to be the same as that of an animal or common object, some tribes think it necessary to give these animals or objects new names, so that the use of the former name shall not recall the dead man to memory. This usage leads to a perpetual change of vocabulary, which causes much difficulty to the missionaries, especially when such changes are permanent. ... an important consequence of this process of suppression is that these peoples possess no tradition and no historical memory, so that any research into their early history is faced by the greatest difficulties.[23]

This very obstacle to writing history is linked by Freud to this linguistic reserve, in other words to the wish to confuse matters, or more radically, to cover over the tracks, to prevent the establishing of any archive, something which the missionaries, elsewhere such great historians, evidently ran up against.

The problem of the changing of names is dealt with rather briskly· in the course of Freud's elaboration, but it would open onto the immense question of the proper name, of its translatability, or even of the right to pronounce it. As you know, the Name *par excellence*—to the extent that today Chouraqui makes it into his principle

23 *SE* 13:70.

war-horse in his translation of the Bible—is the true name of Adonai, which can be written, but which can be neither uttered nor, of course, translated. Names, says Freud, have, for certain people, the full 'meaning of a thing' or 'thing-meaning' (*volle Dingbedeutung*). 'For certain people', that is to say 'primitives and children'; and, he adds, to 'psychoanalysts'; and for my part, by way of completion, I too would add: to translators. The proper name, like the dead person, is untranslatable: it could only be exchanged, in a rigorous sense, for the person himself.

What, then, does it mean to change all the names? It could be said that it draws the necessary consequences from the limitation of mourning. All the attributes of the dead person can be reworked: but his name is untouchable, impossible to *metabolize*. Thus the impossibility of doing a history of these societies. But is it not our tendency, we psychoanalysts, to wonder whether the *result* of a process is not its unconscious *goal*? I will thus propose the hypothesis that it is in order to prevent even the possibility of a history that this happens. *Post hoc ergo propter hoc*: this is one of our familiar arguments in psychoanalysis. Even if societies with a continual and absolute changing of names are at the extreme hardly conceivable, nonetheless, this lets us grasp how, through the taboo on using the name, a space of non-mourning is set up inside which mourning, mourning for everything else, is possible. The taboo thus opens the much larger question: in loss, what is it that can be metabolized, and what cannot?

For Freud, in his moments of all-conquering realism, everything can be metabolized. The taboo would be purely pathological, reducible without remainder to a purely subjective, internal, 'ipsocentric' mechanism. Here, the two linked notions of ambivalence and projection are called to the rescue (I will pursue this question of the taboo slightly further). A dialogue with Wundt (an author completely forgotten today) comes in at this point, whose work might be thought confused, but which is nevertheless illuminating.[24] The initial ambivalence according to Wundt (as he can be reread through Freud's text) concerns the phenomenon itself, or even the word: the word 'taboo' would be ambivalent in itself - sacred and impure, to be venerated and to be loathed. One could even say, in a sense, pre-ambivalent. Wundt includes both aspects in an originary indistinct concept—the 'demonic'—which only later splits into veneration and loathing. On the other hand, for Freud, and this is very important, the two sides—love and hate, veneration and loathing – are from the outset opposed, divided. The ambivalence of the signifier is secondary, for him, to an originary ambivalence of drives. In this there is a sort of prefiguration of the debate in which Benveniste will later come to discuss Freud's text on "The Antithetical Meaning of Primal Words."[25] Primal words, Benveniste will say, do not have "antithetical" meanings. They designate something prior to the splitting into two meanings. The Latin word *altus*, to recall the example shared by Benveniste and Freud, means "high" or "deep" to the translator. But in the original language, *altus* is pre-ambivalent: it indicates only the vertical dimension, prior to the moment when the observer takes up a fixed position, whether at the bottom of a well or at the top; and it is only from that moment that he can say, if he's at the bottom of the well, the well is high; and if he's at the top, the well is deep. Could it not be thought, I would ask for my part, that what is prefigured in Wundt, what Freud could have read there under the term 'demonic', was the original ambivalence—or rather 'pre-ambivalence'—of the

---

24 Even if, at the very moment Freud claims in *Totem and Taboo* that he "listens with attention" to Wundt, he lets out his rage in his letters: "I ... am furious about Wundt," he writes to Ferenczi on 17 October 1912: 'It is a harsh punishment to have to read this rubbish in the evening after eleven hours of work'. *The Complete Correspondence of Sigmund Freud and Sandor Ferenczi*, volume I: 1908-1914, eds E. Brabant, E. Falzeder and P. Gampieri-Deutsch, (Cambridge, MA: The Belknap Press of Harvard University Press, 1993), 411.

25 *SE* 11:155-161. Emile Benveniste, "Remarks on the function of language in Freudian Theory," *Problems in General Linguistics* (1966), trans. Elizabeth Meek, (Coral Gables: University of Miami Press, 1971), 65-75.

message of the other? That which Freud rejects, in his disagreement with Wundt, and under the pretext of obscurity and irrationality, *is a conception in which the dead become demons, reveal themselves in their enigmatic aspect, and being henceforth absent give way entirely to their enigmatic message.*

Freud's objection is simple and profoundly rationalist: demons can in no way be considered to be final explanations, *letzte Dinge*. Quite simply, we don't believe in demons!

> Neither fear nor demons can be regarded by psychology as "earliest" things, impervious to any attempt at discovering their antecedents. It would be another matter if demons really existed. But we know that, like gods, they are creations of the human mind.[26]

By exploring the taboo in the case of the dead, Freud made things easy for himself. Demons already are quite clearly human creations. But the dead do not exist any more than do demons. In one sense, they too are a creation. They thus leave a space entirely open for projection. Projection which, in the last analysis, is that of a constitutional ambivalence of drives. This ambivalence, Freud tells us, is 'of greater or lesser strength according to predisposition'. Now, ambivalence—it is not clear why—is particularly important in primitive peoples (just as in neurotics ...).

This chapter of *Totem and Taboo* includes one of the most comprehensive discussions of projection. Comprehensive in that it presents us with a continuum, going from the projection or so-called projection of bodily sensations, said to be what creates the external world, to paranoiac projection. There again, we see the psychoanalytic psychology (or even ontology) I was condemning a moment ago.

The dead are really dead. It is the limit case. But in this psychology, whether dead or not, the other is first constructed by

26 *GW* 9:34; SE 13:24 [Strachey translates Freud's *letzte Dinge* as 'earliest things'.]

projection. The path of projection will be the one taken by Melanie Klein, which will then engulf her totally. In her view, good and bad are qualities originally projected onto the other. I come back to the case of the enemy: even the enemy, however bad in reality, is not enough to elicit a taboo. His badness is not sufficient for him to be considered a bad object; for him to be a bad object, the projection of my hatred is necessary.

Is there, in Freud's discussion of the taboo, anything which breaks this originary closure, a closure from which the only way out is projection? I find two suggestions, one in *Totem and Taboo* itself, which is only an indirect indication: the mention of an affinity between the taboo and the 'categorical imperative'. For me, this indicates an opening towards the other, towards the message of the other. The superego is not yet present, but is announced; as we well know, the superego will immediately be connected to verbal traces, the traces of the parental 'word'. The other suggestion of an opening onto the originary dimension of the other is not in that text, but it is found in "The Taboo of Virginity."[27] This is one of the few texts which breaks out of Freudian ipso-centrism. The fear of deflowering the woman, Freud tells us, is the fear of castration—but for once it is not entirely projected. The fine excellent discussion of projection is here partially invalidated. I quote:

> Wherever primitive man has set up a taboo he fears some danger and it cannot be disputed that a generalized dread of women is expressed in all these rules of avoidance. Perhaps this dread is based on the fact that woman is different from man (*anders ist als der Mann*), for ever incomprehensible and mysterious, strange and therefore apparently hostile.[28]

27 *SE* 11:193-208 and see *Problématiques II: Castration-symbolisations* (Paris: PUF, 1980), 91-108, 175-8.
28 *GW* 12:168; *SE* 11:198.

A rare, and in every sense extra-ordinary, text. Not only is projection replaced by a centripetal movement, by an originary injection of fear, but the other term in the Freudian explication—that is, ambivalence, the ambivalence of love/hate—is relativized. Nor is hostility seen as a 'last thing', a final element; it is subordinated here to otherness: 'different and thus hostile'. Demons are not a last thing, Freud had objected to Wundt—what is final, what is originary is the ambivalence of love/hate and the resulting projection. Here, in "The Taboo of Virginity," one could say that in a way Wundt answers back. Ambivalence is not a 'last thing'—Wundt seems to say in Freud's voice—what is last, what is ultimate is the demonic, the hidden, the uncanny (*das Unheimliche*), that which is 'otherwise', which comes originally *from* the other, in the mode of the other. It is only secondarily that it is split into good and bad.

Why doesn't Freud find what he notices about the relation to the woman in the relation to the dead person? It is my opinion that he lacks a category, which is neither external reality (real danger) nor the subjective (the projected drives). As far as the relation to the woman is concerned, the lack of this category is not too evident. The woman is there, she is real: it is thus still possible for a real danger to be perceived, scented. Freud, it seems, can appeal from the category of fantasy to that of reality, with no need of a third domain of existence. But the dead person, for his part, is really dead. There is no danger, no otherness to be sensed, except by pure projection. A category is lacking here in Freud, but it is not that of the "symbolic," it is that of the message or the signifier, which is something quite different. A way of approaching this category is to note that in it the difference between the living other and the dead other is relativized. A signifier remains a signifier, even if set down thousands of years ago, and found in the desert or in a pyramid. It could even be said to gain in otherness, as the other who emitted or wrote it is no longer there to support it, to be its guarantor or interpreter.

Mourning

To discuss mourning in Freud is to come up against this same lack, the lack of the category of the message, and in particular, of the enigmatic message. For me, the point is not to re-examine "Mourning and Melancholia," but simply to mark its central aporia concerning mourning.

First, it is an extraordinary invention. Mourning, which seems so obvious, the pain, the time it takes, etc.—all that is only the manifest aspect of a kind of work; a work following the loss of the other and consisting in a *Lösung* or *Ablösung* (I will come back to these terms). But after this brilliant starting-point, the whole analysis will be turned towards the pathological: which is, I would say, in what is barely a play on words . . . quite normal. Mourning is described as the 'normal prototype' of melancholia—it is that which sheds light, and thus that on which there would be no light to be shed: how could light be illuminated? "It never occurs to us," says Freud, "... to refer it to medical treatment;" thus no analysis is necessary, nor even desirable. "We look upon any interference with it as useless or even harmful." Or further: "It is really only because we know so well how to explain it that this attitude (inhibition) does not seem to us pathological." Finally, there is this extraordinary declaration: we relate "melancholia ... to an object-loss which is withdrawn from consciousness, in contradistinction to mourning, in which there is nothing about the loss that is unconscious." And we once again encounter the impressive psychopathological scaffolding of "Mourning and Melancholia:" a scaffolding operating on three ascending levels—that of simple loss, which is mourning; loss + ambivalence, producing obsessional mourning with guilt (already discussed in *Totem and Taboo*); and finally loss + ambivalence + narcissistic object-choice, which produces melancholia. This scaffolding, however, has a fragile base: mourning creaks beneath the burden of all that it is asked to support. Where are we to find mourning which would be only conscious, with no infantile reverberation, no ambivalence and no narcissistic consequences?

The creaking of mourning beneath the weight of the edifice of psychopathology and metapsychology can be heard from "Mourning and Melancholia" onwards. The pain of mourning, Freud tells us at one point, "is taken as a matter of course by us." But then, several lines later: "[it] is not at all easy to explain in terms of economics." If mourning, in fact, entails no narcissistic wound, no breaching of the ego, how can it be understood to be painful? Especially when, in Freudian thought, pain is conceived precisely and above all as breaching. And again, further on: "We cannot even say how mourning achieves its task."

I will leave behind these various creakings, to get to the point of the acknowledgement of failure, that the colossus has feet of clay: it is a year later, in "On Transience." Let us read this lovely passage (lovely because of its anti-climax):

> Mourning over the loss of something that we have loved or admired seems so natural to the layman that he regards it as self-evident. But to psychologists mourning is a great riddle {this is the word that gives the game away,}[29] one of those phenomena which cannot themselves be explained but to which other obscurities can be traced back'. {And a little further on:} But why it is that this detachment (*Ablösung*) of libido from its objects should be such a painful process is a mystery to us, and we have not hitherto been able to frame any hypothesis to account for it. We only see that libido clings to its objects and will not renounce those that are lost even when a substitute lies ready to hand.

What a scandal for Freud! Why not change the object, as soon as the old one has gone and another is at hand? But despite the repetition

29 [Laplanche's aside refers to the French translation of the German word *Rätsel* (in English, and in Strachey, 'riddle') as *énigme*, 'enigma'. For his comments on these riddles of translation, see below, page 191 and footnote 44.]

of this enigma, the passage comes to a halt with an abrupt conclusion, as if impatient to finish: "Such then is mourning" (*das also ist die Trauer*).

It is a scandal for a realist, for whom the dead are really dead. Why is all this work required to change object? Why so much palaver? Now this enigmatic block of mourning is to remain untouchable in what follows, and for posterity. Abraham will seek for a moment to explore mourning, that is, to put Freud to work, but he will be promptly rebuffed.[30] Freud does not like being put to work. Very quickly, mourning will be buried, hidden beneath psychopathology, which little by little re-invests it. See Abraham, then Melanie Klein, even in the article where she analyses her own mourning;[31] and finally, Lagache, whose case entitled "Pathological mourning"[32] perhaps did the most to re-open the question of mourning in its entirety.

There are many routes to re-open that question. Among these, there is one route that is both poetic and linguistic: a patient, when she came to consult me, straight away told me how she had seen her husband off to the war, some years previously. There had been no news! Searches in all the records, in all the camps, Russian or Nazi, proved in vain. It was said that he had escaped, but there was no proof, and already numerous young suitors were crowding round her, demanding that she change her object and remarry. And already . . . you have guessed that it's Penelope. You know of her ruse, the famous cloth. Let us, in turn, allow ourselves to be carried away by the ruse of some words:

στησαμνένη μέγαν ἱστόν (94)[33]
having erected a huge mast.

---

30 Karl Abraham, "A Short Study of the Development of the Libido" (1924), Selected Papers, (London: The Hogarth Press, 1927.)

31 Melanie Klein, "Mourning and its relation to manic-depressive states" (1940), reprinted in *The Selected Melanie Klein*, ed. Juliet Mitchell, (Harmondsworth: Penguin Books, 1986).

32 Daniel Lagache, 'Pathological Mourning' (1956), *Selected Writings*, trans. Elizabeth Holder, (London: Karnac Books, 1993).

33 Homer, The Odyssey, ed. W. B. Stanford, London: Macmillan, 1967, Book II, p. 19.

This requires an explanation, because ἱστόν [iston] will immediately mean, in the next line, a fabric. The link between the two meanings of the word is metonymic. On the weaving loom, as you know, the threads of the 'chain' are rolled onto a baton. Normally, we see a horizontal roll, but on the ancient looms the roll was vertical, the cloth was woven on a sort of mast, an erected baton, with all the associations you may wish.[34]

... ἠματίη μὲν ὑφαίνεσκεν μέγαν ἱστὸν (104)
By day she wove a great fabric
νύκτας δ'ἀλλύεσκεν (105)
And by night, she analyzed it.

(ἀλλύεσκεν, the iterative imperfect of ἀναλύειν, that is to say undo, unweave, or ... analyze).

The last line quoted describes the moment when the ruse is discovered by the suitors. Having begun to get suspicious about this work which never advances, they buy the complicity of a servant, break in one night and surprise Penelope at her work of unweaving:

καὶ τήν γ'ἀλλύουσαν εφεύρομεν αγλαὸν ἱστόν (109)
and we found her in the midst of analyzing her resplendent fabric.

This, then, is Penelope's work; but what is it exactly? Is it weaving or unweaving? The analogy between 'analyzing' and 'undoing' the fabric invites us to attempt to turn the whole process around. We are used to this kind of interpretation. We are told in the manifest tale: a faithful and wise spouse, she wishes to get rid of the suitors, and she weaves with the sole aim of unweaving, in other words to gain time until her Ulysses returns. One can equally well suppose, however, the reverse: that perhaps she only unweaves *in order* to weave, to be able to weave a new tapestry. It would thus

34 A 'cloth' is thus named by the same word as the 'erected mast'. Furthermore, in the line quoted, στησαμνένη [stesamene] (having erected) is from the same root as ἱστόν [iston] (erected mast).

be a case of *mourning*, mourning for Ulysses. But Penelope does not cut the threads, as in the Freudian theory of mourning; she patiently unpicks them, to be able to compose them again in a different way. Moreover, this work is nocturnal, far from the conscious lucidity with which, Freud claims, the threads are broken one by one. This work requires time, it is repetitive (thus the iterative verb form), it sets aside a reserve. One could say, to introduce at this point what has been established about the taboo: it sets aside the reserve of the *taboo of Ulysses*, the reserve of the *name of Ulysses*.[35] There is, however, a possible end. One can imagine that one evening the new cloth, for a while at least, will not be unwoven.

The route opened up with Homer takes us further on, then. Through the very words of the poet, it invites us to enter again into the text of "Mourning and Melancholia." The Greek verb—this point must be stressed – coincides exactly with the German *lösen*, 'to untie', 'resolve'. The *Lösung* of a problem is its 'solution' or its 'resolution'. From this, the German language develops a series of derivatives: *lösen, aeflösen, ablösen, erlösen*. French has a series quite close to this, with words formed on the Latin root *solvere*: *solution* ('solution') (but no verb *soudre*, whence the rather ugly *solutionner*);[36] *resoudre* ('to resolve'), *dissoudre* ('to dissolve'), *absoudre* ('to absolve'); but the equivalences are not exact. Ἀναλύειν [analuein], at any rate, is very exactly *auflösen*, to dissolve, to ana/lyse: what it refers to is a resolution which operates by 'going back over' (*auf*-ἀνα), that is by drawing near the elementary or the originary. 'Psycho-analysis' could have been named by Freud, if he had not wished to choose a Greek term, *Seelen-Auflösen*: disentangling, dissolution or resolution of souls. Terms formed with *lösen* occur very often in Freud and, if one is trying to keep a certain continuity in the French, are extremely difficult to translate. In "Mourning and Melancholia" they appear in particu-

35 The notion of a 'reserve of the name' would perhaps allow the famous question of the 'Name of the Father' to be put to work in a new way.
36 [English has 'to solve' as the solution of this French problem.]

lar in the two forms *lösen* (*Lösung*) and *ablösen* (*Ablösung*). Thus, in the central passage, which is so well known, on mourning:

> Each single one of the memories and expectations in which the libido is bound to the object is brought up [*mis en position*] and hypercathected, and the *Lösung* of the libido is accomplished in respect of it.[37]

Two terms here deserve comment. First of all, '*mis en position*' [Strachey's 'brought up'], corresponding to the German '*einstellen*'. It is a question, very precisely, of the 'positioning' of a piece of cloth on a machine, in order to begin some work on it. In an old translation, we had proposed 'put on the loom', which was a more direct evocation of the 'weaving loom'.[38] One can only marvel to see Freud, who nowhere alludes to Penelope, coming close to the same image for the work of mourning.[39]

The term *Losung* could also have taken us towards 'unweaving', the disentanglement of the libido; this nuance is certainly present in the German word, but, unfortunately, it is gradually effaced in the course of the article, in favor of *Ablösung*, which skews things towards detachment, the slipping of moorings, or rather the breaking of links. What prevails in Freud is clearly the detachment of the libido from

---

37 *GW* 10:430; SE 14:245 [Strachey has 'detachment' for *Losung*.]

38 And, of course, Boileau: 'Twenty times on the loom you begin again your work' (*Art Poétique*).

39 So much the more striking is Freud's other intuition, leading him to ascribe to woman the invention of weaving, seeing in it a sort of perfecting of the pubic hair which, according to him, masks the absence of the penis (in the *New Introductory Lectures*, *GW* 15:142; SE 22:132). Numerous paths open up from this starting-point:

- That of Greek etymology, such as it is reflected in Homer's text, where ἱστόν [iston] is at once the penile mast of the loom and the cloth which is rolled onto it, veiling it. In the same way, the pubic tissue is at once what veils (*verhüllen*) and, symbolically, what is veiled (see 'Medusa's Head', *GW* 17:45-48; SE 18:273-274).
- A questioning of the privileged relation of woman to, at the same time, weaving-unweaving, mourning and melancholia.
- The setting up of a relation between the lost object, in mourning and / or melancholia, and the lacking or lost penis.

the object or, more precisely, from the representation of the object. This does not surprise us as the object is constantly defined by him as 'what is most variable in the drive', so that the change of object, once the object has disappeared, seems to be a matter of course, save for any neurotic complications.[40] Whence, perhaps, the fact that Freud does not see that mourning as a work of unweaving, while being the prototype of melancholy, can also be conceived as that of psychoanalysis: unweaving so that a new fabric can be woven, disentangling to *allow* the formation of new knots.[41]

What are the threads that are unwoven by the work of untying?[42] Freud spoke of 'memories' and 'expectations' attaching us to the other. What he doesn't take account of, but which is rarely absent—precisely in the fabric, the *context* of those memories and expectations—is the place for the *message* of the other. For the person in mourning, that message has never been adequately understood, never listened to enough. Mourning is hardly ever without the question: "What would he be saying now? What would he have said?" hardly ever without regret or remorse for not having been able to speak with the other enough, for not having heard what he had to say.

Eric Toubiana, in his work on *The Psychopathology of Inheritance*, shows this well.[43] The struggle for succession is not only a material struggle for the property of the deceased. The fury which breaks out around the will (that of Caesar, for instance) perpetuates

40 On this point, see J. Laplanche and J.-B. Pontalis, *The Language of Psychoanalysis*, trans. Donald Nicholson-Smith (London: The Hogarth Press, 1973), the entry under 'Object'.

41 Freud gave a clear expression of the spontaneous character of 'psychosynthesis' in the patient in analysis in "Lines of Advance in Psycho-Analytic Therapy" (1919a), SE 17:160-161. The 'reconstruction' of the patient, at least in the analysis of neurotics, is not done by the analyst.

42 The French language brings together untying (Fr. *déliement*, Ger. *Lösung*) and unbinding (Fr. *déliaison*, Ger. *Entbindung*) in a way that German does not. At the same time, the relation between the unweaving of associative threads and the unbinding (unchaining) of libido should be stressed.

43 *L'héritage et sa psychopathologie*, (Paris: PUF, 1988.)

a speech—enigmatic, traumatizing, violent, or even deadly: the voice of the other. A voice no doubt related to the superego, but which is not entirely merged with it.

Enigma

When I hear talk of enigmas, I prick up my ears. Despite using "enigma" to translate the German term Rätsel (from the verb *erraten*: to guess), an enigma is not just a simple riddle [*devinette*.] An enigma, as I understand it, is to be distinguished just as much from a riddle as from a problem to be resolved, or from a mystery.[44] When we hear enigmas talked of, I propose this procedure: to move from the enigma *of*, to the enigma *in*, and then to the function of the enigma *in*.[45] Let me explain: when one speaks, to take up Freud's terms, of the enigma *of* femininity (what is woman?), I propose to move with Freud to the function of the enigma *in* femininity (what does a woman want?). In the same way (but here Freud does not make the move), what he terms the enigma of the taboo points back to the function of the enigma in

44 One is entitled, to be sure, to equate these terms; for my part, I try to differentiate them. An enigma, like a riddle, is proposed to the subject by another subject. But the solution of a riddle in theory is completely in the conscious possession of the one who poses it, and thus it is entirely resolved by the answer. An enigma, on the contrary, can only be proposed by someone who does not master the answer, because his message is a compromise-formation in which his unconscious takes part.

To speak of the 'enigma' of natural phenomena (the enigma of 'black holes') is, in our sense, incorrect, unless one supposes a demiurge with an unconscious. To say that the baby offers an enigma to the adult, just as much as the other way round (see D. Houzel, in *Journal de la psychanalyse de L'enfant*, 1990, 8, p. 289) is to suppose that the psychical apparatus of the human infant is immediately split between 'unconscious' and 'preconscious-conscious', a constitutional split to my mind inadmissible. As for mystery ... let us leave to theologians the task of situating it in relation to the categories of the message and the signifier!

45 This 'in' has no topographical connotation here, and does not situate the enigma on the 'inside' of the psychical apparatus. If one had to situate the enigma, it would be on the contrary as a surface entity, first implanted in the skin of the body, then in the outer surface of the ego (see the schema for primal repression, New Foundations for Psychoanalysis, (New York: The Unconscious in Translation, forthcoming.)

the taboo. And even more clearly, the enigma of mourning points to the function of the enigma in mourning: what does the dead person want? What does he want of me? What did he want to say, to me?

The enigma leads back, then, to the otherness of the other; and the otherness of the other is his response to his unconscious, that is to say, to his otherness to himself. I used the title of this paper, 'Time and the Other', as a kind of approximation. On the one hand, it did not completely correspond to what I wanted to say; and on the other, I realized that it duplicated the title of a work by Levinas, of some years ago now.[46] A work which doubtless would not be the most adequate way to stage a debate between what I am arguing and the thought of that author. Unfortunately, the best title would have been rather too sophisticated: something like 'Time and the other(s)' [*Le temps et l' / les autre(s)*], in other words the different 'others'. In Freud, there are at least two domains of 'the other': *der Andere and das Andere*. In German, *der Andere*—the masculine noun—means 'the other person'; and *das Andere* – the neuter noun—*or das Andere Psychische,* means 'the other thing' or 'the psychical thing.' The 'other thing' is quite simply the unconscious. There is no reason to deny this 'other thing' the characteristics of timelessness and above all the absence of negation. The absence of negation, the absence of discursivity from the diachronic point of view, and the absence of 'value' (in the Saussurean sense of structural opposition) in the synchronic. On the other hand, as I indicated a moment ago in my criticism of a point in Freud's theory of perceptual time, the unconscious cannot in any way be considered the kernel of our being, the *Kern unseres Wesens,* in the sense of an *intimior intimo meo* ['something more inward than my inwardness']. Far from being my kernel, it is the other implanted in me, the metabolized product of the other in me: forever an 'internal foreign body'.

46 Emmanuel Levinas, Time and the Other (1948), trans. Richard A. Cohen, Pittsburgh: Duquesne University Press, 1987.

"The Other Person"

The other person is primal in relation to the construction of human subjectivity (level III of time), in other words, of sexual and temporal subjectivity. I would like this to be understood, for a moment, in relation to all the 'mechanisms' described by psychoanalysis. Take processes like introjection and projection, for instance: since Freud, this pair has had a lot of success particularly in the hands of Melanie Klein. Melanie Klein has been criticized, and in one sense not unjustly, for the primacy she accords to projection. I recalled this in relation to taboo: in Klein, but already in Freud too, the object is bad, primordially, through projection. Is it therefore a question of opposing projection with introjection as that which is originary? Are we not faced with the problem of the chicken and the egg: which comes first? Projection? Introjection? The only way not to get lost in this absurd quarrel over priority, this quest for a perpetual motion of self-engendering, is to *escape* from the dilemma. What I wish to say, fundamentally, is that introjection, just as much as projection (as well as repression, defense, identification, etc.), is a mechanism whose subject, the subject of the verb itself, is the individual in question: 'I introject'; but equally—for I am not setting in opposition mechanisms in the 1st, 2nd or 3rd person—'you repress', 'Pierre or Sigmund identifies'. All these processes are 'conjugated' with the person in question; caught in the trap of ipso-centrism, psychoanalysis can only run after mechanisms in which the subject would still be active, all the while *pretending* to be passive.[47] Let us take the mechanism of disavowal, in which it is me without being me, who wishes to know nothing about it, yet all the same knows. Even Lacan's 'foreclosure' is caught in this trap: introduced following an

47 An exact reversal of, but also correlative to, Cocteau's famous formula: "Since these mysteries are beyond me, let's pretend to be the one who organizes them" ("Les maries de la Tour Eiffel," in *Theatre de Cocteau*, tome I, (Paris: Gallimard, 1949), 57). Clearly, I would say: "Since this *enigma* ..."

admirable condemnation of the 'indestructible percipiens' underlying the whole conception of hallucination as purely projective, it constitutes, nonetheless, a veiled return to ipsocentrist positions which it was thought to have surpassed.[48] Foreclosure, refusal of entry to the symbolic, we are told ... but *who* 'refuses entry', if not President Schreber as the 'indestructible' subject of the process? *Who* 'forecloses' the Name of the Father ..., if not Daniel-Paul himself, *in person*? Can one not therefore propose a fundamental inversion: the originary mechanisms are not 'in person', but 'in otherness', to be formulated starting from the other: *he* implants, *he* intromits ... into Pierre, Jacques or Sigmund?

I will return now to my central theme, that of temporalization; exactly that which Heidegger describes as stretched between its three *ekstases*: present, future and having-been. At this starting-point of the description I have no quarrel with this 'stretching out'. I indicated just now that my analysis is not located in *the wake of* Heidegger's, but certainly *on the same terrain* of being. My criticism does not therefore concern the tension between these ekstases, but the way they are linked together, and the priority to be established between them. My target here is not only Heidegger, but the whole of hermeneutics, including the vast hermeneutical movement which is nowadays invading psychoanalysis, and which we are not sufficiently aware of in France: not sufficiently present in the debate which is establishing itself, in the heart of the psychoanalytic movement, with hermeneutics. Heidegger and hermeneutics give priority to 'being for', as Ricoeur has recently restated: Heidegger asserts "the primacy of the future in the [course] of the articulated structure of time."[49] The originary vector is the future, the 'to-come' [Fr. *l'a-venir*, Ger. *Zu-kunft*], the Orient (*Woraufhin*) towards which the subject throws himself reso-

48 Jacques Lacan, "On a question preliminary to any possible treatment of psychosis" (1955-6), *Écrits*, trans. Bruce Fink (New York: Norton, 2006), 445-488.
49 [Paul Ricoeur, *Time and Narrative*, vol. 3, trans. Katherine Blarney and David Pellauer, (Chicago: University of Chicago Press), 1988.]

lutely. One knows the Heideggerian term *Entschlossenheit,* translated either as 'decision', as 'resolution' or as 'resolute decision'. It is with the same resolute decision that Freud, for his part, goes towards the past. And here I have no argument, there is nothing there that I wish to reformulate. Analysis is a movement towards the past, a going back over – the *Lösung* ['solution'] is an *Auflösung* ['dissolution'], a term which clearly indicates the movement. What should be added emphatically, however, is that it is a going back over which dissolves, which resolves, and not a going back to the so-called ultimate formula of my being. Beyond translations and past constructions, beyond the weavings it undoes, analysis goes back along the threads of the 'other': the other thing of our unconscious, the other person who has implanted his messages, with, as horizon, the other thing in the other person, that is, the unconscious of the other, which makes those messages enigmatic.

I speak of a fixed mover of temporalization, in a certain way repeating the Aristotelian image. But rather than theorizing on this subject, I would like to come back to the little story of the admirer of women. The anecdote is apparently limited to the relation between two scenes: the child at the breast, the adult in the presence of the breast. There are only two protagonists, the individual in question and his 'object', the breast. In this story of 1898, Freud, who has abandoned the theory of seduction, forgets or rather scotomizes *the nurse,* in whom he refuses to see a new version of the 'perverse adult' of the letters to Fliess. Here, she is hardly anything more than the support of an object without enigma, an object to be consumed. But what object, what consumption, is at issue here? Is it the milk which is to be ingested? Is it the breast which is to be... sucked ...? Incorporated ...? Caressed ...? Stimulated ...? As for the nipple, precisely the erogenous part of the object, it is cruelly absent, as is any reference to the pleasure the other seeks there.

Here, then, is what is missed, in the imperfect, unfinished conceptualization of après-coup, just as in the Freudian theory of infantile sexuality, and even in the theory of leaning-on:[50] beyond the movement which carries it to a so-called primal scene, 'the child at the breast', analysis (the unweaving of that scene) opens onto the activity, the implantation, the message and also the enigmatic sexual pleasure of the other. Thus, perhaps, there emerges a way out of the dilemma which troubles our practice, caught between pure determinism and the pure attribution of meaning. A primal 'to-be-translated', if it contained, like a seed, the whole of meaning, would be an 'open sesame' to be discovered, a master-key to open all doors. But, conversely, a primal 'to-be-translated', if it had the obtuseness of brute fact, would be open to all meanings, and from then on any attribution of meaning would be purely arbitrary. A primal 'to-be-translated', if it is a message unknown to itself, coming from the other and implanted by the other, first sets in motion the movement of translation-detranslation, which is that of human temporality.

50 [Freud's *Anlehnung* translated by Strachey as 'anaclisis'.]

Temporality and Translation

Toward Making the Philosophy of time Work Again

Debate on "Temporarility and Translation"

Temporality and Translation

Toward Making the Philosophy of Time Work Again

Where is the question of time in today's philosophical thinking? Did Freud bring anything new to the question? And since Freud, has psychoanalysis been able to make a decisive contribution to our thinking about time, or is it obliged, as just another form of empirical knowledge, to adapt itself to one or another of the philosophical accounts on offer?

These three questions are linked, and each is far-reaching. They are interlinked because in outlining a psychoanalytic philosophy of time one is necessarily "après-coup" (we will see the special significance of this), situated in the après-coup of successive waves of philosophical thought—bearing the names of Kant, Hegel, Dilthey, Bergson, Husserl, and Heidegger—but also in the après-coup of Freud's discoveries.

1. The modern philosophy of time begins with Kant. We will not be so foolhardy as to attempt a summary of that philosophy, but we should note a number of decisive philosophical advances made by Kant and by those who followed him.

   1.1. One decisive step was the uncoupling of the philosophy of time from the question of cosmic time, to which it had been bound since Aristotle. One could put this differently by saying that temporality thus became independent from time. This uncoupling appears to be generally accepted, though it does entail problems. For, since Kant, cosmic time, if one dares use so bold a phrase, has itself not led a quiet life, and today we are a long way from the old clockwork universe. A theory such as that of relativity, or more recently the idea that the physical universe has an absolute beginning and end, opens the door to new philosophical speculation. Bergson already tried to tackle the famous paradox of Langevin's traveler, and he did so quite effectively.[1] Since then, however, so-called rational cosmology has seen a blurring of the boundaries separating it from the imaginary cosmology of science fiction, a convergence or, rather, a rebalancing of powers that would not have surprised or alarmed Kant.

1.2. In another decisive step, temporality became disconnected from the universe of physics (in the broadest sense) and found itself linked to "subjectivity" in the most various and vague of senses: transcendental subjectivity in Kant and Husserl, the historical subjectivity of the spirit in Hegel, "being there" or situatedness in Heidegger and Sartre. Among the various possible "subjects" of time, the term "life" should be noted: the full ambiguity of this term can be seen in Dilthey and Bergson, where the differences between the life of a living being and the "life" of the spirit all but disappear within an all-encompassing vitalism that includes organisms, human individuals, evolution, and even culture—recall Benjamin likening the posthumous evolution of a great work to the evolution of life. So we need to be careful about using the term "life." In fact, we should adopt the following fundamental rule: a theory of subjective time must always distinguish between the time of the "living" subject and the time of the human subject.

1 According to Paul Langevin's 1911 paradox, a traveler able to move at a speed close to the speed of light would, following calculations based on the theory of relativity, grow old one hundred times more slowly than someone who remained on Earth. [See E. Gourgoulhon, *Special Relativity in General Frames: From Particles to Astrophysics* (Berlin: Springer, 2013): 40–43.]

1.3. A third advance has been the linkage of temporality to temporalization, that is to say, to the human being's way of creating, of secreting—*sit venia verbo*—his or her own time. The idea of an active temporalization will certainly find elaborate expression in Hegel on the one hand and in Husserl and Heidegger on the other. But it was Kant who first paved the way for the idea, above all with the notions of "transcendental imagination" and "schematism": it is the idea of time as movement that drives putting the categories of pure reason to work.

1.4 In the end, for all the crucial differences between Hegelian dialectics and phenomenological *ekstases*, in this reference to temporalization, we see the same effort to theorize the onward movement as a three-way dialectic of past, present and future, with the future usually privileged (as synthesis or as being-for). Temporalization is thus conceived of as governed by its end, even if not in an explicitly theological sense of some infinite finality. In addition to clarifying many things, this three-way conception of time risks a facile jettisoning of the category of causality as that category bears on human beings.[2] We will have to come back to this point when we challenge an exclusively end-oriented conception of the temporal dialectic.

2. Having seen so much progress with Kant and the post-Kantians, in many respects returning to Freud may seem like a major philosophical step backward. But let's examine things rather more closely.

2.1. It is undeniable that Freud, albeit with a degree of bad faith, claims to be a nonphilosopher. A few simple and naïve metaphysical claims, such as the unexamined notion of an external world, are enough for him. On the categories of space and time, he explicitly endorses the ideas of Kant—or, rather, a crude

2 Or else it implies merely falling back on the old Aristotelian opposition between material and final causality, with the latter held to be the only kind of causality relevant to human beings.

version of Kant, a sort of ready-to-wear Kantianism that was available to Freud at the end of the nineteenth century. Time and space are thus thought of, according to vague formulas, as "necessary forms of thinking"; even the distinction between the forms of feeling and the categories of understanding has disappeared, not to mention the schematism that connects them. And the distinction between the transcendental and the empirical subject is no longer even visible, let alone something one might criticize. For Freud the subject of time and space is thus quite simply an empirical subject. Now, in fact, from our own point of view, this is not entirely a bad thing—one of its benefits being that it stops Freud from taking the easy path of emptying the transcendental subject by envisaging it as a purely logical, abstract subject. In addition, what we could call Freud's elementary Kantianism allows him to bring about some truly brilliant conceptual reversals—as when he folds the condition of extension (which he never confuses with that of space) back onto the "psychical apparatus": "Psyche is extended; knows nothing about it."[3] Space would thus be the projection of an original, primordial *Ausdehnung* or psychical extension. And the same is true when, almost despite himself, Freud gives the impression that the only thing-in-itself, the only thing truly *in* itself, is the internal world, in other words, the unconscious. This is, of course, only my interpretation; but it is based on Freud's remark about what he calls the "transformation" of metaphysics into metapsychology—namely, that it relates not only to the soul, resituated by animism in the external world, but also to the Kantian thing-in-itself that is posited as behind the externally perceived world.

3 [*Psyche ist ausgedehnt; weiss nichts davon*: Freud's full posthumous note translates as follows: "Space may be the projection of the extension of the psychical apparatus. No other derivation is probable. Instead of Kant's a priori determinants of our psychical apparatus. Psyche is extended; knows nothing about it" (*GW* 17:152; *SE* 23:300)].

In my view, the most coherent way of linking these two kinds of "metaphysics" appears in the following passage:

> The psychoanalytic assumption of unconscious mental activity appears to us, on the one hand, as a further expansion of the primitive animism which caused us to see copies of our own consciousness all around us, and, on the other hand, as an extension of the corrections undertaken by Kant of our views on external perception. Just as Kant warned us not to overlook the fact that our perceptions are subjectively conditioned and must not be regarded as identical with what is perceived though unknowable, so psychoanalysis warns us not to equate perceptions by means of consciousness with the unconscious mental processes that are their object.[4]

What Freud describes here through the analogy between an external and an internal thing-in-itself can be seen as part of the same "repatriation" that comes up in *The Psychopathology of Everyday Life* (*GW* 4:278–88 [SE 6:258–9]): Why, after all, should the "transformation of metaphysics into metapsychology" be limited to religious ideas (specifically, that of the "soul") and not apply to the *true* metaphysics of the thing-in-itself?

All of this leads us back to the idea that the only thing-in-itself is the unconscious: the "thing-representation" that is turned into a "representation-thing" by the process of primal repression. It is, thus, a *secondary* thing-in-itself.[5]

---

4 S. Freud, "The Unconscious" (*GW* 10:270 [*SE* 14:171]).

5 See J. Laplanche, *The Unconscious and the Id*, trans. Luke Thurston and Lindsay Watson (London: Rebus, 1999): 79–80 and 118–9; *New Foundations for Psychoanalysis*, trans. J. House (New York: UIT, 2016): 34-35.

2.2. Let us go back to the question of time (though we will return to this discussion of the psychical thing-in-itself in section 3.3 below). Freud managed to come up with a theory—though it was an idea he long held back, even kept secret—of the origin of time. I quote from the principal expression of that theory below:

> This agrees with a notion which I have long had about the method by which the perceptual apparatus of our mind functions, but which I have hitherto kept to myself. My theory was that innervations for investment are sent out and withdrawn in rapid periodic impulses from within into the completely pervious system *Pcpt.-Cs.* So long as that system is invested in this manner, it receives perceptions (which are accompanied by consciousness) and passes the excitation on to the unconscious mnemic systems; but as soon as the cathexis is withdrawn, consciousness is extinguished and the functioning of the system comes to a standstill. It is as though the unconscious stretches out feelers, through the medium of the system *Pcpt.-Cs.*, towards the external world and hastily withdraws them as soon as they have sampled the excitations coming from it. . . . I further had a suspicion that this discontinuous method of functioning of the system *Pcpt.-Cs.* lies at the bottom of the origin of the concept of time.[6]

This fascinating model would thus base the perception of time on the function of external perception. The latter is seen not as continuous but intermittent, like a light constantly going on and

6 S. Freud, "A Note on the 'Mystic Writing Pad'" (*GW* 14:8 [*SE* 19: 231-2]). [Translation modified.]

off. The reason for this periodicity is to be sought in two factors. Firstly, consciousness, so as not to be overburdened with its contents, must always empty itself of representations in order to remain open to new perceptions, and secondly, since external perceptions are simply too powerful for the system, it must diminish their intensity in order to receive them at all. We perceive something for only one tenth of a second, closing ourselves off for nine tenths of a second: the equivalent of dividing by ten the intensity of perception.

Thus, Freud sees rhythm as involved with external perception, and we also find it in his discussion of internal perception, where it has to do with pleasure (and it is odd that Freud doesn't link the two). When he wonders about its significance in terms of energy in the pleasure-unpleasure principle, he rapidly loses patience with that notion, contradicted by experience, according to which all unpleasure corresponds to an increase in tension and all pleasure to its decrease. We thus have to postulate the existence, in the qualitative perception of pleasure, of a function (in the mathematical sense) of increasing or decreasing tension, a function that would not be purely proportional: "The factor that determines the feeling is probably the amount of increase or diminution in the quantity of excitation in a given period of time."[7] "Perhaps it is the rhythm, the temporal sequence of changes, rises and falls in the quantity of stimulus."[8]

This explicit theory of Freud's about time has yet to be fully worked out. A few key points will suffice us here:

— In no sense does it amount to a general theory of time or of temporalization. What is at stake is the immediate time of perception in the flow of the present moment.

— This perceptual time, it can be correctly said, is the same

7 *Beyond the Pleasure Principle* (*GW* 13:4 [*SE* 18:8]).

8 "The Economic Problem of Masochism" (*GW* 13:372 [*SE* 19:160]).

in man and in animals. It is the time of the living being immersed in its *Umwelt*, its environment, or reacting to its *Innenwelt*, its inner world, which at this level provides only sensations of pleasure and unpleasure. Freud's striking image of a primitive creature putting forth its pseudopodia is indissociably an elementary model and a prototype: the little protoplasmic animal is both a reality and, with some adjustments, an example of what happens in more complex forms of life. Once again with Freud, the example is the thing itself.

—The essential factor in perception, whether external (sensorial) or internal (pleasure-unpleasure), is *rhythm*. This is a way to defend against the objection that the argument here is circular, with time posited as the self-perception of a function that is itself held to be temporal. At the level of immediate biological consciousness, it is rhythm that provides the *temporality of time itself*. Objective, physical time, experienced as rhythm, must therefore reduplicate itself (in the quasi-mathematical sense of a derivative) in order to become the self-perception of time.

In conclusion, this Freudian theory of time must be put back in its proper context, that of immediate time, apprehended no doubt by the living being, the only time it does apprehend. Animals have a memory bank (in the most modern sense of those words) but no history; on the other hand, they do have immediate time. The model put forward in "A Note on the 'Mystic Writing Pad'" is precisely that of a living being and is not limited to that of a human being who also has historical time.

2.3. To state that Freud does not address the historicity and the temporalization of human beings (and human societies) would be formally correct but unfair. Although Freud never explicitly thematizes this, it constantly resurfaces throughout his work.

Here I will simply draw up a list of the relevant elements of the Freudian theory of time. This is firstly because I don't wish to spend too much time on mere "Freudology"; but also, and above all, because in my view all these elements, to be "made to work again," should be seen within a more general framework, as will be set out in the third section below.

Here is the list then (which is not intended to be exhaustive):

2.3.1. Everything in the theory that emerges from the ordering by time is from an early stage designated by Freud as phases, stages, times, or epochs. The term "period," reserved for the specific notion of a recurrence at regular intervals, is abandoned when Freud's intellectual exchanges with Fliess come to an end. This ordering of time in stages applies not only to the origin of the libido and of the ego but also to the sequence of pathological fixations in ontogenesis and even phylogenesis (the periodization of prehistoric eras, etc.). Complex ideas such as fixation and regression are linked to this ordering of time.

2.3.2. The Freudian theory of memory, or rather of memories, since memory as a mental faculty is effectively absent from his thinking. Memories can be understood only through the opposition between those that are unconscious (unedited, susceptible only to involuntary resurgence) and those that are preconscious. This theory is most clearly seen in its pathological manifestations: illusions or difficulty remembering, false memories, screen memories, and so on.

2.3.3. A third item in this vast inventory would cover temporalization and its strategies, as seen above all in psychoanalytic treatment, with its distinctions between "remembering, repeating and working through" or again with the problem of "analysis terminable and interminable"—and also in the wider clinical field, in strategies of mourning, of delay, of fantasy, or of daydreaming[9].

2.3.4. Lastly, we need to take account of the whole relation between the sense of time as it concerns individuals in Freud and what he says about collective time. We need only think about how much of Freud's work is dedicated to problems of history, of prehistory, of archaeology, of myth, or to reflections on the present ("Thoughts for the Times on War and Death") or the future of culture.

At this point, analysis should account for two oppositions that are dialectically generative—on the one hand, that between history and archaeology,[10] which is at the center of my own inquiries; on the other, that between individual and collective time, interrelated by the double modality of comparison (analogies and differences) and of correlation, since each depends on the other.

2.3.5. To finish this cursory inventory of Freudian thinking about time, we should emphasize our own aim: to put forward a post-Freudian point of view that allows us to open a new perspective on a huge number of elements scattered not only throughout Freud's work but also beyond it, across the whole psychoanalytic account of human beings. Up to this point, for clarity's sake, I have left aside a number of concepts that I consider essential but that Freud didn't sufficiently develop or link together. These are precisely the concepts that are central to our own project: the effect of *après-coup*; translation in relation to interpretation as well as to transference; and finally seduction, an essential ele-

9 These strategies—normal *and* pathological—are in strict continuity with one another. Strategies of time are most evident in neurotic compulsion, whereas hysteria tends to involve strategies of the body, phobia the strategies of space.

10 See "*La psychanalyse: Histoire ou archéologie?*" and "*L'interprétation entre déterminisme et herméneutique*" in *La révolution copernicienne inachevée* (Paris: Aubier, 1992). [English translation by Luke Thurston (New York: The Unconscious in Translation, forthcoming).]

ment of theory that in our view must not be approached in empirical terms but accorded its originary significance as a central element in becoming-human.

3. What follows will no doubt seem as schematic as what has preceded it, since both the summary and the programmatic aspect of this article entail referring to other publications where certain points are more fully elaborated and to future developments.[11]

3.1. Our starting point will be a special experience of human time: the lived experience of psychoanalytic treatment. Without entering into the lengthy discussion required to introduce the analytic situation and the concept of transference,[12] let us get directly to the central issue: interpretation. Interpretation, we commonly say, consists of translating an item—roughly analogous to a text—into another text. That item, for instance a manifest dream, is, according to Freud, linked to latent content. But the dream is not the only manifest phenomenon to be "translated" in this way: there are also symptoms, episodes in a life, bungled actions and so on.

Let me first emphasize something whose significance may not be clear until later on in the discussion: psychoanalytic interpretation is inseparable from a *method*, one that has nothing to do with any vaguely intuitive process. It proceeds step by step, and the essence of its approach is the *destruction* of the seemingly rational constructs of manifest phenomena. Its interpretive approach is thus an inherently *analytic* approach: it breaks things down to elementary particles, each of which is caught up in one or more associative train of thought.[13]

11 Above all, we will be referring to Laplanche, *New Foundations for Psychoanalysis*.
12 See J. Laplanche, *Problématiques V: Le baquet. Transcendence du transfert*.
13 See "Le mur et l'arcade" ["The Wall and the Arcade"], in *La révolution copernicienne inachevée* (Paris: Aubier, 1992). [English translation by Luke Thurston (New York: The Unconscious in Translation, 2017).]

With that in mind, let us consider the great debate on time and psychoanalysis, which was first seen in the conflict between Freud and Jung and of which we still find echoes today in Ricœur's opposition of *arche* and *telos*. It is said, not without some justification, that analytic interpretation is retrogressive: it dismantles present constructions only to reassemble, behind them, lines of force, desires, constructs belonging to the past. We "explain" the symptoms of an obsessional neurotic—but also, possibly, Leonardo's creativity—by referring them back to some lived experience, some trauma, fantasy, or desire that has persisted unaltered since childhood. Psychoanalysis is thus attacked for being a flight into the past, something that can only bolster the natural tendency of human beings to seek escape from the responsibilities and tasks of the present. From almost the beginning, Jungian thinking proposed a forward-looking interpretation as an alternative to this retrogressive one, thereby aiming to confront the human subject with his tasks and his being-for-the-future. Silberer's "anagogic" interpretation, Jungian interpretation, Ricœur's talk of *telos*—they all point in such a direction.

Let us pause for a moment over this debate, firstly to note that it involves, at a fundamental level, different ways of thinking about temporalization, with its three *ekstases*, past, present, and future.[14] The three are explicitly ordered by Freud as follows: the

14 "Creative Writers and Day-Dreaming", in *GW* 7:217 [*SE* 9:145]

The relation of a phantasy to time is in general very important. We may say that it hovers, as it were, between three times—the three moments of time which our ideation involves. Mental work is linked to some current impression, some provoking occasion in the present which has been able to arouse one of the subject's major wishes. From there it harks back to a memory of an earlier experience (usually an infantile one) in which this wish was fulfilled; and it now creates a situation relating to the future which represents a fulfillment of the wish. What it thus creates is a day-dream or phantasy, which carries about it traces of its origin from the occasion which provoked it and from the memory. Thus past, present and future are strung together, as it were, on the thread of the wish that runs through them.

present reawakens a past desire, which then seeks to be fulfilled in the future.[15] Thus, psychoanalytic treatment would follow the same pattern, linking our present acts back to our most deeply buried past motivations, with the aim of . . . what, exactly?[16]

It is here that the objections become unavoidable: *so here's why you always choose a particular type of woman who ends up making you unhappy* [present]; *it's due to such and such a peculiarity of your infantile object choices* [past]. "Well, OK!" the analysand will respond, seemingly not unreasonably, "but what am I supposed to do with this translation of everything into a preexisting infantile desire?[17] Should I abandon this old wish? Put it into action? Sublimate it?" [future].

Thus, the objections made by a Jung or a Ricœur are plausible. But a flight into the future, offered as an alternative to a flight into the past, seems to be an open invitation to teleological illusions, both utopian and mystical. To invert the triad, which moves from present→past→future, to present→future→past is to see the past as a mere historical background made meaningful only by my "project"—this is a modern version of the same old illusion, whether offered under the rubric of a philosophy of value, a philosophy of the absurd, or one of being-toward-death.

In terms of the present discussion of analytic treatment, we should hold fast to the Freudian triad present→past→future. We should link the movement of interpretation to the *initial* moment of the dialectic, where the present is related back to the past. But

15 Ibid., 44 [*SE* 9:150].

16 [Laplanche takes up this question in "Goals of the Psychoanalytic Process," in *Between Seduction and Inspiration:* Man, trans. Jeffrey Mehlman (New York: The Unconscious in Translation, 2015).]

17 [In a footnote Laplanche compares this explanation to that given by the character of the "doctor" in Molière's *Le médecin malgré lui* who explains the muteness of a character's daughter by saying it is caused by the loss of the power of speech, famously concluding, "And that's why your daughter is mute." ("*Et voilà pourquoi votre fille est muette.*") Laplanche quotes this line and adds, "Beyond the inanity of such an explication, it is the inanity of all such explications that is revealed."]

unlike Freud and the whole of classical psychoanalysis, let us not understand that interpretation as a *translation* of the present into the past, and more importantly, let us not see the "text" of the past as containing *more truth than*—or even worse, *the* truth of—the text of the present. Let us instead propose the following thesis: insofar as the analytic process can be understood by analogy with the process of translation, interpretation in terms of the past (the infantile, the archaic) is not a translation but a *de-translation,* a dismantling and a reversal of translation. As the "teleologists" would quite rightly argue, all translation is a movement forward in time. But *analytic* translation involves undoing an existing, spontaneous, and possibly symptomatic translation in order to rediscover behind it what it was so keen to translate—and thus to make possible a *better* translation: one that is more complete, more inclusive, and less repressive.

In enlisting ourselves in opposition to an entire tradition that lays claim to Freud, which is often criticized for "reducing the present to the past" and reckoning that "everything is decided at the age of five,"[18] our duty is to highlight several points in Freud's work that support our thesis. Firstly, if we turn to Freud's late work,[19] we see that he reserves the term "interpretation" not for the "construction" of an infantile scenario supposedly underlying the adult scenario but only for the *analytic* discernment of a connection between an element of the present scenario and an isolated element from the past. The analytic method, as we emphasized above, works with individual chains of meaning, moving as if word by word from one representation to the next, never from a whole phrase to another. Another piece of evidence in support of our thesis—this time concerning the second movement of our triad (from the past to

18 Why five and not four or two years of age or even one month?
19 ["Constructions in Analysis," in *GW* 16; *SE* 23.]

the future)—is Freud's stubborn refusal to yield to the temptations of "psychosynthesis." *You destroy things, you break them into pieces, and they cry reproachfully, thus leaving your unfortunate patient in pieces too.* To which Freud would always reply (as do we) that in fact the individual is all too ready to put things back together, to constantly retranslate and remake a synthetic vision of himself and his future.

To conclude this discussion of analytic treatment for the moment: treatment is not, in its essence, the translation of a present scenario into a past scenario, which the patient would then have to manage—who knows how?—to insert into a project. This movement in time revealed by analysis, in an exemplary and prototypical manner, is that of the *decomposition* of signifying sequences, be they present or past, into elements to allow the analysand to spontaneously develop a new synthesis or translation of them—one that is less partial, less repressive, less symptomatic.

3.2. Psychoanalytic treatment undoubtedly brought something new to the history—as old as human existence itself—of interhuman relations, but it could never have had either meaning or any effect[20] if it were not connected to and correlated with something fundamental that preexisted it in human existence and specifically something having to do with the process of human temporalization. It must be possible to link the temporality of treatment (for brevity and clarity, we must present it in a caricatured fashion) back to earlier aspects of human temporality, such as, on the one hand, those situations that can be seen as rough precursors or equivalents of what analysis was in part able to purify and make effective or, on the other, those which can be seen as foundations—in other words, the basis on which analytic processes themselves, as we understand them, were able to emerge.

20 Even if one disputes the value of its effects, even if one considers them harmful, no one can maintain that psychoanalysis leaves those who engage in its method unchanged.

3.2.1. *Precursors or equivalents*: In spontaneous existence, there must be moments and situations that can be described in terms of de-translation/retranslation. What is crucial is that, as we have argued, there is no way simply to "translate" a translation: the only way back to what must be translated involves a preliminary scouring, a scraping away, of the existing translation. The Latin Vulgate is a splendid moment in the translation of the Bible, as is the Bible of Luther. But Luther had to first *undo* the Vulgate before he could redo the translation, just as a modern translator has to first "undo" both Luther and the Vulgate.

We can find a situation analogous to psychoanalytic treatment in the painful period of mourning. An in-depth exploration of the topic, taking into account the many psychoanalytic studies and observations of it, is beyond the scope of my argument here. Let us merely indicate the main lines of the argument. From the very outset, Freud thought of mourning as a kind of work and a reorganization.[21] However, what we must criticize in his conception of mourning is that he places the emphasis mainly on the detachment of the subject from the loved one (the "lost object"). The work of mourning is certainly far more complex than this: what Freud and doubtless most analysts have not seen is what such detachment involves and its relation to the temporal dialectic.

The three-stage movement of time could be described as follows: I have woven a stable relation with someone; in truth it is a conception of existence encompassing my activities, my hopes, and my dreams. This is the text of the present. Now the sudden loss of the loved one causes the brutal collapse of this whole view of the world. But mourn-

21 S. Freud, "Mourning and Melancholia," in *GW* 10:427–66 [*SE* 14: 237–58].

ing pulls me out of this state of absolute destruction that threatens to sweep me away, and this is where the key notion of work comes in: "Each single one of the memories and expectations in which libido is bound to the object is brought up and hypercathected, and detachment of the libido is accomplished in respect of it."[22] Everything hinges on this notion of detachment (*Lösung*), which Freud, in a wholly inadequate conceptualization, sees as a liberating rupture of the bond with the object and precisely *not* as an analysis.[23] Bereavement forces me, through the agony of thinking, to start unraveling the fabric of my existence, a fabric woven on the loom of the lost other. But in this process, even as I detach a single thread ("That was the spring where we both went to drink. . . .") from the whole, that thread is not, as Freud thought, broken. It is, on the contrary, overinvested, set apart, and thought over, linked back to its history ("Do you recall the first time you met her by that spring?") and, beyond everyday history such as that of a couple, related to a larger and far longer history (". . . and it was beside that same spring that you played as a child, lovingly watched over by your mother. . . .").

Without belaboring the point, I wanted to note how bereavement compels one to work to reorganize one's existence, to develop a new vision that can encompass the absence of the loved one but also include his or her memory. However, this new version or translation is possible only if it is preceded by the painful work of *Lösung*, of ana-*lysing* the old version. As well as being painful, however, such work is also fruitful: it makes every element in the whole history richer, reabsorbing it into a new attempt to live, a new project.

22 *Ibid*, 430 [*SE* 14:245].

23 *Lösen* means both to detach and to analyze, exactly like the Greek λύειν in "ana-*lysis*." Analysis is not the rupture of a thread but the unraveling of threads.

Now, I have no wish to blur the differences between analytic treatment and ordinary mourning.[24] Analysis aims to go deeper, and the archaic elements it seeks are more deeply buried and thus inaccessible without its methods. But surely, if analysis sets out to undo the patient's inadequate translations—be they from everyday life, dreams, or symptoms—there must be something already there in human existence that corresponds to this movement of translation and of de-translation / retranslation.

3.2.2. All of this leads us to conclude that a human being, at every stage, constructs himself or herself only by producing a self-representation, the best possible "theory," "version," or "translation" of that self (that is, the most convenient, most accurate. or, in some contexts, the only possible self-representation.) A translation, though . . . of the self? Analysis has taught us to see this "self" as neither autonomous nor transparent nor even auto-centered.

What is the first thing to be translated? It is here that we arrive at the very foundation of the process of temporalization. We call this primordial to-be-translated the unconscious; but in doing so we do not consider it either as a reservoir of biological drives irreducible to, foreign to, the human world or, conversely, as a "structured" discourse that would simply be something to be deciphered. In my view, the unconscious is the result of repressions that bear on scraps of communication that are thereby estranged from their original context. Unconscious "representations," verbal or nonverbal signifiers, rub up against each other without any organization and without contradicting each other. The unconscious, one might say, is rather like

24 They have often been interrelated, but always in terms of the acceptance of loss, never in relation to the question of temporalization.

"being" as described by Parmenides, except that it is a fragmented rather than singular being and, crucially, one that has taken on the consistency of a being-in-itself or a thing-in-itself only secondarily, that is to say, precisely by the act of repression.

At the very deepest level, the inexhaustible material that every human being, throughout his existence, is ultimately compelled to translate into acts, words, self-representations: this is what we call the unconscious. It is untranslatable, but constantly retranslated—for better or worse, in each case—and the self-theorization of each person nibbles away at it without being able to reduce it in any substantial way. Let us go further: the force of self-translation—that *Trieb zur Übersetzung* or drive to translate, to use Novalis's phrase—derives its power not from the translator but from the thing left untranslated or inadequately translated, that thing always *demanding* a (better) translation.

Here we should return to the question of temporalization. The movement present→past→future is a movement of de-translation/retranslation: it presupposes a prior translation, but also a primordial to-be-translated, which we call the unconscious.

3.3. Can we go further? Can we find a more fundamental origin for this diachronic imbalance between the to-be-translated and the present, inadequate translation, an imbalance that pushes constantly (or at least at each of life's turning points) for a renewed translation? In my view, the "fundamental" does not mean the abstract or the transcendental. What we are seeking, beyond the empirical level of human existence, is a universal and inevitable situation but one that is specifically human, not one involving other forms of life. In that sense, our philosophy remains an anthropology. It could be argued that the same is true of post-Kantian philosophers such as Hegel, Heidegger, and Sartre, even if they disguise the anthropology with more general terms like Spirit, Being, Nothingness, *Befindlichkeit*, or even the transcendental Subject. Indeed, in our view all philosophy must be anthropological: this does not imply a relativism but rather leads us to define universal categories of being-human and becoming-human.

The universal and originary situation I posit at the foundation of all human relations is that of seduction. This term, in the generalized sense I give to it, includes a considerable number of variants, with adults (from being seduced by a lover to the inherently seductive dimension of analysis itself) just as with children (in childhood or precocious seduction).[25] But beyond these situations that are still, despite how common they are, contingent by definition (even the relation to a mother or a father, however common, is contingent), what we are trying to isolate is the essence of the phenomenon of seduction, of "originary seduction." Seduction must be defined as a passive-active relation, in the Cartesian sense: the active position entails something extra, more knowledge, experience, etc., than the passive. And crucially what psychoanalysis adds to the definition of this asymmetry is that in the seducer this extra involves *more unconscious knowledge* than in the one seduced. Seduction is an asymmetrical relation whose prototype is the infant-adult couple. There, an infant is confronted by an adult world that from the beginning sends him messages suffused with sexual meanings (those that are revealed by psychoanalysis), messages that are unconscious for the sender himself or herself, that are sensed as enigmatic, as a to-be-translated.

In terms of our present discussion of temporalization, we should note that this imbalance is itself atemporal or, rather, syn-

25 For the exploration of these ideas, see J. Laplanche, *New Foundations for Psychoanalysis*.

chronic. It is a situation that does not involve time but rather the confrontation of two individuals at different stages of development: a fully grown and fully complex adult with his knowledge and partly unconscious sexual peculiarities and an infant in a state of helplessness in the sense that he has only rudimentary means to translate the messages and excitations that are addressed to him.

This imbalance is the veritable "unmoved mover" of the movement of temporalization: straight away, it gives birth to an attempt at translation, as we put it, an attempt that always partly fails, leaving behind it untranslated elements that form the first basic components of the unconscious.[26] What Freud sometimes calls primal repression is nothing but the result of what is properly called the prototemporalization of the human being: his or her way of immediately self-theorizing, of responding to enigmatic messages with a "worldview" and thus entering into time by means of translation, which is both a moving-forward and a leaving-behind.[27] Rapidly, however, new translations will cover up the archaic to-be-translated. The sequence of phases, infinitely more complex than the official manuals of psychoanalysis declare, is ultimately nothing but a process of de-translating and retranslating what is originary (originary first for the adult, then for the individual unconscious of the infant) according to available idioms: the "languages" of orality, anality, genitality, and so on.[28]

---

26 This idea of an attempt at translation corresponds to what Freud sketches out in the letter to Fliess of December 6, 1896. See *The Complete Letters of Sigmund Freud to Wilhelm Fliess, 1887–1904*, trans. and ed. Jeffrey Masson (Cambridge, MA: Belknap, 1985), 206–215.

27 We use the term "theorizing" here not in an abstract sense but in the sense constantly used by psychoanalysis: the infant explains the birth of a brother with a "cloacal" theory.

28 "Languages" is here understood in a wholly metaphorical or enlarged sense, without any privileging of the verbal.

Let us return to the three *ekstases* of time: past, present, and future. The human being is directed toward the *future* only because he is self-theorizing and self-translating: every important life event (the examples we have given are mourning and psychoanalysis) gives him a chance to call into question again the *present* translation, to de-translate it by turning toward the *past* and attempting a better translation—one more inclusive, less repressive, with new possibilities. The fundamental moments of human temporalization are those in which this reorganization comes about through the effect of après-coup.[29]

Conclusion

1. Though it could be only programmatic and condensed here, our theory aims to reactivate the philosophical reflection on time, left dormant since the advances of the post-Kantians, the phenomenologists, and the philosophers of history. The triad of temporal *ekstases* remains fundamental to all dialectical conceptions. We will conclude by indicating how each of these dialectical movements works—in other words, what temporal *imbalance* puts it in motion.

The Hegelian dialectic seems to situate the imbalance in the opposition between past (thesis) and present (antithesis): the movement thus being past→present→future, even if, by a supreme reversal, the future is itself the truth of the past or even coincides with it.

The dialectic of existentialism (in the broadest sense) privileges "being-for" and therefore the imbalance of present and future, the vision of the past being reshaped by the project: present→future→past.

From its beginning psychoanalysis has privileged a turning to the past from the moment of the present. We are left with the task

29 To put things very briefly, the Freudian term *Nachträglichkeit*, though its invention was a stroke of genius, remains split between two one-way perspectives: that of the deferred action of the past on the present and that of the retroactive comprehension of the past by the present. A dialectical understanding of *Nachträglichkeit* is possible only due to the prototype offered by the process of translation.

of interpreting the sequence present→past→future in the light of a de-translation/retranslation theory of human existence and of connecting this movement, which itself gives rise to diachrony, back to the synchronic driving force that is the originary situation of seduction.

2. Three terms have loomed large in our discussion: time, temporality, and temporalization (and we need to add a fourth term: that of historicity). Each one of these terms is more specific and differentiated than the one before it:

Time operates at the cosmological level of our physical universe.

Immediate *temporality* can be located at the level of animals. Freud's decisive advance consists of relating temporality to perception and its rhythmic quality. We are confident that psychophysiology can offer us support on this topic.

With *temporalization,* we reach the human level. This term describes how a human existence organizes itself in time, attempting to gain a new perspective on itself at every turning point. It is temporalization that we have dealt with here.

Finally, there is *historicity,* which remains partly outside the limits of the present article. It could be the historicity of a people (of a *Masse,* to use Freud's language) or the historicity of humanity. This idea takes us to another level: not only that of the sequence of de-translations/retranslations but also that of their *recapitulation*. We will leave this for another discussion.

Debate on"Temporality and Translation"

Maurice Dayan

I'm tempted to start out by teasing Laplanche, Freud's de-translator–retranslator, who doesn't hesitate to molest the language he loves, to put it to work for the benefit of his own discursive translation and self-translation. But joking aside, it is clear that the model of translation (which the author of the *New Foundations* would "scrupulously distinguish" from a linguistic model) entirely governs this new approach to temporality and temporalization.

Here, by "model of translation" I mean that activity, that practice at which Laplanche excels and that is precisely a linguistic practice (even if not that of a linguist) due to the special investment it carries, and that is heightened when applied to the psychoanalytic text, suggesting a theoretical process directed, through and beyond language, at psychical reality. It is not that the model in question claims that this other reality can be made intelligible on the basis of textual movements between languages. Not only is Laplanche not naïve enough to think that, but he is also very far from giving the category of language any epistemological priority. There can be no return to Lacan for him, and he is not seeking some new way to endow the unconscious with a "structure" like that of a language. He even specifies, for anyone still in doubt, that the signifiers that are repressed, fragmented, and rendered untranslatable can be either "verbal or nonverbal."

All that is clearly stated. Nevertheless, translation is originally a linguistic operation, and the model suggested by that practice inevitably gives rise to a preliminary question: Outside the field of language, is a model derived from translation even theoretically *possible,* and could it have any functional value? In other words, to put it very briefly, is it enough to follow the spirit of Freud's letter of December 6, 1896 (repression as a failure of translation—Laplanche prefers "refusal" to translate *Versagung* here, but let that go), to be able to formulate a process of translation that would not be linguistic in the narrow sense?[1] It is certainly not easy to conceive of a translation without a source and a target language. Regarding the target language, one can accept that preconscious verbal representations correspond to interconnectable elements that can refer to objects or to relations. But as to the source:

1. How can the archaic "to-be-translated" envisaged by Laplanche form part of any kind of language whatsoever?
2. If the unconscious "representations" jostle together chaotically like Parmenidean fragments changing and affecting one another in all manner of ways, how can there be anything translatable in such representations, and what is the meaning of the endless demand for a better translation that is ascribed to them?

Some elements of answers to these two questions can be found in the theory of originary seduction. From the adult world, the child receives messages "suffused with unconscious sexual meanings," messages perceived as enigmatic—that is to say, perceived as to be translated. Let us pause for a moment over this "that is to say": Laplanche claims that what is received as enigmatic demands translation. Doesn't this amount to transposing outside of consciousness and to imputing to "a helpless child" the reflexive perplexity

1 [See *The Complete Letters of Sigmund Freud to Wilhelm Fliess, 1887–1904,* trans. and ed. Jeffrey Masson (Cambridge, MA: Belknap, 1985), 208; for Laplanche's discussion of the letter, see *The Unconscious and the Id,* trans. Luke Thurston and Lindsay Watson (London: Rebus, 1999), 16–17.]

of a *speaking* being standing before the sphinx? Moreover, the child is said to receive both "messages *and* excitations" (my emphasis): Does having to translate the messages also imply finding some way to translate the excitations? And does the "demanded" translation have the same sense for both these aspects of the enigma?

The theory in question considers the imbalance of unconscious knowledge—its excess in the seducer, its lack in the seduced—to be the "unmoved mover" of temporalization, and it likewise locates this imbalance at the root of what is always a partial failure of the translation process. This is the kernel of what Laplanche outlines, his most important step toward "making the philosophy of time work again." The originality of this development and its radical consistency with prior investigations into the intersubjective origins of the unconscious—these are both plain to see. This approach nonetheless calls for some new remarks and questions, which are closely related to those outlined above. I will set them out briefly (I'm sorry there isn't time to develop them more fully), first returning to the premises of the problematic:

1. The Freudian triad present→past→future is correctly opposed to the *ekstatic* triads of the philosophers (whether dialectical or not). This triad is given a vector, following the paradigm of analytic interpretation, which Laplanche sees in terms of translation: the movement from the present to the past does not entail a translation but a de-translation, while that from the past to the future involves, beyond the interpretation itself, a translation that is "more complete, more inclusive, and less repressive." Now, since the whole experience of psychoanalytic treatment takes place in the field of interlocution (however that field may open onto other things), the *model* of de-translation is necessarily language based: one interprets on the basis of utterances, even if only "word by word," stepping across syntactic forms. Another result of this model borrowed by analysis is that the first moment of the analytic triad does not correspond to the *onto-*

logical process of temporalization in the child: that process does not begin with a retrogression of translation.

2. I am happy to support the return of a translation model of interpretation (which has barely been seen except in Melanie Klein's work). But what is not self-evident is that de-translation can be treated as a process symmetrical to translation, in the sense that it would lead back to initial elements "to be translated." The question is worth asking: Does de-translation link up with unconscious representations or else with something completely different, a more or less acceptable linguistic-analytic indexing, which still involves the movement of temporalizing translation?

3. The privilege given by Laplanche to the concept of translation brings with it the disadvantage of constantly extending metaphorically a term with an originally well-defined functional usage. Its advantage (which may in fact be false) is that, in a seemingly symmetrical way, de-translation can be opposed to it. We find neither this disadvantage nor this advantage, however, with the term transposition (*Umsetzung*), which Freud linked in a significant way to that of translation (*Übersetzung*) when he said of the unconscious that "it is of course only as something conscious that we know it, after it has undergone transposition[2] or translation into something conscious."[3] But beyond the lexical problem, it is worth noting that Freud employs the concept of transposition only when it is a question of drives and affects: the transposition of love into hate; the transposition of the psychical energy of drives into affects, especially into anxiety; the transposition of the movement of drives into manifest affect—which repression may succeed in inhibiting; or even the transposition of the choice of a sexual object into a modification of the ego (from object libido to narcissistic libido). All these formulations, with their different trajectories, clearly show that "translation" cannot cover as wide

2 ["Transformation" in Strachey's translation.]
3 [Sigmund Freud, "The Unconscious," in *GW* 10:264; *SE* 14:159.]

a field of fundamental psychical processes as "transposition" can—while the latter, by contrast, can be applied wherever one might have wanted to use the former.

I say that here we are beyond a merely lexical problem, since it is clear that this problematic of the transposition of drives into affects (to stick to the essentials) is absent from Laplanche's conception of temporalization. Should we see the rejection of a notion of the unconscious as a "reservoir of irreducible biological drives" as a way of dealing, briskly and by implication, with that problematic? And should we see in this rejection itself a polemical (and illegitimate) reduction of the Freudian theory of drives? I'm not too sure. To my mind (and in Freud's writings), representation is never the only thing at stake in the temporalizing process of transposition, whereas in a translation-based account of the possible destinies of a person who has been seduced, representation ultimately seems to be fully in charge.

4. The question, raised above, of the possible "translation" of the excitations sent by the adult's unconscious must clearly be linked to Laplanche's idea of what constitutes the source-object of the drive. There are no doubt ways of clarifying this aspect of the activity given to the "unmoved mover" of seduction. But conversely the very idea of the source-object requires some refinement if its author, who has given us so many clever and useful intellectual tools, gives sufficient attention to the question of corporeal excitability. For without the latter, there would be no excitation. And with our more or less happy fiction of the psychical apparatus, isn't our dream surely "quite simply" to account for the way, as Montaigne would say, everyone makes their body and soul work together?

Response to Maurice Dayan

Maurice Dayan follows my work so closely and gets to what is essential so directly that I will limit myself to clarifying a few points.

Concerning the model of translation, in fact I do think—I postulate—that it can have a functional value outside the field of language in the narrow sense of that term. Others have pursued that path before me, not only Freud but also Jakobson with his notion of "intersemiotic translation."[4] It remains true, however—but for me this is a *separate* and much more worrying problem—that the movement of de-translation/retranslation takes a different direction when the subject is confronted by *his own* past translations (in treatment, in mourning, in everyday life) than at the moment of the originary process of temporalization when the individual has to deal with the "enigmatic signifiers" of the other. The latter are enigmatic in that they also demand de-translation but the pathway to it is blocked by the repression of the adult other. I agree absolutely that here we are on the cusp of what separates the empirical from the originary. To speak of "prototemporalization" is another way of envisaging the same transition. But the enjambment taking us from the process within time to what I'm trying to outline as its unmoved mover remains guided or tethered down by the Ariadne's thread of the signifier.

In this sense, my talk of "messages and excitations" conveyed to the child needs to be revised if it doesn't make the following clear: that the excitations coming from the adult are traumatic only because they transmit messages that are "unknown to themselves." As for the "perplexity" of the child, to my mind it is not reflective, nor is it linked to being a subject who speaks in the sense of verbal language. I see the *infans* as confronted by the enigma, which it perceives before it has acquired language.[5]

The attempt to subsume translation (*Übersetzung*) into a category of transposition (*Umsetzung*) that would cover a wider field, notably concerning the relation between drive and affect, reminds me, as if I needed reminding, that Dayan is more Freudian than me by amicably asking me to go back to a more classical Freudian

4 [See Roman Jakobson, "On Linguistic Aspects of Translation" (Cambridge, Massachusetts: Harvard University Press, 1959).]

5 [Infans: Laplanche is referring to the Latin root of "infant," which means "nonspeaking."]

problematic. It is quite correct that my conceptualization of the drive distances me considerably from Freud and brings me closer to a certain Lacan (perhaps). The following formula is no doubt provocative in that it radically reverses some of Freud's ideas: "The drive is the way that the source-object *affects* the body and requires it to work."[6] That affect (and the most basic affect, anxiety) should involve the "body" seems almost incontestable and, indeed, not necessarily anti-Freudian. But it is only on the basis of the passivity of the body in relation to the "internal foreign body" that we can investigate how far affect can consequently be seen as representing, transposing, or translating the drive.

I'm sorry to respond in so brusque and peremptory a way; the questions raised by Dayan call not just for a reply but also, as he suggests, for improvements.

Pierre Fédida

Jean Laplanche presents us, if not with an elaboration, at least with a return to those aspects of his work that bear on what can be called temporalization in psychoanalysis. "[Temporalization] describes how a human existence organises itself in time, attempting to gain a new perspective on itself at every turning point" (p. 221). Temporalization is understood as an *activity* inherent to the analytic process and is the object of an investigation distinct from anything that can be thought of in terms of *time, temporality,* or *historicity*. At the conclusion of his article, Jean Laplanche clearly explains his overall project in its current

6 [In 1915, Freud added the following to *Three Essays on the Theory of Sexuality*: "The concept of drive is thus one of those lying on the frontier between the mental and the physical. The simplest and likeliest assumption as to the nature of drives would seem to be that in itself a drive is without quality, and, so far as mental life is concerned, is only to be regarded as a measure of the demand made upon the mind for work" (*SE* 7:178; translation modified.) Later, as here, Laplanche reverses the understanding and the phrase, saying that drives are the demand for work imposed on the body by the mind—imposed by repressed, unconscious, de-signified signifiers on the embodied subject. The infantile drives, infantile sexuality, are drives to make meaning, to translate, and are what founds the human subject.]

trajectory: "Our theory aims to reactivate the philosophical reflection on time" (p. 220). "From its beginning psychoanalysis has privileged a turning to the past from the moment of the present. We are left with the task of interpreting the sequence present→past→future in the light of a de-translation/retranslation theory of human existence and of connecting this movement, which gives rise to diachrony, back to the synchronic driving force that is the originary situation of seduction" (p. 221).

Using a phrase from Novalis, "*Trieb zur Übersetzung*," Laplanche emphasizes that the drive to translate "derives its power not from the translator but from the thing left untranslated or inadequately translated, that thing always *demanding* a (better) translation." And he continues: "Here we should return to the question of temporalization. The movement present→past→future is a movement of de-translation/retranslation: it presupposes a prior translation, but also a primordial to-be-translated, which we call the unconscious" (p. 217).

Laplanche's whole discussion, and especially the passages I've quoted, raises a number of questions:

1. The analyst's aim to "reactivate the philosophical reflection on time" is at first sight a bold one, but it can best be understood if its task is seen as rather more limited: the clarification of the anthropological roots of psychoanalytic thinking. It is this that is already demanded in the work of Ludwig Binswanger, for whom questions of temporality and temporalization are central to Freud's work, although Freud did not succeed in "awakening" them. A more *general* problematic is thus opened up by temporalization: that of the anthropology of phenomena from Kant to Husserl via Hegel. In other words, any psychoanalytic project to "reactivate" the *anthropological* "reflection on time"—and to do so, in a singular way, by thinking about the movement of temporalization—any such project cannot, in my view, neglect taking account of Husserl's intervention, if only to assess the current state of the debate between phenomenology and psychoanalysis.

2. Another clarification is necessary, and it too involves an existing question. It concerns the recent work of Ilya Prigogine and Isabelle Stengers.[7] The study of irreversible phenomena, fluctuations, points of bifurcation, dissipative structures, and so on cannot remain outside metapsychological theory when it involves temporality and temporalization. (I have work forthcoming on this topic.)
3. The argument sketched out here rests on an "analogy" (a word we should pause over) between the analytic process and the process or way of proceeding of translation. Although such a formulation does not raise any major objections if it is put forward as a *metaphorical* comparison (following the example of Socrates, we look for other kinds of work that might allow us, in a negative sense, to define the work of a psychoanalyst: Is he a doctor? A weaver? An archaeologist? A seducer? A translator? . . .), this is not necessarily the case when it is offered as an *analogy*. It is clear that, from a very early stage,[8] Freud took up the question of translation as a way of understanding the function of memory (or of recollection), the status of mnemic traces, and the organization of hysterical symptoms. But this Freudian question of translation cannot be separated from that of inscription or of reinscription—or, indeed, that of *writing* (whose specific dimension is inherent to psychoanalytic *listening* and the technical paradigm of the dream for that listening). I therefore see the Freudian question of translation as based on a whole cluster of theoretical presuppositions relating to memory and to language, with fundamental implications concerning mythical and phylogenetic hypotheses, languages and the impossible fundamental language, the symbolic (and not symbolism), culture, and so on.

---

7 *Entre le temps et l'étérnité* (1988) as well as the essays gathered under the title *Temps et devenir. A partir de l'oeuvre d'Ilya Prigogine* (1988) from the international conference at Cerisy in 1983.
8 See the famous letter to Fliess of December 6, 1896.

4. Finally, reading Jean Laplanche here—and not hesitating to give this debate an amicably polemical tone—I cannot resist asking this question: What differentiates his position from that of Lévi-Strauss insofar as Lévi-Strauss, notably in *Structural Anthropology,* thought about the interpretation of myth (and mythical interpretation) in terms of translation and retranslation? Some of Jean Laplanche's claims seem to lend credence to such a tricky connection. Could we not say, given that every translation (or "version") of a myth partly *lifts* the repression inherent in the mythical tradition and its transmission, just as it also carries out a reorganization itself subject to repression, that the interpretation of myth takes place on the axis present→past? Of course, the methodology of Lévi-Strauss is in no way comparable to that of psychoanalysis. (It is even its antagonist!) But what Jean Laplanche describes as the "process of temporalization," which presupposes a "first thing to be translated," a "fundamental" unconscious—is that so far removed from the process of *historicization* involved in the translation of myth, which also presupposes a primordial chaos?

These questions are only worth asking to open up or feed into a debate. Since this is a debate involving theoretical practices, my own investigation focuses on how this theory of temporalization/translation came about in Jean Laplanche's work.

The brief remarks I have just made are clearly indissociable from the perspective I am developing in my current research, which I can briefly outline as follows:

—In my article "Passé anachronique et présent réminiscent,"[9] I attempted to develop a new way of approaching time in psychoanalysis. My focus on the site of language in analysis and on the epos [story] of the situation led me to investigate the *anachronic* and thus a past that would not be the anterior horizon of the present. The refer-

9 *L'écrit du temps* 10 (1985).

ence to "the present" in a dream, in transference, and so on involves an act of interpretation that is more local than temporal.[10] For me, in these conditions the present→past axis makes sense only if the categories of representation are freed from the rules of grammar and syntax belonging to manifest discourse.

—It seems to me that it is *analytic listening* (and not only the listening of the analyst) that makes possible the resonance and semantic rebellion of words, which receive the waves of temporality produced by speech in analytic treatment. Temporalization, in my view, involves an intertransferential process and of course also a countertransferential one.[11] I am more interested, paradoxical though it may seem, in the *historicization* of the lifting of repression than in temporalization.

—As for the "future," it seems to me not thinkable as such in psychoanalytic terms (it is a synthetic formation of the same kind as symptomatic ideas). In its teleological dimension, it involves interpretive speech in which the function of interpreting the interaction of the present and the past is in my view inseparable from the effect of displacement and thus the production of new possibilities.

—Finally, my interest in construction in analysis leads me to propose the axis temporality-construction-historicization. To put it very schematically, in my view temporalities relate to a timeless present (places); construction means we have to talk about an anachronic past; while historicization is a theoretical process, the self-theorization of the symptom (see *L'absence*).

I am delighted that Jean Laplanche has taken the initiative to launch this debate, and I am very keen to see it take place.

Response to Pierre Fédida

Pierre Fédida quite rightly confronts me with a range of different approaches to time, not all of which I am equally familiar with.

10 See my work on the theory of places. Pierre Fédida, "Théorie des lieux," *Psychanalyse à l'université* 14, no. 53 (1989): 3–15.

11 See Pierre Fédida, *L'absence* (Paris: Gallimard, 1978).

Regarding the phenomenological approach, the further I go, the more it seems to me that my ideas have a considerable overlap with those of Heidegger, while they have little to do with the concerns of Husserl. The latter in fact remains at the level of perceptual time and its phenomenology and not that of the temporalization of a life. The reflexive-descriptive approaches of Husserl and Saint Augustine, along with Freud and his "mystic writing pad," are concerned with a time where the "soul" is stretched out tight, holding on to the past and reaching forward to an immediate future: a temporality that (we might say, at the risk of disrespect to the human) is common to most living organisms.

As for the comparison with Lévi-Strauss, while I am flattered, I am not sure of its precise relevance here. I can certainly see in Lévi-Strauss, with the notion of groups of transformations, the idea of a sort of reciprocal translation of different versions of a myth. But the group is not positioned in time and is in no way driven by a primordial to-be-translated, whether it is organized or not. Furthermore, moving from the collective (myth) to the individual (the temporalization of a life) seems to me full of risks. When I speak of translation in the individual process of temporalization, I am referring to self-translation as an activity that functions and can be outlined as such, while the "translation" that moves from form N to form N+1 of a myth is carried out by the mythologist alone. Each myth, for Lévi-Strauss, is nothing but the open set of its versions, among which one could never trace any temporal vector of a subject or any de-translation/retranslation process.

What are the presuppositions allowing us to give the model of translation a generalized significance outside of the strict domain of verbal language? As I stated above in my response to Maurice Dayan, such an extension can seek support in the work of a linguist like Jakobson. In any event, using such terminology seems to me far less risky than applying the model of writing to the psychical apparatus. I am well aware that Derrida has widened the Freudian pathway on which the mnemic trace is described as inscription, duly taking it as a metaphor for writing. It is nonetheless the case that writing, in a *prosaic* sense, is to my mind a secondary phenomenon, a *codified* and socialized inscription of verbal language with precise historical (or, rather, prehistorical) origins. Now, one may very well imagine, *nonmetaphorically*, that *before* the invention of writing the child was already confronted by adult messages and the impossible task of translating them. I speak of writing "in a prosaic sense" because Pierre Fédida knows all about my positivist view of prehistory, my desire to free it from all mythical or phylogenetic hypotheses.

I very much hope that Fédida will soon extend this conversation between us.

Jacques Gagey

Laplanche is right to emphasize that Freud's thoughts on time, as they can be linked together in a reading not afraid to make them work a bit, outline a movement of temporalization that starts from the present, dislodges the past clinging to that present, and opens up possibilities for the future. There is no doubt that the three ekstases of time are bound together in the work of interpretation, just as Laplanche puts it. There is, moreover, no doubt that, as he shows, psychoanalytic treatment uncovers and refines a conscious process already at work in mourning, among other processes.

Given all that, could we claim that this "logic" of present→past→future amounts to the definition of a psychoanalytic philosophy of time? It seems to me that the three temporal *ekstases* cannot be deployed in any other order. These ekstases clearly can be given separate names but cannot be taken as independent dimensions capable of entering into multiple combinations. Whether it is a question of the sense of time; of cosmological time (or more precisely, its representation); or of the way temporalization emerges in the subject as living, human, or historical, every relation to time will involve them being linked up according to the 2-1-3 pattern.

It goes without saying that the determination of past, present, and future as the three ekstases of temporalization is not an immediate given. With the double awareness that things no doubt endure (my childhood house is still there, weathering the passage of time) but that they are always getting worse (the house where I was born is nonetheless starting to look old), popular thinking concludes by agreeing with Heraclitus: being is essentially fragile, if not beyond our grasp. We thus make Chronos the agent of the dissipation of all things, the source of epistemologico-existential despair. The pure negativity of this popular conception of time knows no *ekstases*: no present, since it is still happening; no true future, since its advent will be no more than a wafer-thin present in the process of disappearing. As for the past, it cannot be given any status at all: the mere fact of having existed offers no conceivable raft to cling to—there is no underworld not barred by the waters of Lethe.

There can be no temporal ekstases without identifying the formal dimension of *psychical* activity in time, something philosophy gradually realized to the extent that it managed to get a grip both on the ostensible barbarity of Chronos and on its antithesis, which cut away its precritical idealism with its bold but somewhat cursory commitment to the Idea, in other words, to eternal truth. These intellectual developments certainly took place with Kant and Hegel, just as Jean Laplanche says (though perhaps we should be more precise: it was following Luther). At that point it began to become clear that there is or can be some *movement* in being and that the different figures of that movement over the course of individual or collective histories signify not the undoing of things but their unfurling. However, this transition from ontotheology to dialectical philosophy could endow being with temporal *ekstases* only by making reflectivity the source of the movement through which being will henceforth be said to have been given its being. Even these ekstases come to be ordered, each in relation to the others, according to the schema of present→past→future.

If the essential disposition of being is no longer to simply preserve its own being, or at least its being as such, and if it thus loses its condition of being always and forever, it becomes no more than constant non-self-identity. The being of a being becomes a process of self-dialecticization, in other words, a reflective process that temporalizes being. That is to say that being never stops turning its present into a past, breaking up the compact density created by the impact of the past on the present to make possible a future. For the field of what is possible can be opened only by deconstructing the plenitude that prevents its appearance, thus by untying that which in the present merely reiterates the past. It is always from the present to the past and on to the future that things open up through temporalization or reflection.

I am quite sure that Jean Laplanche shares this viewpoint. He knows very well that doing philosophy involves taking a step back, discriminating, and deconstructing an initial set of ideas to undermine their viability and therefore their contemporary relevance, thus consigning those ideas to intellectual history. So he rightly proposes that a psychoanalytic philosophy of time can emerge only in the après-coup of Freud's work. One should note though that, as it happens, this après-coup, referring to a moment before ideas that had been seen as the necessary condition of anything new, brings with it an a priori determination of time, the very same determination that directs the movement freeing one from the present by allowing the impact of the past to become visible. The temporalization of present→past→future is the transcendental condition of reflection, not its object: it cannot be reshaped.

There is no doubt, moreover, that Jean Laplanche sees the philosophy of existence as having failed to recognize a basic truth, lured by the bait of another, more effective way of structuring temporalization. My question therefore focuses on what interest there may be in investigating whether the failure in question has more to do with formulation than with deeper issues.

The enemy of psychoanalysis is not the philosophy of existence as one finds it from Husserl to Ricoeur via Heidegger, Sartre, and a few others, but clearly a persistent rationalism still functioning within the framework of a nondialectical philosophy, as we see today in the natural sciences.

The idea of causality stitches together series of events by making the links between them comprehensible. It reveals diachronic structures, indeed, beings whose nature is to change according to a preregulated order, not in response to historical events. Nature, as the supposedly ordered totality of all such beings, far from being inadequate to time, triumphs over it, but the price of this is being left with a precritical philosophical horizon.[12] What thus takes shape is in effect a myth of all phenomena as impenetrably dense, subject to a transitive causality that allows them to be imagined as purely and simply immanent to the long unfolding of a unique and fully determined reality (and tough luck for Heraclitus if the "ungraspable" flow of his river gives way to statistical grids linking river tides to geographical and climatic factors). Here dialectics and temporalization have been lost—or not yet discovered. There is simply a sealed-off fullness of the world that is never threatened by any loss, that is immune to anything new, and where analytic work can never take place: not because its relevance and effectiveness are unclear but because of an a priori, axiomatic foreclosure.

The fact that classical rationality does not conceive of time, the time of epistemic breaks and of the occurrence of the new; that it empties time out by tightly roping together contingent events (notwithstanding the weakness of many of the links it is thus forced to make); that it covers up this deficiency by using the word "time" to describe a mathematical paradigm consistent with everything that

12 This is a very high price, almost beyond endurance. It amounts, in effect, to surreptitiously setting up a religion of absolute knowledge. The essential lesson of positivism is obliterated by this: if Auguste Comte set out (unsuccessfully, of course) to explicitly set up a religion of international positivism, it was clearly an attempt to block the ideological march of scientific rationalism.

gives rise to structures entirely lacking in temporalization (even that of diachrony): this is what our critique should focus on above all. The very foundation of the human sciences, and of psychoanalysis, is at stake.

Having said all that, I see no major obstacles to such a critique. It should be easy to show how the idea of structures, whether diachronic or not, is only ever of interest insofar as such structures are in fact ways of looking, sites and moments that lend themselves to effects of epistemological rupture, either on their own account or due to a specific action. A contemplative rationality likes to imagine itself taking part in eternity, while an embodied rationality knows that, since it serves human interests and labor, needing to take an active part in the work of unbinding/restructuration, it is itself also a work of temporalization.

It should likewise be easy to show that here reflection can find support in what already takes place at the prereflective level, which also involves biology and neurophysiology, when they don't shut their eyes. The fact that microorganisms are very frequently slow in responding to supposedly causal stimuli, whereas a "correct" causality would have them serve up a readymade response in the *hic et nunc* as part of a strict echo system, clearly shows that they too, in their own way, "take their time."[13] They partly deconstruct a rigorous linkage between themselves and the environment they exist in. To recognize this is not a return to the all-too-classical "fragility" of being; it is merely a sign of its living dimension, with the importance of the delayed reaction linked to the degree of psychical activity in the organisms. Here we are clearly taken right back to Freud's remark, noted by Jean Laplanche, on the periodic investment of excitations and the fact that this periodicity usefully distances the living being from them.

---

13 See J. Gagey, "Brève remarques sur le temps en psychologie," *Bulletin de psychologie* 317: 660–664.

The redirection of criticism that I am suggesting here will not, therefore, lead us to confuse *Homo psychoanalyticus* with some project of being, some being-for-the-future or being-toward-death, of which there has been rather too much discussion since the early twentieth century. It should indeed allow us to define the difference between these two things more accurately: it does not consist in the fact that such projects, unlike the psychoanalytic subject, would heedlessly throw themselves into the future from a present properly rendered into the past. Nor does it come from the fact that they are vertiginously driven by a pure *telos*, by a future oblivious to anything past. A "project" of being exists only due to a step being taken back from the confusion of the present moment, which is weighed down and disorientated by everyday factors. Existentialist reflection thus does not misconstrue the formal structure of temporalization but gives too little weight to the past insofar as it understands it as error or inadequacy. The distancing process we noted above is not an organized series of acts. It could only be so if the future Good were determined in advance, which is not the case and which anyway would take us back to a predialectical philosophical terrain. Confronted by a reflective process that opens up a vast array of thoughts, none of which has any claim to legitimacy, the psychoanalyst's method can be given its full importance, and it becomes possible to understand the encounter between psychoanalysis and the philosophies of reflection in its true, productive sense.

The same thing goes for the hymns to "Life" led by Jung and Bergson. In every one of them, there is a rendering-past of the present as the condition of a glorious future. The difference between this and the work of psychoanalysis—which is a substantial difference —is that this rendering-past, after having outlined its effects on the present, overvalues the past. Vitalism holds as sacred the forces it sees working for a long time, if not forever, on the present and urges us to yield ourselves to them in the future even more than we do today, to yield ourselves "religiously" due, yet again, to the lack of a method to "retranslate" that past (in Jean Laplanche's expression, which I am happy to endorse).

At a fundamental level, all of this does not separate us from Jean Laplanche's perspective, the aim of which is to show in what sense interpretation is essentially a method that makes it possible for the analysand to retranslate an enigmatic past. Perhaps it is not out of the question to hope that, by focusing attention on the method that governs temporalization more than on its structure, there will be room for many more thought-provoking comparisons. For there are clearly relevant elements of method in other disciplines, notably the disciplines of history.[14]

Response to Jacques Gagey

Despite my hasty overview at the beginning, my perspective is not that of a historian of philosophy. It's true that I don't subscribe to the idea that every way of relating to time, and every reflection on time, must always discover the *ekstases* connected up in the order present→past→future. As I said in response to Pierre Fédida, my investigation occupies the same terrain as Heidegger's. Now, Heidegger—as has recently been restated by Ricoeur—affirms "the primacy of the future in the course of the articulated structure of time." The originary vector is the yet-to-come (*Zukunft*), the Orient (*woraufhin*), toward which the subject is decisively thrown. Regarding that *Entschlossenheit* or "sure decision" of the "being-for," I oppose it with another decision, no less sure: Freud's decision to deliberately throw himself back into the past. But what I am trying to develop on this point is the fact that this movement does not head toward some sort of cipher to be interpreted, and which would be its "archetype," but rather it is a movement of unbinding, of de-translation, which thus connects up with the living force of a fundamental to-be-translated.

14 I am thinking of course especially of epistemology, whose function is clearly that of retranslating into successive cultural contexts the *activum* of rationality, that stimulus, itself also enigmatic, that makes us creators of knowledge that is always simply partial.

I pictured myself, a minute ago, as a stray sheep helped into the fold by Maurice Dayan in the role of a Freudian Good Shepherd; the same can be said of Jacques Gagey ushering me into the fold of the "philosophy of reflection." With one difference, however, which is that I have never dwelt in that second sheepfold. And also that, in all of the explanations of how that philosophy works, I find no trace of the methodical and definite process of ana-lysis, such as I conceive of it. "Starts from the present, dislodges the past clinging to that present, and opens up possibilities for the future"; "constant non-self-identity"; "never stops turning its present into a past", etc.: these formulations are certainly descriptions of the functioning of the "perception-consciousness system" of which Jacques Gagey notes, not without relevance, that it "takes its time" as it "already takes place at the prereflective level," in other words, in the animal. But what I am trying to describe through the dialectic of successive versions of a life is situated in a completely different domain.

Lastly, I cannot avoid restating that, in my understanding, what is enigmatic is not the past in general but what is inherent to the subject's originary relation to the adult other and what "transcends" it: the originary relation of seduction.

BIBLIOGRAPHY OF WORKS BY JEAN LAPLANCHE

The following is incomplete is several respects. A complete list of Laplanche's writings, collected and uncollected, of all translations of his work and of all video and audio recordings is being prepared and will be available on the web site of the Fondation Laplanche.

1960 ***L'Inconscient : une étude psychanalytique*** in collaboration with Serge Leclaire. Presented at the VI Colloque de Bonneval. Proceedings of the Colloque *L'Inconscient* were published by Desclée de Brouwer, Paris, 1966 in a volume containing other interventions by Laplanche.

Republished in *Problématiques IV. L'inconscient et le ça*. Paris: P.U.F., 1981.

E: ***The Unconscious: A Psychoanalytic Study*** Trans. Patrick Coleman. *Yale French Studies*, no. 48, 1972.

1961 ***Hölderlin et la question du père***. Paris: P.U.F., 1961.

E: ***Hölderlin and the Question of the Father***. Ed. and trans. Luke Carson. Introduction by Rainer Nägele. Victoria, BC: ELS Editions, 2007.

1964 ***Fantasme originaire, fantasmes des origines, origines du fantasme*** in collaboration with J.-B. Pontalis. Les Temps Modernes, #215, Volume 19, April 1964.

1985 Republished in the series T*extes du XXe siècle* with a new introduction by the authors. Paris: Hachette, 1985.

E: ***Primal Fantasy, Fantasies of Origins, Origins of Fantasy,*** trans. Jonathan. *Laplanche*, Dominique Scarfone, New York: Unconscious in Translation, 2015.

Fantasy and the Origins of Sexuality; International Journal of Psychoanalysis, vol. 49, 1968. [Reprinted in *Formations of Fantasy*, ed. Victor Burgin et al, Methuen, 1986; also reprinted in *Unconscious Phantasy*, ed. Ricardo Steiner, London: Karnac Books, 2003].

1967 ***Vocabulaire de la psychanalyse*** in collaboration with J.-B. Pontalis. Paris: P.U.F.

E: ***The Language of Psycho-Analysis***. Trans. D. Nicholson-Smith. New York: Norton, 1973.

1970 ***Vie et mort en psychanalyse***. Paris: Flammarion, 1970.

2nd edition 1971, includes *Dérivation des entités psychanalytiques*

E: ***Life and Death in Psychoanalysis***. Trans. J. Mehlman. Baltimore: Johns Hopkins University Press, 1976. Includes *Derivation of Psychoanalytic Entities*

1970-73 Lectures given at the *Sorbonne-Université de Paris VII*, for his course within the UER des Sciences Humaines, published in the journal *Psychanalyse à l'université*; and then in ***Problématiques I. L'angoisse***. Paris: P.U.F., 1980.
1970-1971 : L' « Angst » dans la névrose
1971-1972 : L'angoisse dans la topique
1972-1973 : L'angoisse morale

1973-75 Lectures given at the *Sorbonne-Université de Paris VII*, for his course within the UER des Sciences Humaines, published in the journal *Psychanalyse à l'université*; and then in ***Problématiques II. Castration. Symbolisations***. Paris: P.U.F., 1980.
1973-1974 : La castration, ses précurseurs et son destin
1974-1975 : Symbolisations

E: Extract: **Lecture 20 May, 1975**. Trans. Arthur Goldhammer. *Literary Debate : Texts and Contexts*, Ed. Dennis Hollier and Jeffrey Mehlman. New York: The New Press, 1999.

1975-77 Lectures given at the *Sorbonne-Université de Paris VII*, for his course within the UER des Sciences Humaines, published in the journal *Psychanalyse à l'université*; and then in ***Problématiques III. La sublimation***. Paris: P.U.F., 1980.
1975-1976 : Pour situer la sublimation
1976-1977 : Faire dériver la sublimation

E: Extract: **To Situate Sublimation**. Trans. Richard Miller. *October*, No. 28, Spring, 1984.

1977-79 Lectures given at the *Sorbonne-Université de Paris VII*, for his course within the UER des Sciences Humaines, published in the journal *Psychanalyse à l'université*; and then in ***Problématiques IV. L'Inconsient et le Ça***. Paris: P.U.F., 1981.
1977-1978 : La référence à l'inconscient
1978-1979 : Problématique du ça

E: ***The Unconscious and the Id***, Trans. Luke Thurston with Lindsay Watson, London: Rebus Press, 1999.

1979-84 Lectures given at the *Sorbonne-Université de Paris VII*, for his course within the UER des Sciences Humaines, published in the journal *Psychanalyse à l'université*; and then in ***Problématiques V. Le baquet – Transcendance du transfert***. Paris: P.U.F., 1987.

1979-1980 : Le psychanalyste et son baquet
1980-1981 : Le descriptif et le prescriptif
1983-1984 : La transcendance du transfer

1987 ***Nouveaux fondements pour 1a psychanalyse***. Paris: P.U.F., 1987.

E: ***New Foundations for Psychoanalysi***s, trans. David Macey, Oxford: Basil Blackwell, 1989.

New Foundations for Psychoanalysis, trans. Jonathan House and Robert Stein, New York: Unconscious in Translation, 2016.

1989 ***Traduire Freud***. In collaboration with A. Bourguignon, P. Cotet, F. Roberts. Paris: P.U.F., 1989.

E: Extract: **Translating Freud**, trans. Maev de la Guardia and Bertrand Vichyn, in *Translating Freud*, ed. Darius Gray Ornston, New Haven: Yale University Press, 1992.

1989-90 Lectures given at the *Sorbonne-Université de Paris VII*, for his course within the UER des Sciences Humaines, published in the journal *Psychanalyse à l'université*; and then in ***Problématiques VI. L'après-coup***. Paris: P.U.F., 2006.

1989-1990 : La « Nachträglichkeit » dans l'après-coup

1991-92 Lectures given at the *Sorbonne-Université de Paris VII*, for his course within the UER des Sciences Humaines, published in the journal *Psychanalyse à l'université*; and then in ***Problématiques VII : Le fourvoiement biologisant de la sexualité chez Freud suivi de Biologisme et biologie***. Paris: P.U.F., initially published in 1993 by Synthélabo .

E: **The Temptation of Biology: Freud's Theories of Sexuality**. Trans. Donald Nicholson-Smith. New York: Unconscious in Translation, 2015.

E: Extract: **Exigency and Going-Astray**. Trans. Vincent Ladmiral and Nicholas Ray. *Psychoanalysis, Culture and Society*, 11, 2006, pp. 164-189.

1992 ***La révolution copernicienne inachevée (Travaux 1967-1992)***. Paris: Aubier, 1992.

E: **The Unfinished Copernican Revolution**. Trans. Luke Thurstson, New York: The Unconscious in Translation, forthcoming.

E: English translations of works contained in this volume

1968 **Interpreting [with] Freud** *(Interpréter [avec] Freud)*. Trans. Vincent Ladmiral and Nicholas Ray, *Psychoanalysis, Culture and Society*. vol. 11, 2006.

1979 **A Metapsychology put to the Test of Anxiety** *(Une métapsychologie à lépreuve de l'angoisse). International Journal of Psychoanalysis*, vol. 62, 1981.

1984 **The Drive and its Object-source: its fate in the transference** *(La pulsion et son objet-source. Son destin dans le transfer).*

Trans. Martin Stanton *Jean Laplanche: Seduction, Translation and the Drives*, ed. John Fletcher and Martin Stanton, London: Institute of Contemporary Arts, 1992.

Trans. Leslie Hill. *Essays on Otherness*, ed. John Fletcher, London: Routledge, 1999.

1987 **Specificity of Terminological Problems in the Translation of Freud** *(Spécificité des problèmes terminologiques dans la traduction de Freud). International Review of Psychoanalysis*, vol. 18, 1991.

1988 **The Wall and the Arcade** *(Le mur et l'arcade)*. Trans. Martin Stanton. Op. cit.

1989 **Psycholanalysis, Time and Translation** *(Temporalité et traduction. Pour une remise au travail de la philosophie du temps)*. Trans. Martin Stanton. Op. cit. New translation, Luke Thurston, in *Après-coup* ed. Jonathan House, New York, The Unconscious in Translation. Forthcoming.

1990 **Implantation, Intromission** *(Implation, intromission)*. Trans Luke Thurston, *Essays on Otherness*, ed. John Fletcher, London: Routledge, 1999.

1990 **Time and the Other** *(Le temps et l'autre)*. Trans. Luke Thurston. *Essays on Otherness*, ed. John Fletcher, London: Routledge, 1999. Revised translation by Luke Thurston in Après-coup ed. Jonathan House, New York, The Unconscious in Translation. Forthcoming.

1991 **Interpretation Between Determinism and Hermeneutics: A Restatement of the Problem** *(L'interprétation entre déterminisme et herméneutique: une nouvelle position de la question)* Trans. Philip Slotkin. Essays on Otherness, ed. John Fletcher, London: Routledge, 1999.

1992 **Masochism and the General Theory of Seduction** *(Masochisme et théorie de la séduction généralisée)*. Trans. Luke Thurston. *Essays on Otherness*, ed. John Fletcher, London: Routledge, 1999.

1992 **Transference: its Provocation by the Analyst** *(Du transfert : sa provocation par l'analyste)*. Trans. Luke Thurston. *Essays on Otherness*, ed. John Fletcher, London: Routledge, 1999.

1992 **The Unfinished Copernican Revolution** *(La révolution copernicienne inachevée)*. Trans. Luke Thurston *Essays on Otherness*, ed. John Fletcher, London: Routledge, 1999. *Essays on Otherness*, ed. John Fletcher, London: Routledge, 1999.

1997 *"The Theory of Seduction and the Problem of the Other."* Trans. Luke Thurston. *International Journal of Psychoanalysis*, vol. 78, no. 4, 1997.

1998 *"From the Restricted to the Generalized Theory of Seduction."* In *Seduction, Suggestion, Psychoanalysis*. Ed. Jose Corveleyn and Philippe Van Haute. Leuven University Press and Duquesne University Press, 1998.

1999 ***Entre séduction et inspiration : L'Homme***. Paris: P.U.F., 1999.

E: ***Between Seduction and Inspiration***. Trans. Jeffrey Mehlman, New York: Unconscious in Translation, 2015

E: Other English translations of works contained in this volume

1992 ***Notes on Afterwardsness***. Trans. Martin Stanton *Jean Laplanche: Seduction, Translation and the Drives*, ed. John Fletcher and Martin Stanton, London: Institute of Contemporary Arts, 1992. Taken from a recorded conversation with Martin Stanton. Later augmented by Laplanche and published with the same title in *Essays on Otherness*, ed. John Fletcher, London: Routledge, 1999. Also, in a French version in *Entre séduction et inspiration : l'homme*. Paris, PUF 1999

1992 **The Unfinished Copernican Revolution** (*La révolution copernicienne inachevée)*.

1992 **Seduction, Persecution, Revelation** *(Séduction, persécution, révélation)*. Trans. Philip Slotkin. *The International Journal of Psychoanalysis*, vol. 76, no. 4, 1996

1994 **Psychoanalysis as Anti-hermeneutics** *(La psychanalyse comme anti-herméneutique)*. Trans. Luke Thurston. *Radical Philosophy*, no. 79, Sept./Oct., 1996.

1995 **The So-Called 'Death-Drive': a Sexual Drive** (La soi-disant pulsion de mort : une pulsion sexuelle). Trans. Luke Thurston. *The Death-Drive*. Ed. Rob Weatherill, London: Rebus Press, 1999. Reprinted in *The British Journal of Psychotherapy*, vol. 20, no. 4, 2004.

1996 **Aims of the Psychoanalytic Process** *(Buts du processus psychanalytique)*. *Journal of European Psychoanalysis*, no. 5, Spring/Fall, 1997.

1996 **Psychoanalysis: Myths and Theories** (La psychanalyse: mythes et théorie.) Trans. *Psychoanalytic Quarterly*, vol. 77, no. 3, 2003.

1998 **Narrativity and Hermeneutics: some propositions** *(Narrativité et herméneutique: quelque propositions.)* Trans. John Fletcher. *New Formations*, no. 48, Winter, 2002/3

1999 **Sublimation and/or Inspiration** (Sublimation et/ou inspiration.) Trans. John Fletcher. *New Formations*, no. 48, Winter, 2002-3

2006 ***Problématiques VI: L'après-coup***

E: **Après-coup**, this volume.

2007 *Sexual : La sexualité élargie au sens freudien 2000-2006*. Paris: P.U.F.

E: ***Freud and the Sexual: Essays 2000-2006***, ed. John Fletcher; trans. John Fletcher, Jonathan House, Nicholas Ray. New York: Unconscious in Translation, (IPB) 2011

E: Other English translations of works contained in this volume

2000 **Sexuality and Attachment in Metapsychology** *(Sexualité et l'attachement dans la metapsychologie.)* Trans. Susan Fairfield. *Infantile Sexuality and Attachment*. Ed. Daniel Widlöcher. New York: Other Press, 2002.

2000 **Closing and Opening of the Dream: Must Chapter VII be Rewritten?** *(Rêve et communication : faut-il réécrire me chapitre VII?)* Trans. Mira Reinberg and Thomas Pepper. *Dreams of Interpretation: A Century down the Royal Road*. Ed. Catherin Liu et al. Minneapolis: University of Minnesota Press, 2007.

2003 **Gender, Sex, and the Sexual** *(Le genre, le sexe, le sexual.)*" Trans.Susan Fairfield. *Gender and Sexuality*, vol. 8, no. 2, 2007.

Index

Elise Yihan Chou (Editor) studies comparative literature at Columbia University. She is a Scholastic Art and Writing Awards medalist and a 2013 New Jersey Scholar.

Jonathan House practices psychiatry and psychoanalysis in New York City. He teaches courses on Freud and Laplanche in the Psychoanalytic Studies Program of Columbia University's Institute for Comparative Literature and Society, and is a Training and Supervising Analyst at Columbia's psychoanalytic institute. At Laplanche's invitation, he agreed to serve on the Conseil Scientifique of the Fondation Laplanche.

In 2010 he founded The Unconscious in Translation, a publishing house dedicated to translating and promoting the work of Jean Laplanche and of other important French psychoanalysts whose work would not otherwise be translated into English. He remains its General Editor.

Luke Thurston is Senior Lecturer in Modern Literature at Aberystwyth University and Director of the David Jones Centre. He is the co-editor of the *Routledge Handbook to the Ghost Story* (2017), and has published widely on psychoanalysis and literature. He studied with Jean Laplanche at L'Université de Paris VII in the 1990s and is the translator of Laplanche's *Essays on Otherness* and *The Unconscious and the Id*. He is currently translating Laplanche's *The Unfinished Copernican Revolution*.